GOD-LIFE

DISCOVERING HOW TO LIVE A CHRIST-LIKE LIFE

Ernest J. Kelley

Dr. Ernest J. Kelley

Xulon PRESS

God-Life
Discovering How To Live A Christ-Like Life
by Dr. Ernest J. Kelley

Printed in the United States of America

ISBN 978-1-60791-427-3

www.xulonpress.com

A Word about GOD-LIFE ~

"As I have traveled around the world, there is one desperate need that jumps out at me. It is the need for believers to fully comprehend the depth of their relationship with Christ and the power that is at their disposal through Him. Ernest Kelley has hit the nail on the head with *God-Life*.

Understanding the meaning of the new birth and the provision God has made for us to proceed into Christ-likeness is a strategic journey for the believer. *God-Life* will clearly and compellingly chart the course for that journey. I commend these pages to every believer with the prayer that each one who reads them will complete this journey, which God has planned."

James T. Draper, Jr., President Emeritus
LifeWay Christian Resources

"I have known the author, Ernest Kelley for over thirty years. Through our close friendship, I have observed his intimate relationship with God and seen the visible evidence of God-Life in him. In this book, he writes profound truths and sound theology in communication so clear that anyone, young or old, experienced in faith or inexperienced in faith, religious or irreligious can understand the realities of God's nature and how God can be alive in us.

This writing is lively and energetic, filled with poignant illustrations and Scripture texts relevant to the theme. He encourages the reader to react to the text with thoughtful questions throughout. I was inspired, challenged, and greatly encouraged in my faith in God through reading this great work. While reading, I was impressed

that every agnostic, every seeker, every new believer, and every matured Christian who needs to be informed by a fresh word about God should read this book."
J. Robert White, Executive Director
Georgia Baptist Convention

"If you are looking for a book that is full of sound theology about the nature and unlimited power of Almighty God, then you would do well to read and study *God-Life*. He has absorbed the Scriptures from cover to cover as a deep thinker, and has proven himself time and again as an insightful teacher and preacher of divine truth. After the prompting of friends and associates, Dr. Kelley has finally put his research and reflections in book form. Good for him and good for everyone who reads *God-Life*!

I love Dr. Kelley's concept of the name of God—"I WILL ALWAYS BE WHO I HAVE ALWAYS BEEN." May I add that the thought provoking questions throughout the book are probing and stretching for all students of Scripture. This is truly an insightful, well-written book. I commend the book and with genuine enthusiasm in doing so."
B. Carlisle Driggers, Executive Director-Treasurer Emeritus
South Carolina Baptist Convention

"The work, *God-Life*, by Dr. Ernest Kelley, sets forth in a very clear manner how our relationship with God ought to be. Dr. Kelley has addressed a key need in our spiritual walk and is easily incorporated into daily devotional material or in a Spiritual Formation course at a college or seminary. The book could also be used for personal devotion, Sunday school or discipleship curriculum, and a preaching series. All of us, individually and corporately, need to be drawn closer to God and *God-Life* encourages us to do just that."
Dr. James Flanagan, President
Luther Rice Seminary

"This wonderful book is packed with insightful applications of Scripture which come only from a devoted, disciplined, and reverent study of the Bible. Dr. Kelley's lifetime of study and application of these biblical principles is obvious on every page. Pastors, church

leaders, and lay followers of Christ will be challenged by this well-researched and deeply convictional book."
Martin F. King, Associate Executive Director
Illinois Baptist State Association

"*God-life* [can be used] as a guide for preachers preparing a sermon or teaching series. This exposition is bolstered with relevant Scripture and biblical story-pictures. It will find its way into my study and prayer time as I seek God's guidance in the work of preaching... it is intriguing and has stirred my heart.

It would be a useful book study in small group setting on campus or in homes. It ought to be a catalyst for personal prayer time as the preacher/teacher/s heart is prepared for ministry. "Water-walkers" is a term that grabs the mind's eye and allows one to see what believing looks like. "Faith to faith" accentuates the journey aspect of the believer's life. The "work of faith" in light of faith vs. works, draws proper attention to the call to live out one's faith vs. the idea that "faith" if a ticket that provides free passage on the train to glory.

You are a true friend, whose life has exemplified "God-faithed" living. I thank God for blessing me with your friendship."
Dr. Robert P. Jolly, Pastor
First Baptist Church, Cumming, Georgia
(Dr. Kelley's pastor)

GOD-LIFE is dedicated and committed
to the glory of God
who inspired and guided me
to put into writing
what He placed upon my heart.

CONTENTS

ACKNOWLEDGEMENTS

First, to Eleanor, my wife, who has been a blessing to me in so many ways. She has been an enthusiastic encourager and supporter of the *God-life* project from the beginning. Her belief in me has been a strength, without which I could never have completed this book—a valued consultant and a tireless proofreader for the many rewrites.

Our daughter Susan spent endless hours typing, editing, and proofreading. She has been invaluable arranging and adjusting the material. Her ability and commitment to *God-life* has been a constant support, I simply could not have completed the project without her.

Our daughter Karen typed some of the first hand-written drafts, and spent many hours proofreading. Many times when we were involved and too tired to prepare a meal, she brought dinner. Her cheerful and bright spirit is always a delight.

I would like to extend heartfelt gratitude to the men who supported, encouraged, and took time from their busy schedules to read and offer an endorsement.

Dr. Carlisle Driggers, a close friend, was the first person outside of my family to encourage me to put the concepts of *God-life* into a book. He is an author, a recognized leader among Baptists, and an effective preacher. His creative leadership has given to Southern Baptists the strategy of "Empowering Kingdom Growth."

Dr. James (Jimmy) Draper is a mentor in my life. Not only to me, also to countless numbers, he is a hero of the faith. He is a highly respected and creative leader among Southern Baptists. He was a beloved pastor and an inspiring president of LifeWay Christian Resources.

Dr. Robert (Bob) White, a treasured friend, is a strong Christian leader and a respected voice among Southern Baptists. His commitment to growing "Healthy Kingdom Churches" has contributed to the effective development of hundreds of churches. His warmhearted encouragement has been a blessing.

Dr. James Flanagan is a widely known administrator and Bible scholar. He's an outstanding seminary president, and has pioneered new and imaginative ways to train students. After discussing a general outline of *God-life*, he warmly urged me to put it into print; he was a great encouragement to me.

Martin (Marty) King is a colleague and dear friend. He is a gifted writer and administrator. A deeply committed Christian, Marty is well respected by all who know him. He is the kind of friend that you call upon in your hour of need.

Dr. Robert (Bob) Jolly is my pastor. He has a caring heart, is an inspiring preacher and spiritual leader. An effective pastor, he has led The First Baptist Church through a number of growth cycles to its current significantly strong ministry and witness.

Sincere appreciation to two who provided professional help in the course of the project.

Jennifer B. Rosania, writer/editor, was invaluable in the early writing. She contributed both spiritual and professional guidance.

Carol Pipes, Publications director/editor, *On Mission*; assisted proofreading and formatting the final draft.

A Word from the Author ~

As a young pastor attending a Bible conference, I had a life-changing experience. In large letters on a banner that hung across the front of the auditorium was the conference theme for the week, "To Live Is Christ." We were challenged *to live Christ*! This gripping quest has never left me—to allow the fullness of Christ to be manifest in my daily life.

For the last several years, the manuscript for *God-life* has consumed my thoughts and a large portion of my daily study time. The magnitude of the concept of living a God-life is overwhelming. It means to take seriously, *It is no longer I who live, but Christ lives in me* (Galatians 2:20).

Think about it. If Christ is the Son of God, and He is; if you have put self to death, and Christ lives in you, then you are empowered to live a "God-life." This is the clear intent of God for you as a believer.

Again, and again, the authority of the Word of God enjoins (commands or directs or instructs or urges) Christians to evidence Christ in their everyday living.

Some of the Scriptures that challenged me were:

"Walk in newness of life." (Romans 6:4)
"Christ lives in me." (Galatians 2:20)
"To live is Christ." (Philippians 1:21)
"Abide in Me, and I in you." (John 15:4)
"Christ in you, the hope of glory." (Colossians 1:27)

"Your life is hidden with Christ in God." (Colossians 3:3)
"The image of the One who created [you]." (Colossians 3:10)

Your commitment should be to live so that these Scriptures will be fulfilled in your life. By God's grace, you can be a partaker of His divine nature; it is God's precious and magnificent promise to you (see 2 Peter 1:2-3). God made every provision for you to be successful in this venture; in fact, He fully expects you to live Christ—to manifest a God-life.

It is easy to offer excuses as to why living a God-life is impossible. No matter what your life situation or challenge may be, you can choose to let Jesus be the essence of your life. Too many Christians go through life with a low self-esteem, always focusing on why they can't live a God-life. Or, mired in the busyness of daily life, they don't take the time to seek a deeper walk—the life God wants you to have.

Forget the past and your current obstacles, and determine today to let Christ live your life—denying self, *let Christ live through you.* Living God-life is up to you. Let's begin the journey.

SECTION ONE

GOD-BIRTH

"Who were born not of blood,
nor of the will of the flesh,
nor of the will of man, but of God."
(John 1:13)

"O God, I thank You that You are Eternal and are eternally the same." I can still remember that dear saint's voice echoing in the rural church in Tennessee where I pastored as a college student. For a young preacher, it was an invaluable truth for me to ponder. Eternal and forevermore the same—our Everlasting God is unlimited in magnitude and completely, unchangingly faithful. What a wonderful way to begin a prayer!

And it's an excellent place to begin our understanding of God-life. We live our lives in relation to time and space (when and where)—these are two dimensions used to describe our human experience. We measure our lives by beginnings and endings—birth, death, hours, days, and years. Our finite minds process events in reckonable quantities.

Contrast that with *ELOHIM*, the majestic *ETERNAL GOD* of the Bible, with whom "one day is as a thousand years, and a thousand years as one day" (2 Peter 3:8). He is the ever-present God; He is absolutely unconstrained by time or space. Unlike you and me, God measures eternity as an ever-present now.

ELOHIM, ETERNAL GOD

He introduced Himself to Moses as, "I AM WHO I AM" (Exodus 3:14). Because the Hebrew used here is timeless, another translation could be, "I WILL ALWAYS BE WHO I HAVE ALWAYS BEEN." Past, present, and future, He is ceaselessly our consistent, ageless, enduring, Eternal God.

He is the self-existing One, and "all things came into being through Him" (John 1:3). This is fundamental and key to understanding God-birth. I would like you to comprehend that you have been birthed by Almighty God who is eternal and beyond any human experience of existence.

- **Take a moment and reflect: Eternal God, who existed before time began, who spoke the earth, land, sea, and sky into existence is your ever-present God today!**

—Chapter One—

Eternal God of the Bible

W hen you received Jesus as your personal Savior, you became a child of God. "As many as received Him… [they] were born… of God" (John 1:12-13). This is *God-birth*, a miraculous, supernatural birth giving you eternal life. In this chapter, you will discover what happened in your God-birth, and gain a deeper understanding of the Heavenly Father who gave you a new life, an eternal life.

Meeting Eternal God

How do I get to know Eternal God? Throughout history, there have been compelling theological and philosophical ways to *think* about God, but the Bible is the only authoritative and revealing way to *know* Him. The Holy One revealed in its pages is above, beyond, and outside the limitations of history and geography. He is the Everlasting, Eternal God, "'I am the Alpha and the Omega,' says the Lord God, 'who is and who was and who is to come, the Almighty'" (Revelation 1:8).

ALPHA AND OMEGA, THE ALMIGHTY

When I was a boy, I heard someone refer to an elderly man as "older than the hills." That's about as old as a person can get, don't you think? The wonderful thing is that God is ageless and timeless, and this prayer by Moses affirms it; "before the mountains were born, or Thou didst give birth to the earth and the world, even from everlasting to everlasting, Thou art God" (Psalm 90:2). God is not just older than the hills; He has no beginning and is timeless. He is the I Am!

God is the starting point of all that exists, while He Himself has no beginning. The Bible consistently asserts the eternal, timeless existence of God. In fact, Paul speaks of His activity "before the ages" (1 Corinthians 2:7), and Jude praises "the only God our Savior...before all time and now and forever" (Jude 25). God is His own self-cause, which means His existence is within Himself. That characteristic sets Him apart from anyone and everything else in the universe. All other things have a cause for their existence outside of themselves—someone created it or them. Eternal God was not created, He is!

Acknowledging Eternal God

Recently I viewed a photograph of the earth taken from space by an astronaut. Perhaps you've seen one like it: one brilliant moment, in the midst of rotation, that beautiful sphere captured with the vast universe as its backdrop. The striking picture brought a myriad of emotions to me. In some ways, the earth seemed lonely and small—in other ways, teeming and grand. However, what struck me most was that I could not see a foundation for the earth—no guide wires to keep it suspended, or underpinnings to hold it in place. I realized that its foundation is the word and will of our eternal Creator God—He Himself keeps it secure in space.

When everything in the universe was formed, God was there—a powerful and imaginative Creator unencumbered by time or other limitation. Genesis recounts how Almighty God spoke the universe, and all that's in it into existence through His absolute authority and creative ability.

"I AM, let time begin!" This is my concept of God's creational greeting in Genesis. There you'll find the Creator's name is *ELOHIM*. This is a plural noun and gives us our first understanding of the unity of the God-head in the blessed Trinity. You may wonder why this is important. It's important because each member of the Trinity—Father, Son, and Holy Spirit—is vital and involved in your God-birth.

Before God spoke the world and its inhabitants into existence, He envisioned a way for your God-birth. "He chose us [you] in Him before the foundation of the world, that we [you] should be holy and blameless before Him" (Ephesians 1:4). The eternal life He provides for you was no afterthought—He created you to receive it through *God-birth*. And, He determined before time that a Savior would be necessary for you to know Him.

- **How does it make you feel knowing that God was making plans for you before time began?**

Serving Eternal God

When I read the Bible, I find it is filled with accounts of faithful believers joyfully worshipping and serving God. In faith, they accepted the reality of the Lord God who is eternal. They understood that God is the eternal I AM, that it is His nature *TO BE*, and that all things came into being because of Him (see John 1:1-3).

For example, Father of the Faithful, Abraham, trusted "the name of the LORD, the Everlasting God" (Genesis 21:33). Here you will find God's name is *EL-OLAM*—the *ETERNAL GOD*, or the *GOD WITHOUT END*. Abraham knew that he could count on God. "When he was called, [he] obeyed by going out to a place which he was to receive for an inheritance; and he went out, not knowing where he was going" (Hebrews 11:8).

EL-OLAM, ETERNAL GOD, GOD WITHOUT END

God has no human frailties, His wisdom is unfathomable, and you can trust Him today as confidently as did Abraham. No matter what you are facing, you can turn to God who doesn't change, and who will always be strength to you. The psalmist declared, "Thou [God] art the same, and Thy years will not come to an end" (Psalm 102:27). The literal language here is, "You are the ever unchangeable I AM!" The same God who kept His promises to Abraham will keep His promises to you.

Hebrews 1:10-12 also strongly affirms that God, your heavenly Father, and Christ, your High Priest, are unchangeable and eternal. "Jesus Christ is the same yesterday and today, yes and forever" (Hebrews 13:8). In other words, what was true of God before time began, will be true when time is no more. He is consistent and faithful; He will never fail you.

Understanding Eternal God

A high school teacher asked the geometry class to find the beginning of a circle on a test page. Various answers were received. One student wrote, "Impossible. The circle has no beginning or ending." This, of course, is the correct answer; a circle has no point of origin or conclusion. And, it's a good illustration of God's infinite, perpetual, eternal nature.

Unquestionably, the most unique quality of God is that He is Eternal. He neither begins nor ends. Every other being is created; the natural life cycle as human beings includes death. This originates with Adam whose home was the Garden of Eden—a paradise of indescribable blessings and provisions. Regrettably, Adam's sin of disobeying God brought devastating changes—death and separation from God. God told Adam: "you are dust, and to dust you shall return" (Genesis 3:19). Because of Adam's sin, we share in his fate of death. "Through one man [Adam] sin entered into the world, and death through sin, and so death spread to all men, because all sinned" (Romans 5:12).

Why am I talking so much about the eternal nature of God? Why is it so important for you to understand it? To comprehend God-birth, you must understand your own limited, death-bound destiny.

Rejoice that through Jesus Christ, you can exchange the *perishing* nature of Adam for the *eternal* nature of God. You can have God-birth. God wants to birth you with eternal life.

- **Have you considered there is an alternative to your limited, death-bound destiny? Or, more importantly, have you accepted Jesus Christ as your Savior and experienced God-birth?**

Chapter Two

A New Birth

Just as the beginning of human life requires a human-birth, the beginning of eternal life requires a God-birth. In the third chapter of the Gospel of John, Jesus shares the necessity of this new birth with Nicodemus, a man seeking answers about life and death.

"Unless one is born again, he cannot see the kingdom of God" (John 3:3). Jesus emphatically stressed, "You must be born again" (John 3:7). This new, regenerated, eternal life is accomplished by God-birth. You aren't alone—everyone shares this need. Jew and Gentile, man and woman—everyone needs to be born again to have eternal life.

~~~~~~~~~~~~~~~~~~~~~~~~~~

"You must be born again."

~~~~~~~~~~~~~~~~~~~~~~~~~~

"Good news of a great joy" was the message the angel of God brought to the shepherds on Bethlehem's fields (see Luke 2:10). When Eleanor and I learned we were to be parents, we had great joy over the good news. The weeks that followed were filled with excited activity preparing for the birth of our first child. Baby clothes, a crib, a decorated room, and names for our baby, all expressed our joyous expectation of a new birth. A range of emotions consumed the weeks and months of expectantly waiting—laughter and tears, joy and wonder, anticipation and anxiety. The transition from being a couple to becoming a family was not only a physical reality, but an emotional event as well.

God Wanted A Family

Have you considered the emotional extremes God must have experienced as He prepared for your God-birth? Imagine, if you will, the smiles and tears, the joy and heartache of God as He prepared and waited for us—His family. Yes, God wanted more than angels, seraphim, cherubim, and other celestial beings; He wanted a family. The first chapters of Genesis tell of God's intricate and miraculous preparation for His first family. He created day and night, land and water, vegetation, and animals of every description—all in preparation for His family.

Albeit, God knew the future, and He knew when His family faced temptation they would make poor choices. Their sin would separate them from His presence. He must have felt a profound sadness knowing His family would intentionally disobey requiring judgment and discipline. But God still wanted a family, even though they would choose to believe the lies of Satan and rebel against Him. It was a time of joy and sadness.

When all was ready, God created human life. I believe God smiled and laughed with joy when He made His family in His own image. He took the first couple, the fountainhead of His family, and placed them in a perfectly prepared garden. I have treasured reading the scene when God walked in the Garden of Eden in the cool of the day with His family (see Genesis 3:8). God enjoyed and fellowshipped with His family. How His heart must have been broken when Adam and Eve yielded to temptation. As a consequence, He ordered them out of the beautiful garden; and sadly, they were separated from God.

But God *still* wanted a family. As a parent, I cannot possibly imagine the unequaled love provision God made—the sin payment, the death of Jesus, His only begotten Son at Calvary. "God SO loved...He gave His only begotten Son" (John 3:16, emphasis mine).

Now, God can have the joy and fellowship of a family through the new birth, your God-birth. If you have faith in and accept the sin payment of the crucified Christ, you will not perish, but have eternal (everlasting) life. You can't have God-life without God-birth. Being a member of God's family begins by accepting God's Son as your personal Savior.

Physical Birth vs. Spiritual Birth

Don't confuse a physical birth with a spiritual birth. This was Nicodemus' dilemma when he questioned Jesus. "How can a man be born when he is old?" A spiritual birth, or God-birth, cannot be achieved through human efforts. Good works, being a good person, and having an active church life are commendable lifestyles, but altogether, they are not enough. Rather, you must be "born of the Spirit" (John 3:8).

Remember, from before time began, God knew that you would perish in your sin and be helplessly lost unless He did something about it. So He made a way of salvation for you through the sacrifice of His Son on Calvary. "Christ... has loved us [you] and given Himself for us [you], an offering and a sacrifice to God" (Ephesians 5:2, NKJV). Jesus clearly stated His mission: "The Son of Man has come to seek and to save that which was lost" (Luke 19:10).

To do so, Jesus had to confront and defeat *sin* and *death* that entered the world when Adam disobeyed God. Paul affirms that "as in Adam all die, so also in Christ all shall be made alive" (1 Corinthians 15:22). Jesus' resurrection from the grave proved that He had accomplished His goal of conquering sin and death and made possible a God-birth for you.

The everlasting, God-born, eternal life you receive through Christ is as enduring, imperishable, and eternal as God Himself. In *My Utmost for His Highest*, Oswald Chambers said, "Eternal life is not a gift from God; eternal life is the gift of God." Jesus gave us His personal assurance, "I give eternal life to them, and they shall never perish; and no one shall snatch them out of My hand" (John 10:28).

A Permanent Provision

Augustine, an orthodox Christian bishop in the third century, once said, "Join thyself to the eternal God, and thou wilt be eternal." [i] Through God-birth, you receive everlasting life, which means you receive the eternal life of Eternal God!

Once someone asked me, "Do you really believe in eternal security?" I realized that the real question was: Could you truly have everlasting life through Jesus Christ? So, I responded that because God-birth completely replaces our corruptible nature with God's own life—which is endless and unchanging—it can never be taken away from us (see John 3:16). Your God-birth is as eternal as Almighty God is eternal.

~~~~~~

God-birth is as eternal as Almighty God is eternal.

~~~~~~

Spiritual DNA

Think of it this way: When you were born into this world, you came with your family's DNA—identifying indicators indelibly printed in your cell nuclei. Like everyone else, you can't do anything to change it. God-birth gives you God's spiritual DNA. You lastingly and eternally have God's family identity—one that can't be changed, removed, washed away, or erased. Your God-birth is permanent and eternal.

Recently on television, I watched a nature program featuring a leopard pride. It covered the life cycle including birth. The newborn leopards were so helpless they couldn't see, much less feed themselves. Guess what? Each had leopard spots—they were just like their parents.

When you are born again, guess what? You are just like your eternal heavenly Father—you now have eternal life! The new birth is not a reformation or re-forming the old nature, but a creative act of God, a brand new being with His DNA!

- **Are there distinguishing characteristics in your life that remarkably resemble your new family?**

—Chapter Three—

The Indwelling Holy Spirit

The Holy Spirit "moves in" at the time of your God-birth. Some suggest that you have to say a special prayer to receive the Holy Spirit, but you don't. Nor do you have to engage in dramatic rituals or emotional exercises to receive the Holy Spirit. At the time of your God-birth, the Holy Spirit supernaturally takes permanent residence within you as a gift from God. He "who raised Christ Jesus from the dead will also give life to your mortal bodies through His Spirit who indwells you" (Romans 8:11). God's greatest gift to you is Himself!

Do you realize that the Holy Spirit's interaction with you did not begin with your God-birth? Far before then, He convicted and convinced you of your sin and revealed Christ to you. Jesus promised that the Holy Spirit would "convince the world of sin and of righteousness and of judgment" (John 16:8, RSV). It's through the Holy Spirit's appeal that you came to a saving knowledge of Jesus.

God in You

Perhaps you are wondering or asking: *What does it mean for God the Holy Spirit to dwell in me?* This sounds so very personal and intimate. Exactly! That is the revealing truth of the indwelling Holy

Spirit. The Holy Spirit has one-on-one communication and interaction with you. God "shall give you another Comforter, that He may abide with you forever; even the Spirit of truth… *He dwelleth with you, and shall be in you*" (John 14:17, KJV, emphasis mine).

Intimate Communication

During a recent television interview, I heard a celebrity couple discuss their marriage and unique form of communication. Of the two, she is more reserved and has difficulty verbally expressing love for her husband and their two children. One day, he noticed she put a chalkboard in their kitchen and on it wrote an endearing message to him. Since that time, loving and encouraging notes to each other have become a family tradition. And there are now three chalkboards scattered throughout their house!

Every day, all day, God the Holy Spirit has an intimate word for you. It may be a verse in the Bible that comes alive, or an almost audible word that swells up from your spirit. I pray that you are experiencing and enjoying an intimate relationship with the Holy Spirit who provides daily inspiration for living a God-life.

- **Have you sensed the Holy Spirit communicating with you? Are you listening? How have you responded?**

How Can I Live a God-Life in This World?

Being born-again, or God-birth, is a divine, heavenly, creative act of God. Through your God-birth, the Holy Spirit indwells you and makes God-life possible. From God-birth on, "it is God who is at work in you, both to will and to work for His good pleasure" (Philippians 2:13). A literal translation of this verse is: "God is the One operating in you—both to create the desire in you for His work, and to accomplish His divine will through you."

The Greek word used here for *work* (*energeō*) is a strong word meaning *to be active, work effectively*, or *operate powerfully*. Human energy alone could never accomplish the work of God or fulfill His will. So, if you ever feel like you aren't strong, smart, or skilled enough to do what God is calling you to—you're right! You *can't* do it—but *He* certainly *can* and *will*! Author and preacher F.B. Meyer affirms: "He who works in you to *will*, is prepared to work in you to *do*." [ii]

Isn't it thrilling to realize that you can please God? How? The Holy Spirit prompts you to *will to do*, and enables you *to do*, that which fulfills *God's will*. God is delighted when you completely yield to Him in obedience—allowing Him to do what you cannot do by yourself.

So, how can you live a God-life in a sinful world? God in you will strengthen you, and operate powerfully through you. As you read, you'll find this challenging question is further explored and answered with sound biblical principles.

The Holy Spirit in you prompts and enables you to do God's will.

Obedience to God

Attentiveness to the presence of the Holy Spirit will be expressed by obedience to God. Obedience is not an intellectual assent to a succession of academic propositions, but it is surrender to the One who asks for your trust.

Paul speaks of the "obedience of faith" (Romans 1:5). This obedience of faith is the very essence of God-life; it's the precise act of believing. Obedience of faith is not works, but the distinctive substance of faith. It is receiving and acknowledging Jesus Christ as Lord of your life. You are to take "every thought captive to the obedience of Christ" (2 Corinthians 10:5).

Consider the two essential components of obedience to God: Restraint and Commitment.

Obedience of Restraint
Restraint is what you *stop* doing or *resist* the temptation to do. The price of your God-birth was costly. Jesus "gave Himself for our sins, that He might deliver us from this present evil age" (Galatians 1:4,

NKJV). God doesn't want you to be weak in times of temptation when your deliverance cost His Son so dearly. Jesus came to rescue you and deliver you from sin.

The obedience of restraint or resistance requires wearing the full armor of God—truth, righteousness, the gospel, shield of faith, helmet of salvation, sword of the Spirit. Only then can you stand firm against the schemes of the devil (see Ephesians 6:11).

Bear in mind this is not just a defensive armor, but with the sword of the Spirit (Word of God), you are to be the aggressive victor. You are encouraged to actively resist the devil and his influences and be obedient to the Lord of your life. Resistance is not passive, but an active triumph over sin.

James clearly states: "submit [be obedient]... to God. Resist the devil and he will flee from you" (4:7). Submit, obey, subject yourself to the authority of God, wear the armor, and exercise restraint. This calls for a vigorous unyielding defense against all of the attacks that the devil may muster. Resist implies firmness—planting your spiritual feet—refusing any and all attacks of the evil one.

Obedience of restraint is all that's required to repulse Satan's assaults. While the attacks may be multiple, victory is assured, "he will flee from you." It is God's promise to you; the devil cannot win.

• **Are you exercising restraint in times of temptation?**

Obedience of Commitment

Commitment is what you *will to do*. How do you choose to live your life? Someone has said, "A belief which does not involve commitment is no belief at all." Commitment may well be the keystone to living a fulfilled and prosperous life. Look at this injunction in the Psalms, "commit your way [life and lifestyle] to the Lord" (37:5). Look again, "delight yourself in the Lord; and He will give you the desires of your heart" (37:4).

Commitment is not to an article of faith, it is the measure of your faith. Joe Namath once reasoned, "If you aren't going all the way, why go at all?" I find this remark regarding life resonating in Scripture. For instance, "every work... he did with all his heart and prospered" (2 Chronicles 31:21). Commitment to God is to be with all of your heart.

An insightful understanding of the obedience of commitment is revealed through Paul's instruction to Timothy. "Retain a commitment to the inspired words you have heard from me, let it be your standard, it is a treasure which has been entrusted to you" (2 Timothy 1:13-14, my translation). The doctrine or teachings Paul had received from the Lord oblige the obedience of commitment to preserve the truth. Guarding, defending, protecting the truth of God requires the empowerment of the Holy Spirit. Such a challenge is more than human strength can accomplish. The indwelling Holy Spirit enables you to maintain a commitment of your way to the Lord.

Your God-birth displays your commitment to good works. Godly or Christ-like deeds and achievements are commensurate with living God-life. Let me emphasize quickly, righteous or benevolent functions are not the basis or means of God-birth (see Ephesians 2:8-9). A desire and commitment to virtuous and godly deeds are a result of God-birth!

As we learn in Ephesians 2:10, "we are His workmanship, created in Christ Jesus for good works, which God prepared beforehand, that we should walk in them." God has a purpose for you—useful, meaningful things for you to accomplish. Are you obedient to committing your life to Him and allowing Him to work through you?

- **If sin brings destruction and Christ gives you a victorious new life, why is it sometimes still difficult to give up sinful behavior? Where is your commitment?**

Chapter Four

Wonder-Working Results of God-Birth

Many miraculous things happen following your God-birth. Of major importance, you are *cleansed*, *sealed*, and *sanctified*. In each experience, your Helper, the Holy Spirit, is your Intercessor, Advocate, and Counselor.

Intercessor, Advocate, Counselor

Cleansed

I am sure you have heard the old saying, "Cleanliness is next to godliness." Though some believe the saying has more ancient origins, others suppose it came from the writings of Sir Francis Bacon. He wrote, "Cleanness of body was ever deemed to proceed from a due reverence to God."

The Bible also relates godliness to cleanliness. "The Lord has rewarded me according to my righteousness; according to the cleanness of my hands He has recompensed me" (Psalm 18:20). The prophet Ezekiel discloses that the biblical concept of cleansing goes much farther than external hygiene.

"I will sprinkle clean water on you, and you will be clean; I will cleanse you from all your filthiness and from all your idols. Moreover, I will give you a new heart and put a new spirit within you; and I will remove the heart of stone from your flesh and give you a heart of flesh. And I will put My Spirit within you and cause you to walk in My statutes, and you will be careful to observe My ordinances" (Ezekiel 36:25-27).

Squeezing the Soap

When Karen, our youngest daughter, was a child she loved to play in the yard but she had an aversion to washing. "Come in now," her mother called one afternoon, "and wash-up for supper." Karen dutifully obeyed her mother and headed for the bathroom. However, when she returned to the kitchen and held up her hands for inspection, they were still grimy with streaks of dirt and water running down her arms. "You will need to wash them again," Karen was told. She held up her hands and said, "But, smell! I did wash them!" Karen had hurriedly squeezed the soap, wiped her hands on a towel, and called them clean.

God's cleansing is not merely outward—you're purified inwardly of all your wrongdoing. Be assured: "the blood of Jesus His Son cleanses us from all sin" (1 John 1:7). In Greek, *clean*, *cleanse*, and *cleanliness* all come from the same word *katharizō*; it means *free from blemish*, *clean*, or *pure*.

Through God-birth, you are washed and cleansed of every transgression. This is the first teaching of Jesus in the Gospel of John. It is an important message. "Unless one is born of water and the Spirit, he cannot enter into the kingdom of God" (John 3:5). The phrase "born of water" does not refer to baptism or the natural birth, but it symbolizes the Word of God as a cleansing agent.

Water is an agent in the physical cleansing process, and water (Word of God) is an integral agent in spiritual cleansing. God, the Holy Spirit, uses the Word of God in the God-birth experience. "You have been born again not of seed which is perishable but imperishable, that is, through the living and abiding word of God" (1 Peter 1:23).

Perhaps my favorite passage regarding cleansing is Ephesians 5:25-26: "Christ... loved the church and gave Himself for her, that He might sanctify and cleanse her with the washing of water by the Word" (NKJV).

- **Are you just "squeezing the soap" by going to church, paying your bills, being a good parent, etc.? Are you being cleansed through the Word of God in your life?**

David, the most prominent king of the Old Testament, was chosen by God to lead the people of Israel. God said: "I have found David the son of Jesse, a man after My heart, who will do all My will" (Acts 13:22). And though David was obedient to God in many ways, he went astray—even to the point of infidelity and murder (see 2 Samuel 11). He committed adultery with Bathsheba and rejected God's authority outright by having her husband, Uriah, killed.

How could such a man find hope of a fruitful life after he so willfully plotted to sin? How could he be made clean after such a moral breakdown?

The answer is found in his heart of confession and repentance. David viewed his actions as transgressions, which means he knew that he had more than crossed the line (see Psalm 51:1). His sins were a revolt against God; they were wicked, rebellious, and an abandonment of the One he served.

David cried out to God: "Wash me thoroughly from my iniquity, and cleanse me from my sin... Purify me with hyssop, and I shall be clean; wash me, and I shall be whiter than snow... Create in me a clean heart, O God, and renew a steadfast spirit within me" (Psalm 51:2,7,10).

David understood the importance of having his heart cleansed by God, because a pure heart is a prerequisite for being in God's presence. "Let us draw near to God with a sincere heart in full assurance of faith, having our hearts sprinkled to cleanse us from a guilty conscience and having our bodies *washed with pure water*" (Hebrews 10:22, NIV, emphasis mine).

No doubt, the reason God used David to write at least 75 of the Psalms was because David recognized his sin and asked God to cleanse him and give him a pure heart, a *God-heart*. David knew the Scripture imperative, "you shall be holy, for I the Lord your God am holy" (Leviticus 19:2).

- **When you lose sight of God, you lose fear of sin and its destructive consequences. Being close to God does just the opposite—it increases your sensitivity to sin and frees you of its bondage. What do you need God to cleanse you of?**

Sealed

It was a typical early morning flight and boarding routine with a hundred or so other passengers—mostly business travelers. We found our seats, stowed briefcases and other baggage in overhead compartments, and settled in. As we taxied down the runway, my thoughts on the day ahead were briefly interrupted by the flight attendant reciting safety and emergency procedures. That's when the routine departure ended.

Abruptly, the plane veered off the runway and came to a grinding stop. You can imagine what that startling jolt did to the atmosphere in the cabin. Once relaxed, drowsy passengers were instantly energized, anxiously looking around to see what had happened.

A voice from the flight deck announced, "An exit door is not *sealed*, the cabin can't be pressurized." In other words, it was too dangerous to take off. A nonpressurized cabin would mean a lack of oxygen and after a certain altitude, the crew could become disoriented and pass out. With no one at the controls, the plane would tragically crash—much like what occurred to the Cypriot airliner in 2005. Dangerous, indeed! When God seals you, it's much more than sealing the door on an aircraft.

The eternal security and assurance of your God-birth is dramatically guaranteed by these resolute words in 2 Corinthians 1:21-22: "He [God] who *establishes* us with you in Christ and *anointed* us is God, who also *sealed* us and gave us the Spirit in our hearts as a pledge" (emphasis mine).

Look again at the three-fold assurance in 2 Corinthians in three critical words: Establish, Anointed, and Sealed.

Establish: "He [God] who establishes us... in Christ."
Establish (bebaioō) is also translated *confirm*. When you are born again, you are established in Christ and confirmed through His shed blood. Your eternal God-birth has been certified and validated in Jesus Christ.

Anointed: "anointed us is God."
Anointed (chriō) means a *sacred separating* or *consecrating*. Through God-birth, God declares you righteous or sacred. He separated you to Himself and gave you eternal life.

Sealed: "sealed us and gave us the Spirit in our hearts as a
pledge."
Seal (sphragizō) is a guarantee of *ownership* and *security*. The seal is the Holy Spirit Himself. This passage could be translated, "He who sealed us for Himself." God the Holy Spirit's presence in you is a seal of authenticity and permanency—guaranteeing your eternal God-birth.

~~~~~~
"Having also believed, you were sealed in Him
with the Holy Spirit of promise,
who is given as a pledge of our inheritance."
(Ephesians 1:13-14)
~~~~~~

Sealing isn't something the Holy Spirit *does*; rather, the Holy Spirit Himself *is* God's seal, or pledge that guarantees your God-born eternal nature. The word translated *pledge* in Ephesians 1:14 is an economic term meaning a *deposit* or *earnest*—that portion of a purchase price that a buyer would give in advance as security for the balance. It's a good-faith promise guaranteeing that the payment will be made in full. God the Holy Spirit is the permanent, irrevocable "deposit" ensuring your eternal God-birth.

The first installment of your birthright—the presence of the Holy Spirit—certifies that you will receive your full inheritance. Rejoice with me, our God-birth is secure and eternal!

Branded and Marked

For years, my wife Eleanor's shop, The Way We Were Antiques, has sold authentically replicated eighteenth-century American Windsor chairs and furniture. The New England maker is an undisputed master of his craft. There are other makers of Windsor chairs, but this craftsman analyzes period pieces, makes exact blueprints, and replicates with meticulous detail far surpassing competitors.

To authenticate, his name is branded under the seat of every chair or on the back of every piece of furniture that he makes. Branded and marked—an undisputed pledge of authenticity. Similarly, the seal of the Holy Spirit authenticates creations of God—the born-again believer who has had God-birth.

You are sealed and given a pledge in the person of the Holy Spirit—a foretaste of your inheritance, your final redemption. John Stott writes that *sealing* and *redemption* are the beginning and ending of the salvation experience.[iii] In between these two fundamental maxims, you are to live a God-life—growing in Christ's likeness and obeying God's will for your life.

Sanctified

In addition to being cleansed and sealed, the third crucial thing that happens when you receive Christ as Lord and Savior is *sanctification*. The word translated *sanctify* (*hagiazō*) in the New Testament means *to make holy* or *set apart*. In 1 Peter 1:15, you're admonished, "Like the Holy One who called you, be holy yourselves also in all your behavior." Holiness is God's intent and will for every

Christian. He wants you to reflect His righteousness, and you do so by being set apart—by being sanctified.

Sanctification is both an event and a process. It's an *event* when you have God-birth: "The God of peace Himself sanctify you entirely" (1 Thessalonians 5:23). The righteousness of Christ is *immediately* conferred upon you through the forgiveness of your sin—you are sanctified.

Also, sanctification is a *continuous* process by which you are perfected. As 2 Peter 3:18 commands, "grow in the grace and knowledge of our Lord and Savior Jesus Christ." Spiritual growth means developing an awareness of God's activity through a daily intake of spiritual nourishment and Christ-like exercise. Through the process of sanctification, your behavior increasingly reflects Christ—you live a God-life. And it comes with a promise, "He who began a good work in you will perfect it until the day of Christ Jesus" (Philippians 1:6). One way to understand sanctification is to recognize it is possessive (established), progressive (becoming), and perfected (completed).

Let's reflect a moment. Your God-birth cleansed, sealed, and sanctified you. Your wonder-working God-birth enabled you to enter into a relationship with the eternal God of heaven. God-birth is the beginning of your exciting adventure to God-life.

- **What are some areas in your life that the Holy Spirit is sanctifying?**

—Chapter Five—

Becoming Like Him

John, a young ministerial student was home on holiday from seminary, and his father, a pastor, asked him to preach one Sunday. The congregation appreciated the sermon, but their comments were more about the young man than about what they'd heard. One said, "He resembles his father." Another responded, "he pronounces some of his words like his dad." Yet another joined in, "I could close my eyes and think I was hearing his father."

Following God-birth, an undeniable family resemblance grows stronger and more evident as you mature. Earlier in this section, we discussed your spiritual DNA. The New Testament says you should demonstrate *godliness*—the state or quality of being godly. "Lead a quiet and peaceable life in all godliness" (1 Timothy 2:2, NKJV). This means you're to devote yourself to conforming to the will of God in order to be more like Him.

Living God-life means exhibiting the qualities of God. How can that be? Read what Paul wrote to Timothy. "Pursue righteousness, godliness, faith, love, perseverance and gentleness" (1 Timothy 6:11). These God-life qualities were displayed in Jesus' behavior throughout His life.

As a Christian, you aren't subject to a vague or speculative philosophy for mirroring your conduct. Rather, as Paul asserts, you live by "the knowledge of the truth which is according to godliness" (Titus 1:1). When you're in Christ and accept the Word of God as truth, you have *His* roadmap to living a godly, mature spiritual life in thought and action. You "grow up" to resemble your heavenly Father, and manifest God-life.

~~~~~~~~~~~~~~~~~~~~~~~~~~~~~~~~

The Bible is a roadmap to holiness.

~~~~~~~~~~~~~~~~~~~~~~~~~~~~~~~~

- **Do you resemble your Heavenly Father? Can others see Christ in you or hear Him speak through you?**

~~~~~~

"Breathe on me, breathe on me,
Holy Spirit, breathe on me:
Take Thou my heart, cleanse every part,
Holy Spirit, breathe on me...
Holy Spirit breathe on me,
Till I am all Thine own,
Until my will is lost in Thine.
To live for Thee alone."
By Edwin Hatch

~~~~~~

A Work in Progress

Driving to work in downtown Atlanta, I noticed heavy equipment moving mounds of dirt and digging a cavernous hole in the ground. A huge, newly painted sign attracted my attention. It read: WORK IN PROGRESS, YOUR COOPERATION APPRECIATED.

Week after week, for over a year, I drove by the project—steel framework was erected, concrete blocks and bricks, then windows and doors were set in place, the parking area was designed and landscaping was planted. One day, finally, a new sign: WORK COMPLETED, THANK YOU!

Many times when I've looked out across a congregation, I've felt that a sign should be posted: WORK IN PROGRESS, YOUR

COOPERATION APPRECIATED. How true it is! We are indeed in the midst of being perfected by the ongoing maturing process of the Holy Spirit.

The believers at Ephesus (like all believers) were "a work in progress." Paul entrusted them "to God and... the word of His grace, which is able to build you up" (Acts 20:32). You are "God's building" (1 Corinthians 3:9); now, how is your building developing? Are you becoming more like Him? Are you a work in progress, becoming a mighty building—yet not you, but *Christ in you*?

God's probing question was and still is: "What kind of house can you build for me (Isaiah 66:1, my translation)? Look at that verse and answer this question: *What kind of house am I building*? Your God-birth gives you an incredible opportunity to become more like Jesus.

Do you ever ponder: *What progress am I making*? Remember the large downtown building? It took time, commitment, and lots of cooperation. Slowly, week-by-week, workers carefully followed the architect's plans, and the building was finally completed. It became what the architect had envisioned from the beginning—the dream for what it could be, even before any work had begun.

The Bible assures that God chose you in Christ "before the foundation of the world." So you come full circle—God, the eternal Architect, dreamed about you before time began. He laid out the plan by which Christ would replace your death-bound life with God's eternal life through the God-birth.

He even sent the Holy Spirit as your Project Manager and His Holy Word as the blueprint to help you develop and mature. It is slow work. It is an ongoing work requiring time, commitment, and cooperation. Through it all, He continues to guide you as a "work in progress" so you can become more and more like Him—what God the Architect envisioned for you from the beginning of the world.

In Galatians 4:19, Paul wrote: "I am again in labor until Christ is formed in you." God-life—Christ living in and through you—is what God envisioned for you, a soul fit for eternity. He'll carry on His supernatural, life-changing activity in you until you see Him face to face and are able to say, "Work completed, my Lord. Thank You!" And He will respond, "Well done!"

God-birth is your starting point to living God-life. God-life is a lifetime journey, not a one-time event or casual activity. It is step-by-step, day-by-day. The following sections explore biblical teachings for your quest of living *not me, but Christ in me.*

- **Close your eyes and quickly review your life this past week, has there been an undeniable family resemblance?**

SECTION TWO

GOD-FAITH

"Faith is the substance of things hoped for,
the evidence of things not seen."
(Hebrews 11:1, KJV)

English philosopher John Locke once said, "Faith is the assent to any proposition, on the credit of the proposer." I begin with his words because he offers an interesting and instructive definition of faith. If you apply this self-evident truism to your relationship with God, faith is an unalterable confidence in the Word of God, because of the character of its Author, the Holy Spirit. Faith is your response to this revelation from the Lord God. In other words, true *God-faith* is a plus-nothing, minus-nothing kind of committed confidence you have in God, and you embrace His word with conviction and certainty because you unquestionably trust Him. God is faith-worthy.

Faith is wonderfully demonstrated in the Bible. Abraham is a classic example of faith—a seeing, persevering faith. "By faith Abraham, when he was called, obeyed by going out to a place... he went out, not knowing where he was going" (Hebrews 11:8). The disciples of Jesus, by faith, responded to the call "follow me." Jesus commended the centurion's faith in His person and word. When the Ethiopian eunuch heard the Word of God, by faith he said, "I believe that Jesus Christ is the Son of God" (Acts 8:37 NKJV). Peter passionately affirms "we did not follow cleverly devised tales when we made known to you the power and coming of our Lord Jesus Christ, but we were eyewitnesses of His Majesty" (2 Peter 1:16). They witnessed God's word proven true and declared Jesus to be faith-worthy.

Theologian Alan Richardson defined faith as confident reliance on God by which each of us, "Lays hold on God's proffered resources, becomes obedient to what God prescribes, and, abandoning all self-interest and self-reliance, trusts God completely."[i]

For some, this may seem too simple. Critics of Christianity conclude that faith is an inferior substitute to a reasoned knowledge. Their flawed interpretation of faith is, "I have never seen it, nor do I understand it, so I'll just have to believe it" attitude.

However, it's wrong to define faith merely as believing what cannot be proven. God doesn't want you to surrender to Him out of utter confusion, resignation, or ignorance. The dismal doctrine of fatalism denies the dynamic nature of biblical faith. "What will be, will be; I can't do anything about it" is not the life-giving, empowering message of God. Faith in "the Everlasting God [ELOHIM], the LORD, the Creator of the ends of the earth" (Isaiah 40:28) fills your heart and life with imperishable hope and unimagined potential.

The Bible consistently dismisses the idea that circumstances limit the outcome of events, and that it is impossible to change a situation or condition. Abraham is an excellent example of this biblical verity. He had faith that God could overcome any obstacle. Abraham had faith (assurance of things hoped for) in God's promise of a son. He had faith (evidence of things not seen) even with no indication that the promise was to happen. And, God was true to His word; it happened, a son was born. In Romans 4:19-21, Paul reflects upon Abraham's victorious faith.

> "Without becoming weak in faith he contemplated his own body, now as good as dead since he was about a hundred years old, and the deadness of Sarah's womb; yet, with respect to the promise of God, he did not waver in unbelief, but grew strong in faith, giving glory to God, and being fully assured that what He had promised, He was able also to perform."

Abraham knew that at age 90, Sarah was well past childbearing age yet, amazingly and faithfully, that didn't prevent him from believing God. To his credit, Abraham fought the lure of fatalism by realizing that God is greater than any natural reality.

In the following pages, let's look at a biblically based understanding of faith, God-faith. Faith is to be your spiritually maturing way of life. "God's righteousness [God-life] is revealed from faith to faith, just as it is written: 'The righteous will live by faith'" (Romans 1:17, HCSB). Your life in Christ has two components, God, and you. God's is "grace upon grace" (John 1:16); and yours is "from faith to [unto] faith" (Romans 1:17). I encourage you to take your Bible and carefully explore the life-altering challenge of God-faith. The next chapters will guide you in maturing your God-faith.

—Chapter One—

Temporal Realities vs. Faith Realities

You observe a breathtaking landscape and admire the towering trees and lush meadows, but its beauty can be quickly diminished through mudslides, fires, or storms. You touch a piece of period furniture and admire the patina on its surface and classic design, but woodworm can damage it. You hear moving and inspiring music, the laughter of happy children, the wind rustling through leaves, but a loss of hearing can bring silence. You breathe the fresh aroma of newly mown hay, but rain can quickly produce a sour, rotting smell. All are temporal realities, and all are insecure and transitory.

It's natural to respond to your temporal surroundings and interact with the world through your five senses: seeing, touching, hearing, tasting, and smelling. But you've also witnessed how quickly your perceptions of reality can change. The idyllic landscape of Mount St. Helens was altered by a volcanic eruption. The towering New York skyline was set ablaze and marred forever by terrorism. The beautiful Thai beach was rendered chaos by a tsunami.

It all has to do with the temporal nature of the world you live in—*temporal* defined as, "relating to time... or relating to earthly life." It also means, "relating to secular concerns" and has the same root as *temporary,* conveying the idea of transience or short-lived.[ii]

The problem comes when building your life on what is temporal—what you can see, touch, hear, taste, or smell. This describes the lifestyle for the vast majority of humanity. Consider the limited nature of your senses because, as Paul reminds us "the form |manner of life| of this world is passing away" (1 Corinthians 7:31). If you govern your life by social and physical circumstances, you'll always have an ever-changing environment. This variable and transitory surrounding will shape your life, and you'll labor with the unsettledness of a temporal life.

By contrast, God-faith is based upon the unchanging certainty of an eternal God and His inspired, infallible word. Reality is defined as "something that is neither derivative nor dependent but exists necessarily." [iii] This is absolutely true of the Lord God found in Scripture—the Great I AM. He is all-knowing, all-powerful, ever-present, and He is not dependent upon anyone or anything—He is the self-existent, eternal Almighty God. As you recall, this foundational truth was discussed in section one.

God-faith is based upon the unchanging certainty of God.

I was told about a pastor who along with a few church members surveyed their church building and property after a natural disaster had caused tremendous destruction and upheaval in their town. What they saw was shocking and disheartening, the building was gone, and what little remained was flooded. In silence, they looked—then one of the men lamented, "It's gone, all is lost!"

The pastor responded, "What's gone, what's lost?" Looking heavenward, he continued, "God is God, He's on His throne. I'm excited to see what He's going to do."

And God did some unanticipated things. Unsolicited, caring individuals and churches sent financial support, donated a pastor's library, and nearby churches offered their facilities to the homeless congregation. The pastor found that his congregation relocated primarily in two towns that were miles apart. He began pastoring both groups on alternate weeks—the two congregations together have a larger attendance (and growing) than the one before the storm. Indeed, it is exciting to see what the pastor's God-faith realized!

In Hebrews 11:1, a God-faith is "perceiving as real fact what is not revealed to the senses" (AMP). God-faith is described as the substance and the assurance of promises confidently hoped for. It also is the evidence and reliability of things you don't see, with the conviction of their existence based on the faithfulness of God to reward you when you seek Him. Repeatedly, the Bible encourages you to launch out in God-faith and have an assured victory through obedience to God.

~~~~~~

God-faith perceives as fact what is not yet revealed.

~~~~~~

Romans 10:17 affirms, "faith comes by hearing, and hearing by the Word of Christ." Be assured that the realities of faith, as we learn through the Word of God, are profoundly reliable. They are not at all like the tangible things of our natural environment.

Three Essential Truths

Consider three truths of God's Word foundational to God-faith: Almighty God, Jesus Christ, and Eternal Salvation.

Almighty God, The "I Am"

To begin, in order to have God-faith, you must first believe in God. Hebrews 11:6 instructs "whoever would come near to God must (necessarily) believe that God exists" (AMP). This is not on your terms or by the invention of your imagination. Rather, you embrace Him in the way He has chosen to make Himself known.

Paul praised Almighty God as "the King eternal, immortal, invisible, the only God" (1 Timothy 1:17). As we've discussed, He is everlasting and He never changes. Moses, who had seen a multitude of false deities in Egypt, could testify that the God of Israel was genuine. He lifted up his voice with confidence when he proclaimed: "There is none like the God of [Israel], Who rides the heavens to your help, and through the skies in His majesty. The eternal God is a dwelling place, and underneath are the everlasting arms" (Deuteronomy 33:26-27).

God isn't reinvented with each generation; nor can He be fashioned or altered by mankind's hypothesis or opinion. Rather, He's the Creator who reveals Himself to you. Acts 17:25 testifies: "Nor is He worshiped with men's hands, as though He needed anything, since He gives to all life, breath, and all things" (NKJV). Almighty God is the enduring certainty from which all other realities proceed.

Jesus Christ

This brings us to the second anchor, or essential truth of God-faith, Jesus Christ. "In the beginning was the Word, and the Word was with God, and the Word was God" (John 1:1). The Word, Jesus (God incarnate), makes forgiveness of sins possible for a repentant person of faith. Remember, Jesus is not man made God, but God made man.

God chose to reveal Himself through the person of Christ. Jesus taught the disciples in John 14:7, 9: "If you had known Me, you would have known My Father also; from now on you know Him, and have seen Him... He who has seen Me has seen the Father." To have God-faith, you must believe that God exists and accept Jesus as God's way of showing Himself to us. Declare as Simon Peter did, "Thou art the Christ, the Son of the living God" (Matthew 16:16).

Acceptance of the deity of Christ, and Jesus Christ being the exclusive way to heaven is an obstacle for many, even millions of people. Since the days of Jesus, there have been those who questioned the veracity of the gospel—especially Jesus' teaching, "no one comes to the Father, but through Me" (John 14:6). Many prefer to follow martial artist Morihei Ueshiba's idea that, "There are many paths leading to the top of Mount Fuji." In other words, many are okay with believing in God, but prefer to rely on their own idea how to find God.

Doubters often ask for tangible proof that Christ is truly the Son of God. They want something they can see or observe. This isn't so far-fetched considering that even Thomas, the doubting apostle, expressed skepticism regarding the resurrection of Jesus. He wanted to touch and inspect before trusting. He said, "unless I shall see in His hands the imprint of the nails, and put my finger into the place of the nails, and put my hand into His side, I will not believe" (John 20:25). Once in the presence of the resurrected Christ, Thomas bore witness and his unbelief vanished. He affirmed the Savior saying, "My Lord and my God!" (John 20:28).

Thomas' human senses were needed to confirm, to his satisfaction, the reality of the resurrected Christ. He had to see the nail prints in His hands. Today, it is not possible to see, touch, or hear Christ, so it is by faith you believe and accept the resurrected Savior. Jesus had you in mind when He said: "Blessed are they who did not see, and yet believed" (John 20:29). The immutability of the Holy Spirit's inspired Word is the established truth of God, and the authentic good news of the way to eternal life. Faith in the crucified, risen Christ is the reality of your hope of heaven.

Eternal Salvation

A third truth of God-faith is the promise of your eternal life. Once you believe that God exists and He has revealed Himself through Jesus, the Christ, you can embrace the mission for which Christ came: "the Son of Man has come to seek and to save that which was lost" (Luke 19:10). It's only by responding in faith to the gospel that you can be saved from your sin and receive eternal life. It can't be earned, only accepted. Ephesians 2:8 asserts "by grace you have been saved through faith; and that not of yourselves, it is the gift of God."

This can also be a difficult aspect of God-faith, because many want to earn their salvation, or corroborate their salvation with works. Such schemes and efforts fail and will not result in eternal salvation. Your faith in the Savior, Jesus Christ, is the only evidence God accepts. Through the shed blood of His Son, God declares you forgiven; "having been justified by faith, we [you] have peace with God through our Lord Jesus Christ" (Romans 5:1).

Janet's Discovery

This reminds me of a time when a deacon and I made a house call to witness to Janet, a young divorcee. After presenting the gospel, I asked her if she'd like to pray to receive Christ as her Savior. With a downcast face and sorrowful eyes, she responded that the deacon and I didn't realize how messed up her life was. Because of her indiscretions and immoral life, she felt unworthy to ask anything of a holy God.

I asked the deacon, who had once lived a tough life, to pray. We bowed our heads, and as he poured out his heart and tearfully offered sincere thanks for the forgiveness of his sins, she began to sob. Soon, she was crying out to God, understanding that He would forgive her transgressions as well. Weeping her way to God, her faith in Him and in His Word became stronger. There were no dry eyes as she prayed with thanksgiving for the forgiveness of her sins.

Before we left, she was laughing and praising God; completely transformed by His grace and provision. She had the new birth through faith. Though intangible—she couldn't touch or see it—she had overwhelming evidence of God's forgiveness. She had a tranquility that surpassed understanding. As Jesus said to the woman who touched the fringe of His garment: "daughter, your faith has made you well; go in peace" (Luke 8:48).

- **We've been learning about the stark difference between sensory realities and faith realities. One is passing (temporal) and the other is eternal. Where are you? Where is your faith more comfortable?**

Read on; are you a water-walker?

Chapter Two

Water-Walkers

While attending college in Tennessee, I pastored a small, rural church. That ministry was a blessing in so many ways, not the least of which was fellowship with other pastors. In a nearby town, a godly and gifted pastor had significant influence on my life.

One warm summer evening I attended a revival service in his church. A well-known guest evangelist and gospel singer had attracted a standing room only crowd. Faces in the crowd included many from other community churches and denominations, and even townspeople who didn't often attend church. The singing was loud and enthusiastic, the musicians talented, and the sermon inspiring— it was a moving evangelistic service. For the altar call, the guest evangelist made an impassioned appeal to accept Jesus as Savior and many, of all ages, came forward. Some were weeping, others smiling, and many for prayer or counsel.

Etched in my memory is when the pastor of the church came to the pulpit asking everyone to bow their heads. And in that still, quiet, packed sanctuary, his booming voice reverberated: *With faith, you can be a water-walker*! His appealing invitation was for us to have the faith of a *water-walker*. Walk by faith, not by sight!

He continued, "This church and this town need you, yes you, to accept this challenge! Get out of your boat, step out into the aisle, and take the challenge." He further encouraged, "Do for God what only water-walking faith can do; don't look at the water, *look to Jesus.* Come to the altar, get on your knees, and commit your self today to be a water-walker. That's the word of Jesus, Come now!"

He was asking us to attempt *what a God-faith alone could accomplish.* God had given him a clear vision of the potential ministry for that church. The pastor was calling for water-walkers to join him in claiming *what could not be seen.* He envisioned a tabernacle seating two thousand people, a camp for physically disabled children, a regional center for Bible study, hundreds coming to know Christ, and on and on. This visionary pastor would lead the church to accomplish beyond what logic or reason would say is possible. But with God, and water-walkers from that congregation, these and many other outstanding accomplishments were completed. Water-walker faith is the only explanation of God's bountiful blessings on their witness and ministry.

~~~~~~

Water-walker faith defies temporal logic and physical reality.

~~~~~~

"Come! Be a Water-Walker!"

In the New Testament, you discover that Peter was a *water-walker.* Matthew 14 tells how the disciples spent a tiring day with Jesus as He ministered to a huge crowd—teaching, healing, and feeding five thousand men and their families. As the day ended, Jesus sent the disciples on ahead in a boat while He lingered with the crowds. That night a raging storm erupted tossing the humble fishing vessel about on the dark and foreboding waters. The tempestuous sea battered and pounded the boat with each crushing wave. There in the dead of night, the disciples feared for their lives.

Then, just before dawn, still in the midst of the storm, the exhausted disciples were startled by a figure moving across the water. In great fear, they thought it was a ghost. Knowing they were too emotionally distressed and fatigued to understand what they were seeing, Jesus called out to them: "Take courage, it is I; do not be afraid."

Though the storm still raged, the wind still howled, and the waves still billowed; Peter cried out, "Lord, if it is You, command me to come to You on the water" (verse 28). At the word "Come," obeying the command of Jesus, "Peter got out of the boat and walked on the water, and he came to Jesus" (verse 29, AMP). With logic-defying faith, he went to his Savior. Peter was a *water-walker*.

Peter was not a water-walker because he walked on water, but rather, his faith defied the obvious, temporal reality, and logic of the instability of the water that surrounded him. To accurately report what happened that night, Peter actually walked on the substance of faith, not the sea. He walked on God-faith by believing "with men this is impossible, but with God all things are possible" (Matthew 19:26). Peter, the water-walker, was a *faith-walker*.

What of the other disciples? They were believers, they had faith, and they'd all made a decision to follow Jesus. They left their families, businesses, and civic positions to follow Christ. They trusted in Jesus as the Messiah, and demonstrated their faith by service and sacrifice. But, they weren't water-walkers. They had faith, *but not a God-faith*—not yet, not at this point of their pilgrimage.

Sustaining Faith and Sinking Fears

Let's return to Peter for a final observation. Peter's strong God-faith enabled him to be a water-walker. His faith reflected the concept in 1 Corinthians 2:5: "Your faith should not be in the wisdom of men but in the power of God" (NKJV). Sound familiar? Peter, the water-walker, rejected human temporal assessments knowing that God's reality was far more important. Only when he took his eyes off Jesus, and looked at the water, did he begin to sink.

You embrace God's power when regardless of the storms in life you obey His command: "Take courage, it is I; do not be afraid... Come!" (Matthew 14:27, 29). The actual Greek language emphatically says, take courage *I am* (*ego eimi*). The faith at the heart of Peter's request was: You are the Christ, the Son of the living God; empower me to walk on water as you do. In other words, Peter was exercising God-faith. The power of God is on display when you truly believe that HE IS—that HE exists—and that no tempest could possibly affect His will.

Seeing the Lord, Peter had an overwhelming desire to live a God-life and do exactly what Jesus was doing. So he stepped out of the boat in a marvelous display of faith. Yet, when he saw the elements around him and reasoned with human understanding, doubt entered his mind. Logic reminded him the substance beneath him was merely water, and he began to sink. Jesus quickly identified his real problem, "you of little faith, why did you doubt?" (Matthew 14:31).

> Have you ever felt yourself sinking in despair, crying out, "It's too much; I don't have the strength, I'm afraid"? Jesus says, *Come, walk with Me.*

I suspect that both you and I have been there. After a long and exhausting time of work or service, you are tossed about by some unnerving disturbance and you end up facing the challenge with fear or anxiety. Though you want to believe that God will provide for your needs, you allow temporal surroundings to shape how you react. It's then you begin to sink in the turbulent sea of your own doubts and problems.

However, if you're to be a water-walker, you must have a strong faith that assures you of the things you hope for and take God's Word as the evidence of His promises you don't yet see coming to fruition (see Hebrews 11:1). Stand amidst the tempest, fix your eyes on Jesus, and resolve never to doubt God—He will sustain you no matter how big the waves, or how threatening the storm.

- **Churches are filled with people of faith, but not many water-walkers. Are you a water-walker? Why not?**

—Chapter Three—

From Faith to Faith

"The righteousness of God is revealed from faith to faith."
(Romans 1:17)

The university graduating class, in their caps and gowns were warm on that summer day and anxious for the commencement speaker to finish. Four years of classes completed, they were ready to walk across the stage and get their prized diploma. Soon they would be on their way. Penetrating their thoughts of freedom, adulthood, career, etc., the speaker said: "You have completed a course of study, at best you have learned how to study, and where to find information. However, your education has just begun, this is commencement day; your life will now go from one learning to another learning."

Likewise, the day of your God-birth was your commencement day in Christ! The righteousness of God was conferred upon you. When you accepted Christ as your Savior, it became possible for you to be "the righteousness of God in him" (2 Corinthians 5:21, NKJV). God judicially declared you righteous.

We learned earlier in this section that God-faith has two components; God, and you. God is grace upon grace, and you go from faith to faith in your pilgrimage.

Righteousness, originating in faith, leads to increased faith. Your life in Christ is to be from faith to faith. "The righteousness of God is revealed from faith to faith; as it is written, 'the just shall live by faith'" (Romans 1:17 NKJV).

The phrase, *from faith to faith* tells me that there's an exciting adventure waiting when living a life of faith. Faith is *not only* an initial act of trust, *but also* an ongoing growth and development in the grace of God. Faith is active, it develops and matures. God-faith is ever-increasing, growing, and expanding—it is a new way of life. The Word of God challenges you to grow in your faith, from faith to faith.

~~~~~~~~~~~~~~~~~~~~~~~~~~~~~~~

God-faith is a new way of life.

~~~~~~~~~~~~~~~~~~~~~~~~~~~~~~~

The Increasing of Faith

Faith is not something you have once in a lifetime, and then forget about. Faith is a way of life for a believer. It should be active, progressive, and maturing in your day-to-day life. Let me illustrate this life-centered truth with the biblical view of salvation. Salvation in Christ is inclusive of three tenses (time of action) in the redemptive activities of God in you becoming all He is forming you to be.

From "faith to faith" can be enlightened by the three tenses of biblical salvation:
Past, Present, and Future.

Your salvation is in the past tense.
You have been saved. "By grace you have been saved *through faith* (Ephesians 2:8, emphasis mine). By faith in the crucified Christ, you have been freed from the guilt and penalty of sin. Being born again, (God-birth) is a once-for-all divinely judicial transaction that declared you righteous—justified. You have been "justified by faith" (Romans 5:1). Your justification was your acquittal from sin's guilt by God the righteous judge.

Your salvation is also in the present tense.

Think of faith as a verb; *faithing*, something you currently do. Your daily life as a Christian is to be a present tense of faith to faith, or faithing. Paul says, "work out your salvation with fear and trembling; for it is God who is at work in you, both to will and to work for His good pleasure" (Philippians 2:12-13).

Through the ongoing redemptive work of faith, you are being freed from the practice and power of forgiven sin. You are being delivered, or saved from dominance and habits of sin. Your present tense salvation is a testimony, "The word of the cross is to those who are perishing foolishness, but to us who are being saved it is the power of God" (1 Corinthians 1:18). This is sanctification—the continuous process of judging and eliminating sin, gradually conforming to the image of Christ. You are "constantly being transformed into [His very own] image in ever increasing splendor and from one degree of glory to another" (2 Corinthians 3:18, AMP).

From glory to glory, from faithing to faithing, you are being delivered (saved). Paul's prayer was that "God may count you worthy of your calling, and fulfill every desire for goodness and the work of faith with power" (2 Thessalonians 1:11).

Your salvation is also in the future tense.

You will be saved from the very presence of sin "for salvation [final deliverance] is nearer to us now than when we first believed" (Romans 13:11, AMP). All of the Christian life is from faith to faith. Remember, in the past, by faith you have been justified and your eternal salvation is not threatened. In fact, the Word of God assures that you are "protected by the power of God through faith for a salvation ready to be revealed in the last time" (1 Peter 1:5). God with awesome power protects and guards your faith-based salvation with unchallenged security.

In the Second Advent of Christ (*parousia*), "Christ... shall appear a second time for salvation without reference to sin, to those who eagerly await Him" (Hebrews 9:28).

- **Is faith something you have or something you do? Is it a subject or a verb in your life?**

The Measure of Faith

The heart-wrenching scene on the evening news showed the unimaginable devastation caused by a massive earthquake in China. Homeless and destitute, hungry people lined up for a portion of rice. They came with containers of every sort and every size. Large cups to small buckets, each to be filled with rice. The size of the container determined the amount of rice they received.

The same is true in your life. Jesus said, "according to your faith be it unto you" (Matthew 9:29, KJV). What is the measure of your faith? The measure of your faith, your expectant trust, determines the measure of your blessings.

Think about it; the container always determines the volume it can receive. It's impossible to receive spiritual blessings when you are not spiritually susceptible. When you come to God, you present yourself to Him in a measure of faith, and anticipate, by faith, Him filling you with His power, wisdom, and provision. As the disciples of old, you need to pray, "Lord, increase my faith."

We are in fact dependant upon God for our faith. It's His divine gift to us—the capacity He's given us to believe in Him. The question is: *what measure of faith do you have?*

Romans 12:3 instructs, "do not think of yourself with exalted thoughts, but rather think of yourself with mature judgment, in keeping with the appropriation of faith God has given you" (my translation).

Instead of comparing yourself to others, hold yourself up to His standard. Faith doesn't merely believe in God—it's also being receptive to what He gives you and using it wisely. You will be filled up to the measure of your capacity and submissiveness.

You began your adventure with God by a personal act of faith (God-birth), and a confidence in Him that must mature and increase. The more *faithing* you do, and the more you engage in the adventure God has for you, the more you will grow in His likeness. Remember, in order to receive what God has for you, you must have that measure of faith.

- **When you go to God in faith, do you take a cup, or a bucket?**

Weak in Faith

In Mark 9, there's a moving account of a desperately concerned father whose son was possessed by a demonic spirit. He brought the convulsing boy to the disciples, but they couldn't do anything for him. I'm sure this perplexed the disciples, because just days before they had succeeded in exorcising demons (see Mark 6:13). Yet, they failed to grant this man's request. It wasn't that the disciples lacked faith altogether, it was because their faithing was weak.

Jesus healed the boy, and said to the father: "All things are possible to him who believes" (Mark 9:23). When Jesus assured the man that nothing is impossible to those who have God-faith, "The father of the boy gave [an eager, piercing, inarticulate] cry with tears, and he said, Lord, I believe! Constantly help my weakness of faith!" (Mark 9:24, AMP).

The father faltered in his walk because of inadequate faith, his propensity toward doubt. He believed enough to go to Jesus, but his confidence in God was not sufficient for his son to be healed, his faith had not fully matured.

How many Christians today resemble this man's weak, faltering faith? You see them every day — perhaps even in the mirror — genuine believers who have experienced Christ's saving grace, yet still have a fragile, insecure trust in their Lord in crucial issues and faith's challenges. Don't criticize or belittle them. Rather, you're admonished to "accept the one who is weak in faith" (Romans 14:1). The word *weak* in original Greek is a participle, and is better translated *being weak*. This verse speaks of believers who are being weak and waver or become vulnerable when tested or challenged.

Everyone has times of stress and challenges when their faith is not all they wish it could be. It is a testing time; a crisis for defeat or an opportunity to exercise mature faithing. Call out to God, claim His promise, and by faith, victoriously meet your present need.

- **Is your faith impaired or vulnerable when you face life's challenges?**

Growing in Faith

The reality is that you don't begin your relationship with Christ with a world-changing, water-walking faith. However, your trust in God will be built up and strengthened as you grow spiritually.

The Bible refers to those who are new Christians and undeveloped in their faith as babes (infants) (see 1 Corinthians 3:1). This is an excellent way to think of your spiritual walk because it signals that you're expected to mature. Just as a child eventually becomes an adult, you should not remain a baby in your faith.

Synergistic Faith

When Paul addressed believers in the Corinthian church who were experiencing life as newborn Christians, he said, "we have the hope that as your faith increases, our area [of ministry] will be greatly enlarged, so that we may preach the gospel to the regions beyond you" (2 Corinthians 10:15-16, HCSB).

Paul revealed two astounding revelations. Expansion of the church's ministry was dependent on the Corinthian's developing and growing faith. And, proclamation of the gospel in unreached areas beyond Corinth, was contingent on the spiritual strength of believers. These are important principles.

- **Have you paused to consider that your faith growth (faithing) impacts you, your church, and the world around you?**

Transforming trust in God is not only possible, but it can grow in faithing in ways beyond your imagination. Paul wrote to the church at Thessalonica, "We ought always to give thanks to God for you, brethren, as is only fitting, because your faith is *greatly enlarged*, and the love of each one of you toward one another grows ever greater" (2 Thessalonians 1:3 emphasis mine).

By using the word translated *greatly enlarged*, or *grows exceedingly*, Paul recognized the abundant and thriving spiritual growth of the believers. It was far beyond what he'd expected. Paul wasn't flattering them with his praise, but was expressing deep appreciation for the wonderful work of God in them. Through faithing, *God will build a water-walking God-faith in you.*

Jesus gave the mustard seed as an example of this quality of growth, emphasizing the believer's boundless potential. "The kingdom of heaven is like a mustard seed... though it is the smallest of all your seeds, yet when it grows, it is the largest of garden plants and becomes a tree" (Matthew 13:31-32, NIV). Don't overlook the fact that the mustard seed gave all that it had. It was not a little faith, it was all faith.

~~~~~~

The mustard seed of your faith can yield enormous results
in Christ's hands.

~~~~~~

When Jesus asked Philip how the five thousand were to be fed, I cherish the God-faith response of Andrew, "There is a lad here who has five barley loaves and two fish" (John 6:9). What are a boy and a sack lunch in the face of such a challenge? The measure of a growing faith is faithing a grain of mustard seed or a boy's sack lunch. In the hands of Jesus, spectacular results can occur. Faithing manifests growth by giving to God all you have and letting Him use it, even if it is only a mustard seed or a sack lunch.

- **Is your mustard seed faith growing a strong tree?**

Maturing Faith

As you read the Bible, you may notice that even the most advanced believers were continually learning more about trusting God and developing their God-faith. This is because, as noted in *God-birth*, we are works in progress. Your faith will continue to mature until the day you see Jesus face to face.

Even the father of faith, Abraham, had room to grow in his walk with God. We know that his confidence in God was amazingly strong. Unquestioningly, he trusted God when departing from Ur of the Chaldees, the only home he and his family had ever known (see Genesis 12). Ur, located on the southern Euphrates, was a city of temples, commerce, art, and was well advanced in the conveniences and luxuries of the day. Abraham left all of it for the unknown; believing God's promise to be all the evidence needed to proceed. As courageous as that seems his faith was not perfect, he had some rough moments.

After decades of waiting for God to fulfill His promise of making him the father of many nations, Abraham's faith weakened. He wrongly conceded to Sarah's suggestions, and fathered Ishmael with her maidservant Hagar (see Genesis 16).

Had God forgotten what He'd pledged to Abraham? No! Was God unable to fulfill His promise? Certainly not! God both remembered His covenant with Abraham and was fully able to accomplish His plans. In God's perfect timing, He did! Never forget, God keeps His word: "I will remember My covenant, which is between Me and you" (Genesis 9:15).

Renew your hope in Him by spending time in His Word and allowing His Spirit to fill and strengthen you. That is how you go from faith to faith—and that's how your trust in Him will continue to increase. As you live your God-life, commit to going from faith to faith, in the glorious prospect of becoming more spiritually mature and more like Him.

- **Is faithing a way of life for you?**

—Chapter Four—

The Work of Faith

It was the first day of football practice and the room was filled with hopeful high school freshmen. The head coach quieted the excited and noisy "wannabes" and said in an authoritative voice, "If you make the team, you will have to work hard, you won't miss a practice, and you'll do as I say."

Let's translate this admonition to a faithing life, a God-faith. A faith, which is disciplined, developing, energetic, and obedient, is a God-faith.

God-faith should be neither dormant nor unproductive. A growing, exercised, developing faith is profitable. Paul had an affectionate remembrance of the work of faith by the believers at Thessalonica. In his second letter to this church his prayer was that they would "fulfill… the work of faith with power" (2 Thessalonians 1:11). Faith is viewed as not passive, but an active faithing of the power of God in fruitful service.

The high school football coach knew rigid exercise and practice would strengthen and develop the team. Exercise or work of faith will aid you in maintaining spiritual fitness, and enable you to display God-faith. When you resolve (work, toil, labor) to live a life of faith, the public disclosure is godly fruit, or God-life.

It was early in the morning, Jesus and the disciples were returning to Jerusalem from Bethany for His final week when they saw a fig tree. It was a fully-leafed fig tree giving promise of a tasty snack; but alas, the tree was fruitless.

Jesus condemned the tree, not that it provided no fruit, but because it had leaves suggesting there would be fruit. (Fig trees produce fruit simultaneously with leaves.) It was the tree's hypocrisy, not unfruitfulness that brought the censure of Jesus.

It was then that He turned to the disciples and said that the work of faith, adequate faith, would empower them to cast Mount Zion, the Temple mountain, into the sea (see Matthew 21:18-22). Jesus was teaching them that with their faith, they were empowered and expected to do great things.

R.C.H. Lenski wrote, "We stand in the faith, not like a dead post that has been driven into the ground, but as a living tree that fixed its roots ever deeper into the ground."[iv] Your God-faith will be a continuing work of faith—a growing, maturing trust in God that is both vibrant and active.

When you resolve to live for God, it is commitment to a work of faith. Your work of faith generates good or godly works. Faithing springs from a God-centered focus sustained by your deeply rooted confidence in Him. As noted earlier, good works don't earn or prove salvation; rather, they are the outpouring of redemption, the result of Christ's work in us.

Ephesians 2:10 tells us "we are His workmanship, created in Christ Jesus for good works, which God prepared beforehand, that we should walk in them." You don't choose the fruit you bear; rather, God gives assignments for you to accomplish with your work of faith and the abilities He has given you.

Effectiveness of service is influenced by your communication with Him in prayer and a steadfast conviction that He will empower you to do what He calls you to do. You'll be successful as long as you're deeply rooted in Him. The principle Jesus taught holds true forever "as the branch cannot bear fruit of itself, unless it abides in the vine, so neither can you, unless you abide in Me. I am the vine, you are the branches; he who abides in Me, and I in him, he bears much fruit; for apart from Me you can do nothing" (John 15:4-5).

- **Is your life bearing fruit? If not, why not? How deeply rooted are you in Christ?**

Serving in the Fullness of Faith

When the church at Jerusalem began to grow, the apostles led the congregation to select deacons to help them with church ministries. Among these new deacons was "Stephen, a man full of faith and of the Holy Spirit" (Acts 6:5). He exhibited a contagious confidence in God, and it overflowed with his fullness of faith, or faithing.

The task delegated to Stephen was "the daily serving of food" (Acts 6:1). Although menial, he did it faithfully. It is recorded in Acts 7 that Stephen gave an inspired address to the Sanhedrin. He reminded them how the patriarchs of Israel foretold the Messiah's coming, and then he courageously confronted the Jewish leaders for betraying Christ, the Messiah.

Stephen faithfully served God regardless of the task—whether serving tables, preaching the gospel, or confronting powerful men. Even when Stephen was accused by false witnesses and martyred, his fullness of faith was powerfully demonstrated. We are told that at his death, "Stephen, full of the Holy Spirit, looked up to heaven and saw the glory of God, and Jesus standing at the right hand of God... While they were stoning him, Stephen prayed, 'Lord Jesus, receive my spirit'" (Acts 7:55, 59, NIV). He truly had an indefatigable faith in God, a God-faith.

The guidelines for living in the fullness of faith are well summarized in 1 Corinthians 16:13-14: "Be on the alert, stand firm in the faith, act like men, be strong. Let all that you do be done in love."

Every church has its "Stephen" who stands firm in the faith and serves in love. He's the first one there, unlocks the doors, turns on the lights, and sees that everything is in order for the day. Or, a "Stephen" who is always willing and available to visit the sick, or prospects, and welcomes every opportunity to serve and doesn't ask for recognition.

Faithing is not passive, but active and persistent; and motivated by love for your Savior and for each other rather than by titles or earthly rewards. The result of enduring trust in God is that you are unshakeable from your path to the victorious finish line no matter what task given. Philippians 1:6 (NKJV) promises "He who has begun a good work in you will complete it until the day of Jesus Christ." We know that our faithful service will bring God glory, whether we're waiting tables or preaching the Word. So be steadfast in what He's given you to do—even if it doesn't seem too glamorous—and trust Him to show you His power through it.

- **Are you a "Stephen," serving God where He calls you to serve?**

— Chapter Five —

Living an Untethered Faith

Some years ago, I watched with fascination the swiftness and accuracy of a falcon. This skillful bird, with its long wings and sleek body, would swoop and soar catching with ease and precision a piece of bait thrown into the sky. However, the falcon was tethered to the trainer; it could fly only within the radius of the line that bound him. He couldn't ascend into the distant mountains and be the free falcon God created him to be.

In some ways, we're a lot like that falcon. God's desire is for us to "mount up with wings like eagles... run and not get tired... walk and not become weary" (Isaiah 40:31). The soaring eagle is an image of a bird that is untethered, but can read the wind and fly masterfully. We should be like that majestic bird—not bound with earthly limitations. Reading the *wind* (*pneuma*) or *Spirit*, we should defy manmade limitations and live with an unshackled faith. Sadly, weak unexercised faith can hamper us from mounting up like eagles.

Don't miss the untethered joy of believing in God with a fullness of faith, a faith without limits. Immature faith impedes your spiritual strength and stops you from having the full power of *for to me, to live is Christ* (Philippians 1:21).

A local television station was interviewing an elephant trainer who demonstrated tricks the well-trained elephant could perform. It was quite amazing to see. But what was even more interesting was when the interviewer asked about the tether—the chain connecting one of the elephant's legs to a peg in the ground.

Incredulously, the young reporter asked, "Is this sufficient to restrain this enormous animal?" "Yes," answered the trainer. "But it's only sufficient because the elephant doesn't know its own strength!" If that enormous animal had only understood the great strength it was capable of, it could've been free.

~~~~~~

Untethered faith is freedom to unimagined blessings.

~~~~~~

God-kind of Faith

Seeing the withered fig tree, Peter seemed surprised. "Rabbi, behold, the fig tree which You cursed has withered. And Jesus answered saying to them 'Have faith in God'" (Mark 11:21-22). What are the limits of faith? This statement from Jesus addresses an untethered faith. Most translations interpret the statement of Jesus, "have faith in God." However, the Greek text (*echete pistin theou*) literally says, *have* [the] *faith of God* or *have the God kind of faith*. This is a Greek idiom, in which the genitive (of God) denotes the object. The word *have* in the Greek text is much more emphatic than in English, it asserts that the believer is to retain or hold fast to the *faith of God.*ᵛ

In a matter of a few verses in the eleventh chapter of Mark, you are challenged from the simple (a withered fig tree) to the sublime (moving of mountains). For years, I preached from this text challenging people to trust God in their life's mountain challenges until one day I asked myself, how could this be? Only God could fulfill this promise—to move mountains. Only God! It was then I realized that Jesus was not asking us to summon up our own faith; He was challenging us to exercise the faith *of God*—to have a God-faith.

How can we grasp a God kind of faith? Remember: "all things are possible with God" (Mark 10:27). In the spiritual phenomenon of your

God-birth (possession of divine life), you received the indwelling Holy Spirit (possession of divine presence). God-birth is a one-time experience and the indwelling Holy Spirit is your permanent resident.

The pre-eminence of the abiding presence of the Holy Spirit in your life cannot be overstated. The divine purpose of His presence is to accomplish your sanctification and enable you in fruitfulness. God in you can assure the unfailing purpose of God for you to be fruitful and live with God-faith. God "has granted to us |you| His precious and magnificent promises, in order that by them you might become *partakers of the divine nature*" (2 Peter 1:4, emphasis mine). Or as William Barclay wisely states, "He became what we are to make us what He is." [vi]

An untethered faith is a proven and steadfast faith. "Knowing that the testing of your faith produces endurance |steadfastness|. And let endurance have its perfect result, that you may be perfect and complete, lacking in nothing" (James 1:3-4). The Amplified Version says your faith is tried or tested—that you would be a people "perfectly and fully developed (with no defects), lacking nothing." The divine nature, *Christ in you*, is the source of faithing with an untethered faith.

- **What tethers are keeping you from having a fully free, unimpeded faith in God—a God-faith?**

Believing Is Seeing

God summons that which does not exist into being (see Romans 4:17). He speaks of future events with clarity as though they were already history. The Amplified Bible translates it: "God... speaks of the nonexistent things that [He has foretold and promised] as if they [already] existed."

"Faith is to believe what we do not see;
the reward of this faith is to see what we believe."
Saint Augustine

One of my favorite examples of a mature, tetherless faith is the centurion, whose story is recorded in Matthew 8. You may recall that he asked for Jesus' help because his servant boy was suffering with great pain. Jesus simply said, "I will come and heal him" (verse 7). What a relief—surely a miracle was going to occur!

Wait, the centurion replied, "Lord, I am not worthy that You should come under my roof. But only speak a word, and my servant will be healed" (verse 8, NKJV).

The centurion took Christ's word as incontrovertible evidence, and Jesus recognized his mature, unshakable faith, "'I have not found anyone in Israel with so great a faith... Go. As you have believed, let it be done for you.' And his servant was cured that very moment" (Matthew 8:10, 13 HCSB).

To the centurion, *believing was seeing*—seeing didn't have to come before believing. He went home *knowing* that the sick servant boy would be healed. His God-faith was able to move his mountain. Sadly, for many, "seeing is believing." What about you?

~~~~~~

Don't tell God how big your mountains are,
tell your mountains how big your God is!

~~~~~~

Let's return to the fig tree lesson and the challenge to have "the faith of God" for an additional word. Jesus said faith, a God-faith, "does not doubt" (Mark 11:23). The word *doubt* (*diakrinō*) has the connotation of oscillating between belief and unbelief. A hesitating uncertain faith is not God-faith. Having God-faith means faithing that you have what God has promised.

Jesus made the promise of answered prayer inherently personal, "I say *to you*" (Mark 11:24, emphasis mine). It's accurate to say that the answer to your prayer may be only limited by your own faith. As fifteenth century Flemish painter Sir Anthony Van Dyke said, "Self is the only prison that can bind the soul." [vii]

Believing is seeing. Jesus challenged: "all things for which you pray and ask, believe that *you have received* them, and they shall be granted you" (Mark 11:24, emphasis mine).

~~~~~~

God-faith believes what God promises before seeing it.

~~~~~~

Think of Noah, who was "warned by God about things not yet seen, [and] in reverence prepared an ark" (Hebrews 11:7). For 120 years, Noah labored to build the vessel of his vision without even a raindrop for confirmation. To Noah, believing was seeing, or seeing what he already believed.

Without hesitation, the Father of Faith followed the call of God into a strange new land. Furthermore, Abraham knew that in spite of his advanced age, God would honor His promise to give him a son and make him into a nation. For Abraham, believing was seeing.

Believe That You Have Received

One winter, our daughter Susan drove 800 miles to the mountains of Pennsylvania to visit her college friend, Dianne. While there, Susan became severely ill and bedfast with the flu. After several miserable days and an imminent snowstorm, she decided to drive home. I wanted to go and bring her home, but it was impossible. So I prayed for her protection, as any father would. I prayed that she'd be alert, maintain control of the car, and drive with wisdom. I asked God to be a Daddy to her and bring her home safely.

During my prayer, I began to *thank* God for her successful journey home. I was no longer asking God to *give her* a safe trip; I was praising Him *for* it, as if it had already occurred. I went about my responsibilities the rest of the day without concern. I was confident that her secure return was already accomplished. And it was.

- **Is believing seeing for you? Or, do you doubt if you cannot see?**

Chapter Six

Faith is the Victory

Early in my pastoral ministry, one of the traditional hymns confidently affirmed, "Faith is the victory!" Normally, we celebrate victories after conflicts are won. However, with God, we can have a glorious celebration of victory *prior* to the battle—we can rejoice over our triumphs even *before* the struggle is engaged.

> "Faith is the victory! Faith is the victory!
> O glorious victory that overcomes the world."
> *Faith Is the Victory* by John Yates

There's an ongoing battle between the flesh and the spirit, but you can claim victory over your circumstances, foes, and temptations by faith. "This is the victory that has overcome the world—our faith" (1 John 5:4). You are assured that living a godly life—overcoming temptations and keeping God's commandments—is not a burden (verse 3).

You have been given the power or strength to overcome any and all things that would defeat you from living a Christ-like life. Your faith is the victory. An amazing supernatural power now permanently operates in you, the Holy Spirit. He empowers you to seize the victory.

In John 16:33 Jesus said: "in this world you have tribulation, but take courage, I have overcome the world." Look again at what Jesus said, "you have" and "I have." Because He has won the conquest, you have the victory. When you comprehend the glorious actuality that *Christ lives in you* (Galatians 2:20), you awaken to the reassuring truth that the battle has been won. "This is the victory!" This confirmation is a present tense statement; an assurance that today's conquest is today's victory.

- **Are you living a life of spiritual triumph?**

There is a truly remarkable promise of answered prayer in Philippians 4:19, "My God will liberally supply (fill to the full) your every need according to His riches in glory in Christ Jesus" (AMP).

Your pressing need may be caused by uncontrollable circumstances and require immediate action and supernatural aid. Look to this glorious promise, and claim it with all of your heart. God will give you the faith to believe Him for an answer—and it will produce a God-sized harvest of blessings.

Fearless confidence is grounded in His encouraging Word "do not, therefore, fling away your fearless confidence, for it carries a great and glorious compensation of reward" (Hebrews 10:35, AMP). Do not doubt, but keep trusting Him because His provision is assured.

Fearless Confidence

During WWII, an Air Force bomber was fatally disabled by enemy fire, and it was going down. The pilot, my cousin Edmund, ordered the crew to jump, and they did so with *fearless confidence* in their parachutes. But not the co-pilot. He had a paralyzing fear of jumping because he didn't trust his parachute. He opted to fly the plane solo to the ground attempting a controlled crash landing.

Tragically, he perished, not because of the plane crashing, but because he lacked a fearless confidence in his parachute. With faith, he could have survived like the rest of the crew.

Will you meet the challenge to embrace fearless faith—a water-walking, victorious trust in your all-powerful God? Paul admonishes you to "fight the good fight of faith" (1 Timothy 6:12). Step out with conquering faith in God in every circumstance.

In the preceding section, God-birth, we affirmed that eternal life is from God. It is His life, and you're born again with His nature. Obviously, there is no God-life without God-birth. In this section, you learned God-faith is the activator or energizer of living God-life. With the foundation of God-birth and the faithing of God-faith, you can grow strong in your quest *to live is Christ.* In the next sections, critical areas for developing Christ-likeness are unfolded. Are you ready to "shine" in your God-life?

SECTION THREE

GOD-SHINE

"Arise, shine; your light has come,
and the glory of the LORD has risen upon you."
(Isaiah 60:1)

It was a spectacular sunrise, unlike anything I had ever seen. My host, Harley, a regional missionary in northern Alaska, handed me a steaming cup of fresh coffee and said, "Come with me, you'll want to see this." In the darkness, we waited as the Eastern sky began to turn light grey, pastel pink, and then exploded with colorful streaks of brilliantly hued light. I witnessed a breath-taking sunrise over the pristine snowscape of arctic Alaska. Every frozen ice crystal in this indescribable spectacle glistened and sparkled, innumerable minute prisms all reflecting a rainbow facet of color.

When the light of the sun emerges on the eastern horizon, there's no mistaking the fact that a marvelous change has taken place. A new day has made its appearance. A fresh opportunity in which anything is possible—a time to rise and shine. David, a morning watcher, exclaimed, "Weeping may last for the night, but a shout of joy comes in the morning" (Psalm 30:5). How wonderful! All of yesterday's mistakes and misfortunes are faded away, strength and hope, renewed with the dawning of a new day.

This is even truer at the bright dawn of God-birth when Jesus Christ becomes your Savior and Lord. He brings His radiance to your life because He is the *Light of the World*. In contrast to the darkness when you didn't know Him: "the LORD will rise upon you, and His glory will appear [be seen] upon you" (Isaiah 60:2). God-birth removes all of your sins, and fills you with His presence and radiance.

Isaiah was saying that this new life in you emanates *God-shine*. Arise, shine!" God calls to you, because not only do you receive the light of Christ, you are also to exude Him, actually glow. It's His divine presence in you. Jesus commands: "Let your light shine before men in such a way that they may see your good works, and glorify your Father who is in heaven" (Matthew 5:16).

~~~~~~~~~~

Arise, Shine!

~~~~~~~~~~

When you show God-shine through your words and actions, God is glorified and others see Him through you. Joseph Alexander wrote, "The perfection of the glory promised to the church is not to arise from its contrast with the darkness of the world around it, but from the diffusion of its light until the darkness disappears."[i] What you possess isn't just better than the darkness, it overcomes it! The more intensely the light of Christ glows in you, the less territory there is for the shadows of sin and doubt to enshroud you.

Proverbs 4:18 tells us: "The path of the righteous is like the light of dawn, that shines brighter and brighter until the full day." All Christians have this new life in Christ, but many haven't matured to the fullness of a radiant God-shine. Your life can have a divine God-shine.

- **Consider this: are you radiating God-shine like the dawn of a new day?**

—Chapter One—

Dominion of Darkness

B efore we talk about light, let's address the darkness. On the evening of Jesus' betrayal in the garden of Gethsemane, He addressed the chief priest, captain of the temple, and the elders. He told them, "This is your hour, and *the power of darkness*" (Luke 22:53, KJV, emphasis mine). A diabolical dominion had descended, and Satan ruled in the hearts of those who came to betray Jesus.

A Maleficent Enemy

Although Jesus would have ultimate victory in His hour of triumph at Calvary, there was an ominous darkness in the hearts of men that night in the garden and a seeming defeat for Jesus. While the city of Jerusalem slept, a conflict was taking place far more grievous than that between the Jewish rulers and Jesus. The dominion of darkness taking hold was more portentous than the darkness of the night in which Jesus was arrested. It was an open clash between Satan, the ruler of this age, and God, the Creator of the world. While the smirk of Satan that night may have appeared to be a smile, all was in God's plan. Jesus said, "This has happened that the Scriptures might be fulfilled" (Mark 14:49).

There is still today a malevolent, dark force in the world trying to eradicate hope for mankind—to prevent anyone from knowing the Light of the World. Jesus confirmed this sad truth, "Men loved the darkness rather than the light, for their deeds were evil" (John 3:19).

Perhaps the best example of this was Judas who walked with Jesus daily, and yet betrayed Him. Judas was a disciple of the darkness and in fact, Jesus called him "a devil" (John 6:70). Scripture documents this assertion: "The devil having already put into the heart of Judas Iscariot... to betray Him" (John 13:2).

Likewise, when the Pharisees and others in Jerusalem sought to kill Jesus, He said to them, "You are of your father the devil, and you want to do the desires of your father. He was a murderer from the beginning, and does not stand in the truth, because there is no truth in him" (John 8:44).

Paul gives a sinister and foreboding description of the evil rule of the devil when he calls it "the domain of darkness" (Colossians 1:13). The word translated *domain* in Greek means *authority* or *power of influence*. This passage describes the enemy's unruly force—his tyranny of lawlessness which thrives in the dark wickedness of this world. When imprisoned in the realm of darkness, people live under the diabolical reign of the devil.

The dominion of darkness is monstrously cunning—the power to captivate mankind through deceit. When caught in the beguiling lure of Satan, people who don't know God embrace corrupt lifestyles in an attempt to fulfill an emptiness that only He can satisfy. Lamentably, sin is never finished, it only causes increasing hopelessness. As Asaph declares, "They do not know nor do they understand; they walk about in darkness" (Psalm 82:5).

However, when Paul spoke before King Agrippa, he proclaimed that life didn't have to be that way—people could know God and find their way into the light. Paul gave testimony of his conversion and call to be a witness to the Gentiles saying that his goal was "to turn them from darkness to light, and from the power of Satan unto God" (Acts 26:18, KJV). His message was one of a distinct choice and an opportunity for change.

God-shine is about the glowing difference God has made in your life. Like Paul, you are to shine-forth with a strong testimony to those trapped under the devastating power of Satan. They need to hear about the Light of the World.

- **Do you know people who are prisoners of the dominion of darkness? What are you doing to lead them to the light of Christ?**

The Devil Made Me Do It!

In the early 1970s, a popular television comedian entertained audiences with his offhand sense of humor and hilarious skits. He would say, "Funny is an attitude." His outlook worked well. Keeping audiences laughing, his variety show was popular for several years.

One of his most comical routines involved dressing up as a sassy, flashy character named "Geraldine Jones" who was loosely based on Prissy from *Gone With the Wind*. Whenever Geraldine would get into trouble she'd say, "The devil made me do it!"

This laugh line always struck a chord with audiences. Perhaps somewhere inside we recognize that we do things that we don't think we are capable of doing, and don't understand why. That's because the devil, by lies, deceit, and enticements, sometimes tricks us into wickedness. He cajoles us into relying on ourselves and other sources of security instead of God.

Peter said Satan is "like a roaring lion, seeking someone to devour" (1 Peter 5:8). He's a committed and corrupting enemy of God, and to you as well. The devil's strategy is more understandable when you realize that his name *diabolos* means *false accuser* or *slanderer*. Satan is master of deception—not only a fraud, but also the "father of lies" (John 8:44). This false accuser aggressively combats the Word of God and the salvation of the lost. He also stands against you—trying to stop your radiating God-shine.

He is indescribably cunning and dangerous; the Enemy knows your weaknesses and insecurities, which means he knows how to tempt you and make you vulnerable to sin. That's why you're warned to "have no fellowship with the unfruitful works of darkness, but rather expose them" (Ephesians 5:11, NKJV). Stay strong, and shine brightly, God will be glorified through you!

- **Have you ever thought to yourself, "the devil made me do it"? Then consider: why are you taking orders from the enemy?**

Who Is This Ruler of Darkness?

Ezekiel 28 tells the story of how Satan was formed, and what he was like before he rebelled and was cast out of heaven. Created by God, he initially was typologically called Lucifer: "light-bearer," "shining one," and "morning star" (see Isaiah 14:12, NKJV). In Ezekiel 28, he was "anointed cherub" (verse 14) and "full of wisdom and perfect in beauty" (verse 12). Again, "[He was] perfect in [his] ways from the day [he was] created until iniquity was found in [him]" (verse 15). Satan began to love himself more than he loved God. He sinned against God by self-centered ambition, he wanted to make himself like God, the Most High (see Isaiah 14:14).

J. F. Strombeck tells us, "When Lucifer rebelled against God and said that he would set himself above the stars of God and be like the Most High he was… permitted to set up a kingdom of his own over which he became the supreme leader."[ii]

However, the realm he set up is destined to fail—Lucifer's self-centered, rebellious spirit will bring his demise.

Our enemy [Satan] fell from heaven because of his *pride, self-deception*, and *rebellion* (see Isaiah 14:12-15). These three sins can be identified in the lives of those who allow Satan to rule over them. They believe the Deceiver's lies—that God is keeping something good from them—and that if they submit to God, He'll prove to be a harsh taskmaster.

These are the same falsehoods that the serpent told to Eve in the Garden of Eden (see Genesis 3:1-5). As Paul Powell insightfully states, "The whole social structure of this world is controlled by a prevailing principle of life that is foreign to God and leads people away from Him."[iii]

- Knowing that Satan's main strategy utilizes pride, self-deception, and rebellion, do you steer clear of these traps?

Witness of the Dominion of Darkness

With advancement of medical procedures and modern resuscitative techniques, many statements have been collected from people who have had near-death experiences. A renowned cardiologist, Dr. Maurice Rawlings, has carefully recorded accounts of many declared clinically dead but through medical resuscitation returned to life.

He suggests, "Resuscitation is something that affords a... peek into one's future... perhaps a glimpse of glory, a glimpse of hell." [iv] People who encountered a near-death "twilight" state reported varied experiences. Some told of a "glimpse of glory," bright lights, peaceful feelings, ecstatic happiness, and seeing loved ones. But, not everyone. Others, when resuscitated, had an entirely different account.

Dr. Rawlings reports, "The encounter with a light seems to be the most common event noted in most near-death experiences." However, for some, the light was accompanied by a fearsome darkness. Those who had this kind of near-death experience, were unbelievers, and witnessed a counterfeit light and the terrifying darkness of the Enemy's dominion.

Frightened witnesses told him: "The darkness was so real you could touch it and it would burn...The darkness of hell is so intense that it seems to have a pressure per square inch. It is an extremely black, dismal, desolate, heavy, pressurized type of darkness. It gives the individual a crushing, despondent feeling of loneliness."

Dr. Rawlings reports, "If there is a hell, if the Bible is true, if these patients had a sighting of hell instead of glory, then we must each decide for ourselves, *is it safe to die?*"[v]

The imperative question is: *Have you prepared for what follows this life*? Or, are you ready for what Dr. Rawlings calls "life after life"? Your God-birth assures you that in death you will be in the presence of His glory. What about your family, friends, neighbors, and co-workers, are they assured of a home in glory?

~~~~~~~~~~~~~~~~~~~~~~~~~~~~~~~~~~~~~~~

"Jesus is Victor! The battle is Won!
We can do nothing, for all has been done;
Jesus is Victor! The foe from the dust
Never can rise again if we trust."[vi]

~~~~~~~~~~~~~~~~~~~~~~~~~~~~~~~~~~~~~~~

The only way the devil can win is by convincing you to deny the love of God and the atoning death of Jesus Christ—or at least be silent about it. Don't ever forget, you have God-shine to illuminate your path, it is *Christ in you, the hope of glory* (Colossians 1:27). Will you allow Him to shine through you?

- **Heaven is real. So is hell. Is your God-shine creating a desire for others to know the Light of the World?**

—Chapter Two—

The Light of Life

Rain had come in squalls all afternoon that Sunday and when we arrived at church, attendance was significantly diminished because of the turbulent weather. Still, we were committed to pressing on because this was the closing service of the Summer Revival. We began despite thrashing winds and an unrelenting downpour.

As the service proceeded, we could hear the storm becoming increasingly more severe. At times, the crack of lightning, and the loud booming thunder drowned out the enthusiastic singing of favorite revival hymns and choruses—"Revive Us Again," "Rescue the Perishing," and "Down At The Cross." Then, no more than five minutes after I began my sermon, simultaneously, a blinding flash of lightning and a deafening thunderclap shook the building and we were emerged into complete darkness. Many gasped. No one moved. In an instant, a shroud of oppressive darkness blanketed the sanctuary—so real, it seemed you could touch it.

I continued in that totally lightless church despite the almost overwhelming darkness. The sermon was an evangelistic message entitled "Jesus, The Light of the World," it was not by chance, it was God's leadership some days before.

As if prearranged, two men brought in flickering altar candles and placed them on either side of the pulpit. A soft, shimmering glow dispelled the intense darkness and illuminated the sanctuary. Then came the planned invitation verse: "Through the tender mercy of our God; whereby the dayspring from on high hath visited us, to give light to them that sit in darkness and in the shadow of death, to guide our feet into the way of peace" (Luke 1:78-79, KJV).

What started out to be a rainy Sunday night church service became a once-in-a-lifetime worship celebration! God provided a tangible object lesson of what He did for us; light in the darkness. The movement of His Spirit was incredible; lifting that overpowering blanket-like shroud, and showing us that deliverance from the darkness of sin is available through Jesus Christ.

Life-changing decisions were made, some coming forward to pray with renewed commitment to God, and others confessing Christ as Savior for the first time. It was a service to remember, when *His* light dispelled the darkness.

God is Absolute Light and Genesis of Life

From the first chapter of the Bible forward, light and life are associated with God—they flow from the same divine source. We are told in the very beginning, the Spirit of God moved over the formless surface of primeval earth, and God said, "let there be light" (Genesis 1:3). Following light, God populated the earth with life, with living things. Light and life go together. When all things that are known to mankind began, Light and Life, the eternal I Am, already was.

The absolute Light was the Life; and there in, you find the genesis of all life. "All that came to be was alive with His life, and that life was the light of men" (John 1:4, NEB). Literally, His life is the source of light for all humanity. Or, behind the absolute Light is the eternal Life, the Lord God of the universe. Divine Light is God's self-revelation, so believers will not stumble in the darkness.

God doesn't just create light—He is *absolute* Light. In Him, there is complete absence of darkness. Light is an attribute of His holiness, it's who He is, it's His God-shine. "This is the message we have heard from Him and announce to you, that God is light, and in Him there is no darkness [evil] at all" (1 John 1:5). God's unquestioned, never changing, supreme moral goodness is affirmed by apostle John. Light versus darkness is not simply the contrast of knowledge and ignorance; it characterizes good versus evil. Look again at verse five; John states he received personally his information about God "from Him," from the Lord Jesus Christ Himself.

Jesus is Light and Life

The Son of God, Jesus Christ, is the incarnate light and life of God. Jesus came "to shine upon those who sit in darkness and the shadow of death" (Luke 1:79). The Greek text indicates Jesus came to give light, to shine, and His light is *ongoing* and *timeless*. The radiance of Jesus is as bright today as in Luke's day. Jesus is "the Sunrise from on high" (Luke 1:78).

Again, life follows light—this is a repeated sequence throughout Scripture. In fact, light and life are particularly dominant themes in the New Testament—especially in the Gospel of John, which begins by declaring that Jesus is the light and life. John's stated purpose of his gospel was "believing you may have life in His name" (John 20:31).

I am often struck by how the first chapter of the Gospel of John associates the coming of Christ with creation: "All things came into being through Him, and apart from Him nothing came into being... the light shines in the darkness" (verses 3, 5). Compare these verses to the account of creation. We're told that "The earth was formless and void, and darkness was over the surface of the deep" (Genesis 1:2). The literal translations of the Hebrew words *formless* and *void* (*tōhû* and *wābōhû*) are *worthless* or *empty,* and *uninhabitable*.

But God changed all of that when He said, "Let there be light!" Because after light came life. With one command, the Lord created endless possibilities for the earth and made it useful, worthwhile, and fruitful—a living thing.

As the apostle John points out, the same is true in the human heart. People who don't know Christ sit in the darkness of condemnation and spiritual desolation. But, when Jesus, the Light of the

World is invited to shine into the emptiness and void of a person's being, He creates a vibrant, meaningful life—a God-shine.

"Ed's" Story

Ed, a church planter, had joined me for breakfast. It was a warm day, and Ed had on a short-sleeved shirt. I guess I was staring at a large tattoo on his arm when he said, "Oh, that's a leftover from my former life." Ed grew up in foster homes; he was a large, strong kid known as a troublemaker. Given the choice of jail or joining the Army, he chose the Army. He didn't do well there and got out as quickly as he could.

Then, he met a girl opposite in every way from him—a dedicated Christian. She invited him to her church's singles group, where in time he committed his life to Christ. From darkness and desolation, he found the Light of Life. You guessed it; the girl is now his wife, and they both have a wonderful God-shine. They have committed their lives to reaching lost people with the message of Jesus, the Light of the World.

You see, from the beginning, there's been a spiritual battle raging between light and darkness—or you might say, between good and evil. God knew that mankind was lost, condemned to spiritual death and in need of a Savior. John 3:19 testifies: "This is the judgment, that the light is come into the world, and men loved the darkness rather than the light; for their deeds were evil."

It makes sense. Human nature is bent toward sin—it compels people to do bad things. Though you may control yourself, nonetheless, I'm sure there are things you do of which you aren't proud. Even the apostle Paul confessed: "I am of flesh, sold into bondage to sin. For that which [what] I am doing, I do not understand; for I am not practicing what I would like to do, but I am doing the very thing I hate" (Romans 7:14-15).

Whether there are things you do, or that are done to you, you try to keep them hidden, or concealed in darkness. Tragically, the more you turn inward—keeping secrets and masking your real self—the more easily darkness takes hold of you.

However, "nothing in all creation is hidden from God's sight. Everything is uncovered and laid bare before the eyes of him to whom we must give account" (Hebrews 4:13, NIV). That's why Jesus came to earth, so that you wouldn't have to hide in darkness and fear any more. He understood the helplessness of those blinded by sin and stumbling in darkness when He said, "no longer do you have to wander in darkness."

~~~~~~

"I have come as light into the world, [so] that everyone who believes in Me may not remain in darkness."
(John 12:46)

~~~~~~

Jesus is the light and life of mankind. Light and life are joined inseparably in nature; so also, they are united in the spiritual realm.

Life is the antithesis of death, and light is the opposite of darkness. Jesus straightforwardly announced, "I am the light of the world" (John 8:12). The "light" was not in reference to the radiance that is seen, but the Luminary Himself from which radiance emanates. His is the life and light of the universe, there is none like Him.

Let's look at another insightful verse, "The light shines in the darkness, and the darkness did not comprehend it" (John 1:5). The word *shines* is in the present tense—Jesus *continues to give light* from the days of His ministry on earth until now. I like to translate this grand truth as "Jesus goes on shining." This wondrous truth is indeed good news for lost humanity. Even a more glorious truth, "The darkness [does] not comprehend it (Jesus, the light of the World)." The word comprehend (*katalambánō*) means to *apprehend, overcome*, or *overpower*. The world in its darkness has not dissipated or extinguished the light, the divine light of the World. The corrupt world loves darkness; but Jesus, the light, continues to shine so that those who accept Him will not remain in darkness.

To God be the glory! The divine Luminary has not been affected in the least by the darkness that is in the world. The light and life of Christ is eternal, unquenchable, and triumphant. Darkness can never snuff out or eclipse the light. Christ will always overcome the darkness because it can't resist Him. He is always victorious!

A fitting summary to Jesus the light is from William Barclay: "Although men did all they could to obscure and extinguish the light of God in Christ, they could not quench it. In every generation the light of Christ still shines in spite of efforts of men to extinguish the flame."[vii]

Follow the Light

Late one Saturday night, I heard our daughter scrambling down the hall. She burst into our room and exclaimed, "George is on the roof!" This recently rescued young cat had pushed out the window screen from her upstairs bedroom, jumped onto the adjoining kitchen roof and disappeared in the night.

Grabbing a couple of flashlights, I joined Susan circling the house looking for the wayward cat. It was a moonless night and the only source of light were the beams from the two flashlights. We circled the house calling him and shining the beams of light along the roofline. It was then that I saw him.

He was sitting on the very top of the second story roof, next to the chimney. We called out to him and he moved toward us with a loud, plaintive cry. He had lost his way back to the bedroom window, he was upset, scared, and confused.

Now, dangerously close to the edge of the roof, he was thinking about jumping from the second story. In a quiet, calm voice, I spoke reassuringly to him. Keeping his attention and talking to him, I put the beam of light in front of him and moved it slowly along the roof. He followed the light back over to the kitchen roof and over the top to the front of the house to the upstairs window where Susan was waiting.

You have a light and a still quiet voice to lead you through your difficult times when you are upset, scared, and confused. The light of Christ will lead you to safety.

Jesus came to set those in the darkness of sin free—to provide hope for those sitting in death's shadow, and salvation to whosoever will accept Him as their Savior. Jesus is "The authentic (true) light, the incarnate Christ, who came into the world, enlightens every one in the world" (John 1:9, my translation). Nothing can extinguish the God-shine of Christ in you—or take away the eternal life of your God-birth. Finally, the new day has dawned.

Reflections

Light is a penetrating, invasive, phenomenon that overcomes the adverse darkness. The Bible announces, "God is light" (1 John 1:5). Light is His very nature. He is the unquestioned victor over all opposition and no darkness can successfully challenge Him because He is Supreme Light.

Reflected Light

Along coastlines there are silent sentinels guarding ships and warning them of dangerous and rocky shores—lighthouses. In darkness, their powerful and piercing light is visible from great distances. This brilliant beam of light is a welcome sight to a ship's captain. Do you realize the radiant light from a lighthouse is a reflected light? Mirrors faithfully and effectively reflect the light source and provide safety for seamen.

When reading Philippians 2:15, I envision believers as lighthouses: "In the midst of a crooked and perverse generation, among whom you shine as lights" (NKJV). Like a lighthouse, you are to be a reflector of light, the Light of the World. Also, like a lighthouse, you are to faithfully reflect light in all kinds of conditions. It is one thing to emulate a God-shine at church, but quite another to radiate

God-shine in an evil-disposed and perverse world. But, to reflect in the darkness, that is precisely where God-shine is needed most.

To mirror a God-shine, you cannot allow your life to become smudged with sin, with worldliness. Provide a clear, irreproachable reflection of the Lord by being blameless and without fault. The lighthouse keeper regularly cleans the giant lens; likewise, you must faithfully and routinely carry out a refreshing cleansing. Activate 1 John 1:9 daily in your life. Only then, can your shine provide a clear, visible, dependable reflection of the Light of the World. You are to be a heavenly light in a sinful world.

"If we confess our sins, He is faithful and righteous to forgive us our sins and to cleanse us from all unrighteousness."
1 John 1:9

Light is to be seen. Jesus made this truism very clear in His Sermon on the Mount. "Let your light shine before men" (Matthew 5:16). He gave a graphic picture of what we are to do, and not to do with our light. We are not to hide or obscure it, like putting a candle under a basket—but we are to let it shine like a candle on a lamp stand (see Matthew 5:15). You have an incredible opportunity to be a reflection of Him who is light. *He is the light of your God-shine.* As reflected light, you are God's light in a darkened world of sin and degradation.

- **Is your life reflecting a God-shine?**

Making Holes in Darkness

In *A Child's Garden of Verses*, Robert Louis Stevenson recalled a time when as a child he was at his bedroom window watching a lamplighter. Faithfully moving from lamp to lamp, the man would raise a pole with a flickering flame to each street lamp, lighting the way for pedestrians. When the young Stevenson was asked what he was doing, he replied, "I'm watching a man making holes in the darkness." That's it! Reflecting the light of the world, you make holes in the foreboding darkness of this world.

A commonly used interpretation for you being "the light of the world" (Matthew 5:14), is that of the moon *reflecting* the light of the sun. The moon isn't the source of illumination, rather it mirrors the source; the luminary is the sun. Likewise, you are to have God-shine, reflecting attributes of God as seen in the life and teachings of Jesus.

You may ask: *How in the world can I do that*? Look at Moses when he returned to the Israelites after an intimate conversation with God on Mt. Sinai, "The skin of his face shone because of his speaking with Him" (Exodus 34:29). God's luminous radiance remained on Moses' face—everyone could see Moses had been in God's presence. He actually *reflected* the glory of God, who is absolute light.

~~~~~~~~~~~~~~~~~~~~~~~~~~~~~~~~~~~~~

Your God-shine reflects God's glory!

~~~~~~~~~~~~~~~~~~~~~~~~~~~~~~~~~~

No one can stand before God without being affected. The question is: *Will you be a reflection*? When you spend time with Him, basking in His radiance and awesome presence, you will exhibit God-shine that reflects His image. "Whenever a man [person] turns to the Lord, the veil is taken away... But we all, with unveiled face beholding as in a mirror the glory of the Lord, are being transformed into the same image from glory to glory" (2 Corinthians 3:16, 18). Moses' appearance was different when he came from the mountain summit, everyone could see the shine on his person. Living a God-life, in intimate communication with God, will emanate a resplendent God-shine.

God-shine is possible for you because God "has caused his light to shine within us, to give the light of revelation—the revelation of the glory of God in the face of Jesus Christ" (2 Corinthians 4:6, NEB). Fantastic!

"I See Me!"
An ever-doting....grandpa warmly welcomed his two-year-old granddaughter as she climbed into his lap. She loved to sit with him and affectionately rub foreheads—it was their unique way of

being close and showing love. However, this time, the little girl held her grandpa's face in her small hands and peered curiously into his happy eyes. With a giggle she exclaimed, "I see me!" She saw herself reflected in her grandpa's eyes.

Our eyes reflect an image of what we're seeing. Your God-shine works in much the same way. If you're "fixing our [your] eyes on Jesus, the author and perfecter of faith" (Hebrews 12:2), Jesus will be reflected in everything you do. If you're faithful to follow Him, when you finally meet Him face to face He'll say, "Well done, I saw Me in your life!"

As an authentic Christian, you're being changed—a new image is emerging—a God-life. "All of us... continue to behold and to reflect like mirrors the glory of the Lord, are constantly being transformed into [His very own] image in ever increasing splendor and from one degree of glory to another; [for this comes] from the Lord [Who is the] Spirit" (2 Corinthians 3:18, AMP).

This transformation is to be a present tense reality—you are being changed in a continuous, ongoing way into another form. You are in the process of mirroring Him more accurately each day with your God-shine.

The Revised Standard Version interprets this verse: "We all... are being changed into his likeness from one degree of glory to another." Your transformation isn't only a journey, but it's also your future destiny—you are to grow continually in His likeness resembling Him more and more. In fact, the proposed destiny of all Christians is to be conformed to the image of the Lord Jesus Christ (see Romans 8:29).

- **Are you reflecting Jesus in your daily life?**

Chapter Four

God's Image

Charles Wesley gave the world over six thousand hymn texts, but none more clearly presents the gospel than the Christmas hymn "Hark the Herald Angels Sing." Hear again the powerful prayer in the fourth stanza: "Adam's likeness now efface, stamp Thine image in its place: second Adam from above, reinstate us in Thy love." Wesley addressed the transformation we've been discussing—how we should continually be changing into the likeness of Christ.

The God-shine of His Image

We know that in the beginning when mankind was formed, it was God's intention that you and I would bear His image. "God said, 'Let Us make man in Our *image*, according to Our *likeness*'... God created man in His own image, in the image of God He created him; male and female He created them" (Genesis 1:26-27, emphasis mine). In Hebrew, the word *image* means *resemblance* or a *representative figure*. The word *likeness* means *similitude* or *visible likening*. You are to be God's representative with a family likeness—as mentioned in God-birth, His DNA.

From Genesis on into the New Testament "image" is a prominent theme. Paul stresses "just as we [you] have borne the image of the earthly, we [you] shall also bear the image of the heavenly" (1 Corinthians 15:49). Here, the word *image* (*eikōn*) speaks of the *derived likeness* to Christ that you should resemble more and more. [viii] Notice, in addition to God's image, this verse reminds us there is an earthly appearance you are to discard or cast off. This resemblance you are to cast off is that of Adam—the first man and the father of humanity—who by his sin brought sin and death to all. "Through one man sin entered into the world, and death through sin, and so death spread to all men" (Romans 5:12). You are Adam's heir through natural birth, and you inherit your sin nature through his bloodline. However, Christ has provided a way for you to have a God-birth, to receive His atonement and forgiveness of your sins.

A wonderful comparison between death in Adam and life in Christ is portrayed in Romans 5:12-21. You can be delivered from the death of the natural Adam-birth through the supernatural God-birth that Christ offers. And, it's through this God-birth that you're capable of moral and ethical living—capable of imaging Christ's divine likeness, a God-shine.

The probing question remains: *How can I genuinely reflect the image of God, a God-shine, when God alone is holy and good?* In fact, during His earthly ministry, Jesus said, "No one is good except God alone" (Mark 10:18). In a beautiful praise song by Moses we read "I proclaim the name of the LORD; ascribe greatness to our God! The Rock! His work is perfect, for all His ways are just; a God of faithfulness and without injustice" (Deuteronomy 32:3-4). Do you recall that God said, "I am God, and there is no other; I am God, and there is no one like Me" (Isaiah 46:9). How? That's the question: "How can I have God-shine of His image in my life?"

As mentioned when we talked about reflection, Moses reflected God's glory visibly after spending time with Him. The answer further unfolds in Matthew 5:48 when Jesus issues a challenge that "you are to be perfect, as your heavenly Father is perfect." The word *perfect* means to be *complete* and *mature*.

Think about it. God has many qualities—such as self-consciousness and freewill—to which you can relate. Unlike all other creatures, you were created capable of moral living, which is a reflection of God. Ethical consciousness sets you apart in the animal kingdom.

However, it is only in Christ that you are able to make the same principled decisions as He would make. How? It is affirmed that as a saved person you can know the Lord and He can instruct you—because you have the mind of Christ. Intrigued? This is fully discussed in Section Seven.

In reality, you cannot be perfected or mature on your own. Even when you strive to become the best version of yourself, you're still flawed and lacking.

~~~~~~

"Put on the new self who is *being renewed* to a true knowledge according *to the image* of the One who created him [you]."
(Colossians 3:10, emphasis mine)

~~~~~~

A Workable Plan

You still may be thinking: *How can I possibly become more Christ-like?* For years, I've worked with groups implementing long-range planning. A decision to formulate future planning is an admission that you want change—to go from where you are to an improved position.

Let's find the answer to your important question of how to fulfill the imperative of Colossians 3:10 by using a good planning model.

Challenge: How do you get from where you are, to where God wants you to be?

Objective: To be renewed and conformed to the image of Christ
The objective is the long-term destination that incorporates your commitment and desire to live a God-life. Living God-life is a pilgrimage, a lifetime journey.

Goal: To put on a new self, *No longer I who live, but Christ lives in me* (Galatians 2:20).

The goal is time-sensitive involving the questions "when" and "what." By time-sensitive, I mean to set specific, calendar-dated goals for your spiritual maturation. For instance, by (day/month), I will have completed a word study of Colossians. Measurable progression is chronicled as you are becoming more of Christ and less of you.

Action plan: To continuously, day-by-day, be renewed *in the process of being made new* (Colossians 3:10).

Action plans answer the question "how," and define specific actions that move you closer to your goal. Gather tools for your study—a commentary on Colossians, your Bible, and a notebook. Schedule daily time and weekly goals; faithfully dedicate yourself to your action plan.

Take a moment and let's think again about the word *renewed* (*anakainoō*) to *renovate* or *make new* (Colossians 3:10). God wants to make you into something you never were before, to have the radiance of God-shine. This is a process. I find encouragement in my journey of faith from 2 Peter 3:18, "I am to develop in the grace of and increase in the perception of my Lord and Savior Jesus Christ" (my translation).

Let's return to an operative plan, being renewed into the image of Christ.

Tactics: Dedicated prayer, meditation with God, disciplined Bible study, fellowship with mature believers, and a personal commitment to be conformed to the image of Christ (see Romans 8:29).

Evaluation: "The measure of the stature which belongs to the fulness of Christ" (Ephesians 4:13). How are you measuring up?

The Radiance of God's Attributes

God-shine in your life obviously means God's attributes are shining through you. Do you wonder: *What attributes of God can possibly be seen in me?*

Three moral attributes are a must for God-shine: Truth, Love, and Holiness.

Truth

For many in this post-modern world, truth is relative; there are no absolutes. For them, truth changes and shifts as their whims and conveniences may dictate. Albert Einstein once quipped, "No amount of experimentation can ever prove me right; a single experiment can prove me wrong." He was ever in flux. But, there *are* absolutes—non-debatable, unchanging, ever the same, truths. God is Truth!

To God, truth is His identity. John 17:3 proclaims that He's "the only true God."

God is *absolute* truth—He's the source of every reality. And His intentions, actions, and plans all originate from His person, and that person is Truth.

Likewise, Jesus declared, "I am… the truth" (John 14:6). Jesus wasn't just saying, "I am the One who tells the truth," even though, He was always honest and forthcoming in every situation. Rather, He was saying, "I am the source of truth." He's the One who leads you to absolute truth, which is unconditional now and forever, it's the God-shine of truth.

An Arrow Into the Sky

It is like yesterday, I've never forgotten when truth failed me as a child. My father had a few inflexible rules: Don't tell stories (lies), don't sass, and do my chores. When I was in the fourth grade, my favorite birthday present was a child's bow and arrow set. Dad showed me how to use it properly, and strongly cautioned me to always aim at the target he placed on the side of the garage, never otherwise.

There were three arrows and each had a suction cup on the end. After practicing on the target, I then "killed" all the trees, fence post, garage door, etc. A car went by our house and I "killed" it. The arrow stuck on the fender, but the car never stopped.

That evening, Dad asked about my bow and arrow set, and why I only had two arrows. "I lost one" I told him. "Did you shoot it at a car?" he asked. "Oh no, I just lost it." Then he produced the third arrow. The driver of the car saw Dad at the store, gave him the arrow, and told him the story. After Dad took me to the garage, I was reminded of the importance of telling the truth.

God is Truth, thus believers have the "hope of eternal life, which God, who cannot lie, promised" (Titus 1:2). You reflect God, and have God-shine when you are known as a person who tells the truth—the unenhanced, unembellished truth. Truthfulness and honesty are hallmarks of God-shine. When Christ is at the core of all you say and do, He'll be seen in you in an amazing way and you'll radiate God-shine.

Love

"Love" may be the most overused and misused word in our vocabulary. In one breath we say we love apple pie, the beautiful morning, the family pet, our spouse, and our cell phone. People "fall in love" and marry, then "fall out of love" and divorce. Where is unconditional love? Unfortunately, "love" today is often as provisional and conditional as is situational truth. The Bible asserts that unqualified love is the very essence of God. God is unconditional love. It's His identity, the very fabric of His being.

~~~~~~~~~~~~~~~~~~~~~~~~

God is unconditional love.

~~~~~~~~~~~~~~~~~~~~~~~~

First John 4:8 announces: "God is love." When I was a child in Sunday school, this is one of the first verses we memorized. Yet, it wasn't until adulthood I began to understand the depth of its meaning. When the Bible speaks of God's love (*agapáō*), it's not an abstract concept—it's real, unconditional, inexhaustible, and reflects

His trustworthy character. God's love overcomes every obstacle, because He's unwaveringly committed to loving you.

God deliberately chooses to love you, and He doesn't fall in and out of love with you. When the Bible proclaims that God loves you, it's with an active, accepting love. Consider this: He doesn't love you for what He can get, but for what He can give.

Well-planned Travel

My co-worker, an executive with responsibilities and pressures inherent to his position, traveled extensively both domestically and abroad. His wife often traveled with him even though she was confined to a wheelchair. His love and care for her was a model for everyone. He would make detailed travel arrangements in advance for her convenience and comfort. Restaurants, overnight reservations, and tourist attractions were screened ahead of time to ensure her wheelchair could be accommodated.

Someone mentioned to him the endless details of his planning: "You really go overboard in caring for your wife's every comfort, don't you?" Puzzled, he said, "How could I do less? I love her." That's it, unconditional, unqualified love.

When I think of Calvary, I wonder, how God could love us to the utmost extent, sacrificing His own Son? I can hear God say, "How could I do less?" "I love you." God's love for you is independent of how you feel or respond to Him. Romans 5:8 reveals, "God demonstrates His own love toward us, in that while we were yet sinners, Christ died for us." Before you were born, Jesus became sin and gave His life for you.

> God doesn't love you for what *He can get*,
> but for what *He can give*.

The God-shine of love is unconditional and unreserved love. This radiant attribute of God seen in you is for others, not for you. It is even for those who may be difficult and unlovable. You stand apart when you have a God-love for those who say things that hurt you. What about the workplace? Do you have a God-shine of love with an unreasonable boss or troublesome co-worker? Perhaps a neighbor who makes your life miserable, an unruly child, or a trying parent, do you have a radiant God-shine?

The God-shine of love embraces other believers, because you are instructed "beloved, let us love one another... if God so loved us, we also ought to love one another" (1 John 4:7, 11). Similarly, Matthew 19:19 commands "love your neighbor as yourself." Just as you seek for your own good, you should be committed to pursuing the best for others.

A challenging and God-honoring command is to "love your enemies... that you may be sons of your Father" (Matthew 5:44-45). You have God-shine when you control your emotions and self-interests, and extend a hand of friendship even to those who mistreat you. This is the selfless love of *agapao*, and that is what Christ did for you on the cross.

Holiness

Without question, the most defining attribute of God is His absolute holiness—there's no comparison. In Isaiah 6:3, the angels announce: "Holy, Holy, Holy, is the LORD of hosts." They proclaim it three times to emphasize that He's absolutely holy in His personhood. God faultlessly discerns between right and wrong, good and bad, just and unjust—and makes judgments based on His supreme righteousness. To understand Him, you must grasp that He's absolutely set apart—righteous and holy in all He is and does.

The Bible tells you that integral to having God-shine is emanating holiness. Yes, you! The Lord commanded: "You are to be holy to Me, for I the LORD am holy; and I have set you apart... to be Mine" (Leviticus 20:26). How do you show holiness? You exhibit holiness through purity and obedience to Him. He is the example to follow and there is no acceptable standard for goodness other than the one He set for you.

Purity and obedience is a God-shine of holiness.

Philosopher Johann Wolfgang von Goethe (1749-1832) said, "Behavior is a mirror in which everyone shows his image." Consider this truth—your actions [fruit] show who you really are. That's why you have to separate yourself from worldly lifestyles and socio-cultural standards. Rather, by observing God's commands, you show the world that you bear His likeness in a life of holiness.

For this reason, the apostle Peter made this appeal: "As obedient children, do not be conformed to the former lusts which were yours in your ignorance, but like the Holy One who called you, be holy yourselves also in all your behavior; because it is written, 'You shall be holy, for I am holy'" (1 Peter 1:14-16).

- **Whose image is in the mirror of your life? When others observe your behavior, who would they say that you resemble?**

Smudged Lamps

Have you ever been in a room lighted by oil-burning lamps? Many decades ago, this was a main source of light in most homes. These lamps had oil stored in the base that fueled a burning wick that shone light through glass chimneys.

A continual chore was cleaning the glass chimneys as they became smudged with soot from the burning oil, thus causing the light to dim. The flame would remain bright as ever inside the lamp, but the blackened glass chimney would prevent the light from shining to its full potential.

The same is true when those who have had a God-birth, but smudge their lives with sin by choosing to live carnally. Jesus said: "Walk while you have the light, [so] that darkness may not overtake you; he who walks in the darkness does not know where he goes" (John 12:35). When fleshly appetites appeal to you—rather than the fruit of the Spirit—your light is dimmed, your witness is smudged.

So then, how do you maintain God-shine? "If we walk in the light as He Himself is in the light, we have fellowship with one another, and the blood of Jesus His Son cleanses us from all sin... If we *confess* our sins, He is faithful and righteous to forgive us our sins and to *cleanse* us from all unrighteousness" (1 John 1:7, 9, emphasis mine). When you walk with Him daily, your God-shine can glow brightly to the lost world around you through your truth, love, and holiness. But, what if your life is dimmed or smudged by sin? You must acknowledge and confess your sin so that Christ can cleanse you, and make possible a God-shine.

Confess and Cleanse

Two decisive and operative words in 1 John 1:9 are *confess* and *cleanse*: "If we confess our sins, He is faithful… to cleanse us from all unrighteousness." Biblical confession is vastly different from the kind of confession that emanates from a guilty conscience. Simply saying, "I'm sorry," isn't sufficient.

The word translated *confess* (*homologeō*), is a merger of two words that means *to speak the same thing*. It signifies agreeing with God regarding your sins. Robert Candlish explains, "It is the confession of men 'walking in the light, as God is in the light,' having the same medium of vision that God has; it is continual confession of men continually so walking, and so seeing."[ix]

The second word from 1 John, *cleanse* (*katharízō*) means *to make clean*, *to purge*, or *to purify*. This cleansing is directly dependent upon the confession. Paul told the Ephesians that Jesus, because of His love for the church "gave Himself up for her; [so] that He might sanctify her, having cleansed her by the washing of water with the word" (Ephesians 5:25-26). The word translated *washing* can be translated *cleansed* or *released*. Jesus not only purifies you from the sin, but He breaks its rule over you.

~~~~~~

Jesus purifies your sin and breaks its rule over you.

~~~~~~

How does Jesus do that? He sent the Holy Spirit (John 15:26) to be our helper. First Corinthians 3:17 tells us "the temple of God is holy, and that is what you are." The temple of God is always to be a sanctuary, a sacred place. Your helper, the Holy Spirit is always convicting you of your sin so that you can remain clean and undefiled. Only then can He shine brightly through your thoughts, words, and actions. He makes sure your God-shine radiates with truth, love, and holiness.

This is the ongoing work of the indwelling Holy Spirit, who is sanctifying you—making you holy—by ministering the Word of God in your life. When Jesus was tempted by the devil to turn stones into bread, He responded: "It is written, 'Man shall not live on bread alone, but on every word that proceeds out of the mouth of God'" (Matthew 4:4). He used the Word as His defense against temptation.

Ephesians 6:17 confirms "the sword of the Spirit, which is the Word of God." Here, the *word* (*rhēma*) is specific Scriptures the Holy Spirit calls to mind during a particular time of need. Your first defense for maintaining personal holiness is storing helpful Scripture verses in your mind. In every situation or temptation, there is Scripture you can use to protect yourself, that will aid you in a God-shine of holiness.

- **What is dimming your God-shine?**

- **Are you sharpening the sword of the Spirit by memorizing Scripture?**

—Chapter Five—

Imitators

A well-known and admired actor once told of his humble beginnings as a novice on Broadway. During his first play, he shared the
stage with a world-renowned actor. This situation quickly became
a wonderful learning opportunity for the novice. He studied the
celebrated star—seeking to mimic his moves, voice, gestures, stage
presence, and even his interaction with other actors and with the
audience. Learning the craft by watching other accomplished profes-
sionals, he ultimately became a famous performer himself.

Imitators of God

Ephesians 5:1 admonishes "be [become] imitators of God, as beloved
children." At first glance, this may sound utterly unreasonable. How
can a finite person *know* God, much less try to imitate His infinite
character? He's God, the Almighty—and we, well, we're but limited
mortal beings.

You should know, this instruction by Paul is far more than a
suggestion—it's a *duty* for you as a believer. The verb *be* in this
passage may be translated *become*, or *be brought to pass with
result*. Your God-birth is a one-time event; however, God-shine is
an ongoing process of maturing into a godly lifestyle (God-life).

You have everything you need for God-shine: "His divine power has granted to us [you] everything pertaining to life and godliness" (2 Peter 1:3).

To *imitate* is following another's example—modeling their actions. I'm sure you have heard the saying, "Imitation is the sincerest form of flattery." Think of it, someone admires you enough to imitate your actions or lifestyle. In terms of patterning yourself after God, you're to "pursue righteousness, godliness, faith, love, perseverance, and gentleness" (1 Timothy 6:11). Imitating His moral attributes should be the goal of your life—continually endeavoring to emulate God-shine.

- **How are you modeling God in your life?**

Imitating (following) God requires you to "discipline yourself for the purpose of godliness" (1 Timothy 4:7). This takes effort—it means putting self-centered plans aside for a Christ-centered life. At times, that's more than you may desire, or are even willing to try. It's a choice; your choice to have God-shine.

Matthew 8:1 reminds you: "When He [Jesus] came down from the mountain, large crowds followed Him" (HCSB). I've often wondered about all of the people in that crowd. How many were there because they sincerely believed Jesus was the Messiah? How many actively sought Him and went on to be true disciples? And, how many were there just to be fed and maybe see or even receive a miracle?

What about church attendees today? How many in our churches are true disciples, or are they there for other reasons? Of the faces in the congregation, how many are being transformed by the Word of Life, or are they there to just "get" something else from the service? Too many churches promote services as a "today's feature" or an "exciting special" in an effort to build attendance—entertain a crowd. The purpose of the local church is for worship, to proclaim the gospel, and teach the eternal truths of the Word of God. Oh, that the "crowd" would desire God-shine, what a different world it would be!

Ambition Over Commitment

"Pastor, there's a man waiting to speak with you," came my office assistant's voice over the intercom as I was preparing the sermon for Sunday. I opened the door to my study and a well-dressed man entered. He said that he and his wife had attended and enjoyed services for several weeks. I asked him if they were believers—had they accepted Christ as their Savior? He confirmed they had and told of their church membership in another state.

All of the discussion sounded great until he said, "We've started a new company here in town, and I'd like to establish myself in the community. I've always thought that membership in a local thriving church was good for business." I recognized this ambitious entrepreneur wasn't a true disciple, but one of the "crowd." He wanted to show off the family, get some business contacts, and maybe even make new friends. To the "crowd," church is there for what they can "get" from it.

If your motive for claiming Christ as your Lord and Savior is something other than making Him the focus of your life, then you won't reflect the true Light. Instead, you're attempting to commandeer His identity for your own benefit, and there's a serious warning for you. "Many will say to Me in that day, 'Lord, Lord, have we not prophesied in Your name, cast out demons in Your name, and done many wonders in Your name?' And then I will declare to them, 'I never knew you; depart from Me'" (Matthew 7:22-23, NKJV).

"I am the light of the world; he who follows Me
shall not walk in the darkness, but shall have the light of life."
(John 8:12)

Those who choose to be imitators of God are to show Him vibrantly and visibly in their daily lifestyle. God-shine is the antithesis of self-centeredness. Choosing to be imitators of God is to surrender any self-seeking glory, spotlight, or recognition. God-shine is conspicuous and apparent, *It is no longer I who live, but Christ who lives in me* (Galatians 2:20, RSV).

- **Are you shining His light or seeking the spotlight?**

Imitators of Others

When I became interested in learning how to fly-fish, I went to a sports equipment store seeking help. I asked the clerk if they had a "how to" book that would help me learn the art form of fly-fishing. The helpful clerk gave me wise counsel when he said, "Find an outstanding fly-fisherman, and do what he does."

I did just that, in fact, there was a man in my church said to be the best in the area. I told him of my interest, and he invited me to go fishing. I learned to fly-fish with some success by imitating him.

In 1 Corinthians 11:1, Paul boldly commanded: "Be imitators of me, just as I also am of Christ." This wasn't brash egotism. Rather, Paul could ask others to simulate him because he was doing everything he could to be like Christ. He was committed to the Savior and was allowing Christ to live through him; he had God-shine.

- **Are you imitating Christ? Are you an example setter?**

Nowadays, it's typical to hear the admonition, "Do as I say, not as I do." Not so with Paul. He tells us in 1 Corinthians 9:23, 27, "I do all things for the sake of the gospel, that I may become a fellow partaker of it... I buffet [discipline] my body and make it my slave, [so that]... after I have preached to others, I myself should be disqualified."

Believers at Corinth were having difficulty honoring Christ in their daily living. To help them, Paul told them to imitate his example so they could learn to live like Christ. Paul's passionate concern can be heard in his language: "If you were to have countless tutors in Christ, yet you would not have many fathers; for in Christ Jesus I became your father through the gospel. I exhort you therefore, be imitators of me" (1 Corinthians 4:15-16).

Paul's sincere desire was to let his God-shine be a model for them, and he implored believers to be godly. Likewise, missionaries, pastors, Bible teachers, Christian leaders, and yes you, should exhibit the same exemplary walk. "Remember your leaders, those who spoke to you the word of God; consider the outcome of their life, and imitate their faith" (Hebrews 13:7, RSV). It's worth noting that it wasn't a forgone conclusion that leaders would be worth emulating. Rather, leaders to be followed, must be measured by God's standards of behavior. Are the Christian, professional, or political leaders in your life worthy of following?

Paul tells us *to live is Christ* (Philippians 1:21). This is to be the hallmark of believers who are *example setters*. In his letter to the church at Philippi, Paul calls for you and me to be: true, honorable, right, pure, lovely, and of good reputation (see Philippians 4:8). These characteristics are to saturate your life and distinguish your God-shine from the darkness of the world. As you grow in these traits, you become a spiritual *example setter*. That's because these are Jesus' own characteristics, and when you model after Christ with all of your heart, soul, mind, and strength; only then can you call upon others to imitate you.

An obedient follower of Christ is worthy of emulation. Paul wrote: "You also became imitators of us and of the Lord, having received the word in much tribulation with the joy of the Holy Spirit, so that you became an example [pattern] to all the believers" (1 Thessalonians 1:6-7).

The word *example* (*túpos*) means a *pattern* or *model*. The believers at the church at Thessalonica became an example for the entire region. They had *imitated* Paul, who had God-shine, because he followed the Lord. The result was that the God-shine of the believers at Thessalonica strongly influenced and gave an example to follow for new churches established in Paul's second missionary journey.

You aren't only to look to those with a mature God-walk, but you're to become an example setter as well. Your life should reflect Christ and the Word of God in all situations so others will learn how to honor Him with their lives by watching you. That's the bold challenge for you today.

- **Check out your God-shine. Who is following you?**

—Chapter Six—

Let Your Light Shine

They say that confession is good for the soul and contributes to a strong character. I agree with that, so I'll admit that for years I interpreted Jesus' words in Matthew 5:16 in what I now believe to be a shallow or even an erroneous way. He said: "Let your light shine before men in such a way that they may see your good works, and glorify your Father who is in heaven."

As discussed earlier, most people understand this passage infers the sun/moon concept, the moon not generating its own light, but rather, reflecting the light of the sun. In that vein, we mirror the light of the Son, Jesus Christ. This is how I understood it, and while my understanding was in the mainstream, I now believe that Jesus was talking about much more than simply reflected light.

That's not to say that the concept of reflected light is in any way unimportant or inferior to the concept I'm about to present—it just doesn't fully encompass all that Scripture says about God-shine.

~~~~~~~~~~~~~~~~~~
Let your light shine.
~~~~~~~~~~~~~~~~~~

Consider Jesus' imperative statements in Matthew 5, the heart of the Sermon on the Mount: "You are the light of the world" (verse 14). "Light a lamp… it gives light to all" (verse 15). "Let your light shine" (verse 16).

In verse 14, the word for *light* (*phōs*) means *to shine, be luminous,* or *make manifest by rays.* In other words, we're the ones shining—illuminating the world!

Further, reading on in verse 15, the word for *light* (*kaiō*) is different—it signifies *to burn* or *set fire to, to light.* And, the *lamp* (*lúchnos*) mentioned in this verse was a portable lamp, a brilliant torch that burned oil and was usually set on a stand. The same idea is seen in verse 16—we allow our light to shine, glow brightly, like a fire ablaze.

Notice that in all of these verses you don't see a *reflected* light, but rather, a *luminous light.* Obviously, there's much more here than just a mirror of the Lord's glory. G. Campbell Morgan insightfully notes, "When we received the Essential Light, it was not merely that we might reflect it; it was that it might ignite us and burn in us."[x] You're not only to glow by a reflection, but are charged to have an inner incandescent God-shine. You have an illuminated life when you are crucified (die to self), and are set ablaze by the living Lord Jesus Christ—a luminous God-shine.

Jesus' statement is clear and straightforward: "You *are* the light" (Matthew 5:14, emphasis mine). However, you may be wondering: *How can that be?*

Let's look at it through a progression of logic.

Scripture tells us that Jesus is the Light of the World (see John 8:12; 9:5), and that the Triune God—Father, Son, and Holy Spirit—are one (see Deuteronomy 6:4). So, if one of the Trinity is light, then *all* are light because they are as one.

God's Word proclaims that the Holy Spirit indwells you when you receive God-birth, giving you the potential of living God-life (see 1 Corinthians 6:19-20). He is in [inhabits] you; therefore, the Light of the World is within you.

The importance of the Holy Spirit's presence in your life can't be overstated. He's proof of the grace given to you and of the divine purpose that God has for you. Even so, He also becomes the glory of God in you. Second Corinthians 4:7 tells us, "we possess this precious treasure [the divine light of the Gospel] in [frail, human] vessels of earth, that the grandeur and exceeding greatness of the power may be shown to be of God and not from ourselves" (AMP).

The Holy Spirit is proof of the grace given *to you* and of the divine purpose that God has *for you.*

Jesus' promises are absolutely reliable. In John 8:12, He says: "I am the light of the world; he who follows Me shall not walk in the darkness, but shall have *the light of life*" (emphasis mine). The Holy Spirit makes it possible for you to have the light of life within you. His presence gives you the spiritual capacity to become an ignited God-shine. It's His power and presence by which you are able to conquer the darkness. And Jesus reassures: "Greater is He who is in you than he who is in the world" (1 John 4:4). Be confident, you will have a glowing God-shine because He is shining through you.

- **You *are* the light of the world. Does that make a difference in how you live?**

Luminaries

Do you get excited when you see a "falling star" in the night sky? Do you make a wish? Do you watch it until it disappears beyond the horizon? Even when the canopy of sky is filled with twinkling stars, your attention is drawn to this brilliant spectacle of a single star in space.

Of course, we know that falling stars are actually blazing comets streaking across a blackened sky. They illustrate a beautiful portrait of you as a Christian — you are the light that is to dispel and conquer the surrounding darkness. You are to live with a visible God-shine in your everyday environment.

As we discussed earlier, as a believer, you are not only to walk in light, but are also a source of light—it radiates from you. The illuminating presence or anointing of the Holy Spirit shines in you (see 1 John 2:20, 27). Through the Holy Spirit, God-shine bubbles up and brims over, overflowing to everyone around you.

Jürgen Moltman noted, "It is obvious that no one can 'make' this life, either through asceticism or through discipline. But one can *let it be* and let it come."[xi] The light shines of itself, but we can open ourselves to it and let it shine.

Paul told the Ephesians: "You were formerly darkness, but now you are *light in the Lord*; walk as *children of light*" (Ephesians 5:8, emphasis mine). It's important to emphasize that Paul *did not* say they were *in* darkness and now are *in* light, merely enlightened because of their salvation. On the contrary, they themselves were *literally* darkness and had become *actual* light.

Rejoice! You were *darkness* and became *light*.

Paul speaks again about light when writing to the church at Philippi, he reminded them: "It is *God* who is at work in you, both to will and to work for His good pleasure… that you may prove yourselves to be blameless and innocent, children of God above reproach in the midst of a crooked and perverse generation, among whom you *appear* as *lights* in the world" (Philippians 2:13, 15, emphasis mine). God-shine should be an intrinsic part of your life as a Holy Spirit indwelt believer. It becomes your essential nature as you live life in communion with God.

The word translated *appear* (*phainō*) means *to be seen, to lighten,* or *shine*. And the word rendered *lights* (*phōstēr*) means, *a brilliant luminary*. It has the same root as *phosphorus*, which is a light-bearing substance that glows in the dark. How fitting that you're to be an illuminator in a world that so desperately needs rescue from the darkness.

Incandescent for the Lord

But really, how can you overcome the darkness of the world? As I thought about this critically important question, I leaned back in my chair and looked up at the ceiling of my study. There it was, the answer!

Early that morning, when I first entered the study, it was dark. I flipped the switch on and light appeared, but only after electricity flowed to the filament, energizing it. It burned, but wasn't consumed. The bulb was there, the filament was there, the electricity was there, but nothing happened until I *willed* for it to happen, until I flipped the switch. A single light bulb illuminated the room and dispelled the darkness.

When you *will* for the Holy Spirit to fill your life and determine to be crucified with Christ, you become a luminary with God-shine. A God-shine life will dynamically illuminate the darkness of the world!

How often have you heard the phrase, "Like father, like son?" Sometimes it's used to reflect high morals and strength of character, while at other times it identifies weakness of character or an unbecoming nature.

Through God-birth, you inherit the nature of God. Remember, at the beginning of this study we said God's essence is described as light, "There shall no longer be any night; and they shall not have need of the light of a lamp nor the light of the sun, because the Lord God will illumine them" (Revelation 22:5). He is light and the radiance of God-shine; it is an inseparable part of the new nature He has given to you. *You've become light.*

Sunshine's Name was Connie

A few houses from my parents was a little girl named Connie. She lived with her mother and widowed grandmother, all three subsisting on an irregular and inadequate income. It was a bleak and unpromising beginning for Connie.

I don't know where she got the nickname "Sunshine" but it fit. She always had an infectious smile, a giggle, and a lyrical laugh for everyone. She never asked for much and was excited for anything she received.

Connie had an early love for Jesus. She loved singing children's choruses about Him—"Jesus Loves Me," "This Little Light of Mine," and "I'm a Sunbeam." With an index finger, she would point up, and say, "I love Jesus." Unthinkably, inoperable cancer was discovered—but, cancer is not her story.

"Sunshine" never lost her Son-beam. She never complained. Even when you were aware that she was hurting, she would smile, pointing her index finger up toward Heaven.

Church members, neighbors, and friends came to visit this special little girl—all profoundly touched by her. After the city newspaper featured Connie's story with a picture of a smiling little girl and as always, a pointed index finger, many from outside of the community came wanting to meet her.

A prominent pastor from a large church sat by her bedside—praying and weeping while reading her a story. He said, "Today I learned tranquility." When a neighbor, who was a fireman asked her, "Is there anything you want?" She responded, "A ride on your big red fire engine!" The next day, she did. When George Beverly Shea heard about her and that she loved to hear him sing, he came to see her and gave her a signed album. There were so many touched and changed by the radiant testimony of "Sunshine." Even when it became difficult for her to talk, there was always her smile and upward pointed index finger.

At her funeral, the pastor said, "Connie not only taught us how to die, but more importantly how to live." "Sunshine" was always aglow, shining for Jesus. She was only six years old when she went to be with Jesus.

With that in mind, the invitation of Scripture is to believe and become the child of light that you were meant to be. Jesus said, "While you have the Light, believe in the Light—have faith in it, hold to it, rely on it—that you may become sons of the Light and be filled with light" (John 12:36, AMP).

Believe and *Become* a child of light.

Jesus is saying that by allowing Him to live in and through you, your life will be a holy, luminous example to everyone around you. Therefore, yield to the Spirit of God, and glow with the brilliance of a God-shine. A fresh, new day is dawning, and you're going to be the one who shows others the love of Christ by your God-shine.

- **Are you a light that shines in the darkness? Does your God-life have the brilliance of a God-shine?**

Section Four

GOD-TALK

"Let the words of my mouth
and the meditation of my heart
be acceptable in Thy sight,
O Lord, my Rock and my Redeemer."
(Psalm 19:14)

"Walk the talk." We've heard that phrase a thousand times in conversations and speeches. It comes from the question, "You can talk the talk, but can you walk the walk?" Do your actions match up to your words?

If you talk about your faith, you must be willing to live it. However, just as important as "walking the talk" is "talking the walk." You as a Christian must effectively communicate what you believe.

The first time I heard the expression "talk the walk" was in college when I pastored a church in rural Tennessee. There were two Baptist churches in our farming community. In addition to other fellowship opportunities during the year, it was their practice to visit each other's services during summer revivals. During one such night, the preacher emphasized the need to guard our talk and always speak in a way acceptable to God—in other words, to "talk the walk." Does your talk match up with your professed walk?

Talking is an important activity in the Bible. In fact, the Bible begins, "God *said*, 'Let there be light'; and there was light" (Genesis 1:3, emphasis mine). Likewise, the Bible concludes with Jesus *saying*, "Yes, I am coming quickly" (Revelation 22:20). Between the first and the last book of the Bible, there's a lot of talking—God has a lot to say. And so does everyone else, including an unusually gifted donkey (see Numbers 22:21-35). Throughout the Bible's pages, men speak great prophecies, angels make wonderful proclamations, a promise that one day, "every tongue [will] confess that Jesus Christ is Lord, to the glory of God the Father" (Philippians 2:11).

Knowingly or unknowingly, our world is led by words—words of parents, friends, preachers, teachers, politicians—words that are good and bad, helpful and hurtful. Words can lead to success or failure, inspiration or discouragement, life or death. History records the sad commentary that the masses, like a flock of sheep, can be led into a diabolical path by persuasive words (remember German dictator Adolph Hitler). How invaluable then are words of true wisdom!

How you express yourself is very important. David's prayer in Psalm 19 was on target: the words of your mouth and the meditation of your heart should be acceptable to God. David is asking that both the outer and inner person be in perfect conformity with God's will and thus pleasing to Him. Do your inner (thoughts) and outer (words) communications please God?

What is appropriate talk for you as a Christian? You're challenged to speak and think only about those things that are worthy in God's sight. Further, you're admonished to make sure your actions are righteous, that your mouth doesn't utter evil or hurtful words, and that your heart purges sinful thoughts. Why? Because, your talk is the first and often the most lasting impression others have of you.

Will you join me in discovering acceptable and unacceptable use of our voices, a God-talk?

- **What can people tell about you by how you talk?**

— Chapter One —

Inappropriate Talk

Mother Teresa of Calcutta once said, "Words which do not give the light of Christ increase the darkness." Undoubtedly, that's why the Bible has so much to say about what proceeds from our mouths. You're to be crucified with Christ, and what you do and say should be Him living and communicating through you. That's the very essence of God-talk.

Sadly, many Christians don't honor God in their daily conversations. When I consider "talk," I'm aware that it's far easier to control the actions of the body than to control the tongue. Your talk can create havoc. In James 3:8, we're told "no one can tame the tongue; it is a restless evil and full of deadly poison." And Proverbs 11:9 warns "with his mouth the godless man destroys his neighbor."

In fact, the Bible has much to say about those who misuse the gift of speech to harm others. Jeremiah 9:8 tells us "their tongue is a deadly arrow." In this passage, God condemns His people for their destructive talk. Jeremiah 9:3 explains "'they bend their tongue like their bow; lies and not truth prevail in the land; for they proceed from evil to evil, and they do not know Me,' declares the Lord."

- **Stop for a moment and consider your talk. Do you allow your tongue to become a deadly arrow?**

It's incalculable to know the detrimental effect your talk has on the lives of others. God-life isn't achieved when you use inappropriate talk. To understand what God-talk is, let's first look at what God-talk isn't.

Destructive Attitudes

Words are the venting of thoughts and attitudes. Attitudes fuel your speech. It's true, what you say portrays who you are. You don't use destructive talk about others unless there are underlying destructive attitudes.

Paul encouraged the church at Colossae to embrace a holy life by "seeking the things [which are] above, where Christ is, seated at the right hand of God" (Colossians 3:1). Paul then addressed some un-Christ-like attitudes that would damage the *fellowship* (*koinōnia*) among believers. His admonition was for them to put off completely these detrimental thoughts. Let's look more closely at these ruinous emotional attitudes.

Paul singled out three destructive attitudes: Anger, Wrath, and Malice.

Anger
Anger (*orgē*): a state of excessive emotion or feeling. It's an emotional response to a threat or insult and is often retaliated by heated language. Anger can be a quick passing response or a lasting state of smoldering emotion.

Wrath
Wrath (*thumos*): violent anger and extreme passion that may escalate to revenge. It may desire harm to come to the object of its passionate rage. It says, "I hope that you suffer for what you've said or done."

Malice
Malice (*kakia*): feeling and often expressing an intense or even vicious ill will towards others. This malevolent emotion is deep-

seated and is frequently unreasonable. It says, "I'm going to make you wish you'd never done that."

Little wonder Paul says "put off" disruptive attitudes that would affect the fellowship of the church. He knew these harmful attitudes would ferment into destructive speech. Bear in mind that Paul was writing to Christians—yes, Christians participate in destructive speech!

- **How have you been hurt by another person's words? Why do destructive words stay with you long after they're spoken?**

Destructive Talk

Destructive attitudes produce destructive talk. And, destructive talk will destroy your witness and reputation. The church of the risen Lord suffers and you forfeit an opportunity to live God-life when using destructive talk. Charles Spurgeon said that it is a tragedy if the Christian's mouth is ever "defiled with untruth, or pride, or wrath; yet so it will become unless carefully watched, for these intruders are ever lurking about the door." [i]

~~~~~~
Destructive talk is not so much a mouth problem
as a heart problem.
~~~~~~

Consider commonly used destructive talk: Slander, Lies, and Gossip.

Slander
Defined as intensely destructive talk that discredits, destroys, and vilifies the object of its ire, slander is vicious and scandalous accusations made to besmirch someone's reputation through falsehood or by innuendo.

Look again at Colossians 3:8 (AMP) "rid yourselves [completely] of… slander and foulmouthed abuse." Slander and foulmouthed abuse defames and damages another's very personhood—their character, witness, and ministry.

The word *slander* used in the New Testament is most often the Greek word *blasphēmia* from which we also get *blaspheme*. Realize that when you make derogatory statements about another, you're trying to discredit a person made in the image of God. Serious? Listen to God, "Whoever secretly slanders his neighbor, him I will destroy" (Psalm 101:5). Slander in any form is character assassination. In our court system, defamation of character is prosecuted.

Lies

Guard your lips so that no falsehood escapes. Hebrews 6:18 tells us "it is impossible for God to lie." Therefore, can you imagine how offensive lying is to God? "Let the lying lips be put to silence, which speak grievous things… against the righteous" (Psalm 31:18, KJV).

Satan himself is the father of lies and falsehoods (see John 8:44). When believers speak a lie, untruth, or embellished truth with the intent to deceive or mislead, they're allowing Satan to use their talk to corrupt and taint the witness of Christ. "A false witness will not go unpunished, and he who tells lies will not escape" (Proverbs 19:5).

God is truth, and one of the characteristics of His nature to be actualized in your life is truthfulness—unqualified validity and accuracy in your every statement. I hear people making excuses by calling untruths "little white lies." American physicist Austin O'Malley astutely said, "Those who think it's permissible to tell white lies soon become color-blind."

God-talk manifests a newness of life in Christ by speaking truthfully. "Do not lie to one another, since you laid aside the old self with its evil practices" (Colossians 3:9).

Facing Truth

Recently, I was watching a popular television judge questioning the defendant. He hesitated to answer the judge's inquiries until glancing at the papers on the desk before him. Another question and he fumbled for an answer while looking to the right then to the left. The judge asked him to look at her when testifying, but the defendant continued to have evasive eyes. Again, and more sternly, she admonished him to look at her when speaking. Her reprimand had little effect. Exasperated she said, "Look at me! I can tell if you are lying when you are looking at me!"

Think about it... every word out of your mouth should be true—so true you could look into God's face and say it.

Gossip

Few are more disruptive in our Lord's church than gossipers. They are spreaders of rumors, hearsay, and grapevine tales. Gossips and busybodies are not conformed to God-talk. Paul gives an excellent verbal description of gossips and busybodies "some among you are leading an undisciplined life, doing no work at all, but acting like busybodies" (2 Thessalonians 3:11).

Neither the church nor its erring members are helped when faults and failures are carried from house to house. Busybodies aren't busy in their own matters, but overly busy in the matters of others. Christians are instructed to "make it your ambition to lead a quiet life and attend to your own business" (1 Thessalonians 4:11).

As Paul was mentoring Timothy, he discussed the perplexing problem of gossips in the fellowship of believers. "They go around from house to house; and not merely idle, but also gossips and busybodies, talking about things not proper to mention" (1 Timothy 5:13). What a sad commentary, we are to love and to forgive—not to have an insatiable curiosity in other's business, enjoying idle talk, and spreading rumors with malicious words.

- **Do you remember a time when you yielded to sharing an all "too juicy" story?**

Have you ever been in a group sharing prayer concerns and it quickly became a gossip session? Indiscretion and even well meaning prayer requests can turn into a rumor mill.

I've heard announced aloud in a time of prayer and intercession statements like, "I'd like to request prayer for Joe and Mary, they're in marriage counseling." Another, "They are keeping it quiet, but Beth's son Greg is on drugs again." Often such requests for prayer begin, "I heard... Someone told me... I'm not sure, but I think that."

Gossip can occur so very easily. Take great care when someone is in a personal crisis and confides in you. Protect them and your integrity. Gossip is damaging to the church fellowship and to your witness for Christ.

Peter places busybodies and meddlers in bad company. "By no means let any of you suffer as a murderer, or thief, or evildoer, or a *troublesome meddler*" (1 Peter 4:15, emphasis mine). There's unquestioned agreement that a Christian shouldn't be involved in murder, stealing, or any sort of crime—Peter adds in the mix, gossips, busybodies, and meddlers. Does that surprise you?

Look again at the text. Gossips and busybodies *murder* another's witness and ministry; they *steal* another's reputation; and as *evildoers,* they do the work of Satan. Talebearers are reluctant to give up their choice stories, and by extending the telling of the event, they make it disruptive in the church. Avoid gossips, "he who goes about us as a slanderer reveals secrets, therefore do not associate with a gossip" (Proverbs 20:19).

Gossips and busybodies *murder* witness and ministry,
steal reputations, and as *evildoers,* do the work of Satan.

Unacceptable Talk

Language is a tool of thinking and not merely a means of communication. Your language (talk) reveals your measure of development in God's grace and growth in God-life. The impulse to use base, vulgar, or suggestive language indicates the Holy Spirit is not in control of your mind, thought, or language (talk). It defiles your character and witness.

Cursing

The use of profane or obscene language or invoking the name of God in an oath has no place at all, at any time, in any way, in the life of the believer. It's disgraceful to use profanities to express or give emphasis to an opinion. Not too long ago, there was no cursing on the radio or television. And, in public, when a man uttered a curse word in the presence of a lady, he apologized. How different it is today! All mediums of communication are pushing the limits of foul language in mainstream conversation. There are more and more bleeps on television. How soon before they stop the "bleeps" and allow the language?

Eddie's New Language

Let me tell you about a man I know. Before he was saved, Eddie was a hard-working, foul-mouthed, prolific curser. However, when he came to saving faith in Christ, he was cleansed both spiritually and linguistically. He said smiling, "When I became a Christian, I lost half of my vocabulary. But, praise God! I'm now learning a new one." It was a tribute to God's grace—Eddie gave over his mind, thoughts, and speech to the Lord, and began learning a new language—God-talk.

James 3:10 tells us "from the same mouth come both blessing and cursing. My brethren, these things ought not to be this way." James is addressing the fellowship of believers, the church. The mouth that seeks to praise God and give a witness for Christ on one hand, and utters foul cursing on the other, is immeasurably destructive. Not only is it disruptive within the church, it nullifies your witness (talk) to the unsaved.

Filthiness

Filthiness speaks of general obscenities that are base and shameful—all that is contrary to purity. It is the same word translated *disgraceful* in Ephesians 5:12 where Paul says it's deplorable to mention, much less participate, in dirty talk. Filthiness is a common term including immoral thoughts, obscenities, lustful fantasies, and sexual impurities or abnormalities. Contemporary culture is brimming with those considering obscenities, vulgarities, and off-color stories to be amusing. Keep in your mind that Jesus said: "the mouth speaks out of that which fills the heart" (Matthew 12:34).

Coarse Jesting

Wisecracks or witticism can skillfully twist and turn something said or done, regardless of its innocence, into obscene, suggestive, and filthy talk. As Marvin R. Vincent explains, "The sense of the word here is polished and witty speech as the instrument of sin... lodged in a sly question... in shrewd intimation... a tart irony, in a lusty hyperbole, in a startling metaphor." [ii]

To observe the foulness of coarse jesting, or raillery, tune in to late night comics and talk-show hosts. They never miss an opportunity to turn something of innocence into an immoral innuendo. Sometimes attempting wittiness, even religious leaders engage in borderline jesting. While maybe not originating the off-color jesting, believers sometimes laugh at impure word-twisting innuendos. Guard against laughing at or participating in such jesting.

- **Are the thoughts of your mind and the words of your mouth acceptable to God?**

Useless Talk

Have you been silent in a gathering of people and listened to the chatter, the small talk? It may be chitchat or light conversation at a food court in the mall, a sports-related or other social event. It serves little purpose other than being social. While useless in the long term, it's accepted as a form of communication or relating on a casual level. Sometimes, do you get the feeling that there are those who talk just to hear themselves talk? My father would say, "Empty heads produce useless talk." The older I get, the more I understand what he meant by that.

During a rather noisy discussion at a church meeting, the person leading the discussion turned to an older man and said, "I've noticed that you haven't said anything." His reply was wise and memorable, "When I have something to say, I'll say it." Perhaps his model is one to be followed; useless talk is without profit.

Let's look at two forms of useless talk: Unprofitable and Silly Talk.

Unprofitable Talk

In the oldest book in the Old Testament, Job's friend, Eliphaz, told him his talk had been idle, unprofitable prattle. Job had been so absorbed with himself that he delivered a lengthy soliloquy of useless talk and profitless arguments. Eliphaz observed that Job's useless talk indicated he was devoid of a reverence for God (personal holiness). His irreverence regrettably undermined the faith and reverence of others, and discouraged prayer and meditation (see Job 15:3-4).

Job, a man of faith, should have seized the opportunity to say something more profound about his faith and God; or encouraged his friend to share his own faith. Job wasted an opportunity—when delivering his monologue it was an unprofitable talk. We have all let opportunities slip by to share our faith.

Have you considered your useless talk may not
be useless, the devil may be using it to his advantage?

Silly Talk

The word translated *silly* or *foolish talk* (*mōrŏlŏgia*) is from the same root word (*moros*) from which we get *moron*. Silly talk is moronic buffoonery or foolish chatter that is pointless and stupid. It is more than mere random talk. It may be a vain effort to be cute or funny, but is poor judgment and insensitive.

To live God-life, a holy life, have a sanctified mouth—appropriate God-talk. Keep a strong volition to maintain God-honoring talk at all times. "I will guard my ways, that I may not sin with my tongue; I will guard my mouth as with a muzzle" (Psalm 39:1). God (*JEHOVAH MEKADESH*) is THE LORD WHO SANCTIFIES you (Leviticus 20:8). He is the God of your salvation; joyfully sing of His righteousness. There's a marvelous verse by David that should be your daily prayer-call, "set a guard, O LORD, over my mouth; keep watch over the door of my lips" (Psalm 141:3).

~~~~~~

JEHOVAH MEKADESH, THE LORD WHO SANCTIFIES

~~~~~~

How serious is useless or silly talk? Jesus gives you a clear warning: "I say to you, that every careless word that [people] shall speak, they shall render account for it in the day of judgment" (Matthew 12:36). There's an eternal responsibility for talk.

Pubilius in the first century B.C. said, "I have often regretted my speech, never my silence." I love an ancient Celtic saying that teaches, "Silence, unless the reason for speech, will bear the search-light of eternity." Oh my! Have you considered the eternal effect of your inappropriate talk?

- **Does your talk communicate that you are a crucified believer in whom Christ lives?**

—Chapter Two—

Appropriate Talk

J esus assured believers that the Holy Spirit will give appropriate words to speak: "Say whatever is given you... it is not you who speak, but it is the Holy Spirit" (Mark 13:11). You're to "pray at all times in the Spirit... that utterance may be given |you| in the opening of |your| mouth" (Ephesians 6:18-19). The Holy Spirit will illumine you with the thoughts and words of God. The Word of God becomes your lexicon for appropriate God-talk.

Remembering Sir Winston Churchill
It has been reported that Winston Churchill would labor over every word of a speech making certain it conveyed exactly the thought and inspiration he desired. He took great care that his speeches did not contain useless words. Into the night, he would toil with words and phrases, evaluating them for their meaning and effect. He wasted not one syllable, not one word; he was a master wordsmith of the English language.

In the British House of Commons, there is a larger than life bronze figure of Prime Minister Churchill. With hands on his waist and leaning over slightly, he is obviously speaking. The statue not only captures the distinguishable features of Churchill, it reminds us he is known for his words. No wonder it is said that Britain won the battle of World War II on the words of Winston Churchill.

- **Do you pray for God the Holy Spirit to wordsmith your speech so you'll have appropriate talk?**

Unforgettable Words

Like me, I'm sure you're constantly bombarded by words and ideas; we live in an environment of never-ending talk. But, what of it all? You're remembered for *what* you say — not *how much* you say. Abraham Lincoln is remembered for a dozen lines in his Gettysburg address, which began: "Four score and seven years ago our fathers brought forth on this continent, a new nation, conceived in liberty, and dedicated to the proposition that all men are created equal." John F. Kennedy is remembered for: "Ask not what your country can do for you; ask what you can do for your country." Also memorable is Winston Churchill's appeal to his countrymen: "I have nothing to offer but blood, toil, tears, and sweat." And who could forget Franklin D. Roosevelt's words before Congress following the December 7, 1941 bombing of Pearl Harbor: "A date which will live in infamy." Ronald Reagan initiated the fall of communist Russia when standing at the Brandenburg Gate in West Berlin he said, "Mr. Gorbachev, Tear down this wall!" We remember these men of history for their poignant words.

- **What do you say or not say that may have an effect in eternity?**

The Dead Sea is unique among the bodies of water in the world — it goes nowhere; there is no outlet. There are no fish or life in this sea. To the north, the Sea of Galilee has an outlet; the Jordan River flows through it. It's been a productive fishing area since before the days of Jesus. Let's use these two bodies of water for an illustration for appropriate talk. God wants you to be a "Sea of Galilee," letting His words flow through you. He wants to bless you so you can be a blessing to others. Let God's blessings flow through you.

Wisdom of Socrates

Patrick Mahoney in *You Can Find A Way* tells of a student who once went to Socrates (469-399 B.C.) in order to learn appropriate conversation. In the first meeting with the renowned teacher, the student talked so incessantly that Socrates said he couldn't accept him as a pupil without a double fee. "Why charge me double?" the loquacious student asked. "Because," answered Socrates, "I must teach you two things, one how to hold your tongue, and the other how to speak."

While you don't have Socrates to teach you how to speak, you have someone far greater—the Holy Spirit will teach you appropriate God-talk. The indwelling Holy Spirit enables you to honor God with your voice and speech. He is interested in your words. He produced the words of Scripture by inspiration through the minds of the authors. By illumination, He will give you spiritual and intellectual enlightenment for appropriate God-talk. "To each one [believer] is given the manifestation of the Spirit for the common good... the word of wisdom" (1 Corinthians 12:7-8).

Three meaningful ways express appropriate words to God, to the unsaved, and to your fellow believers—Praise, Witness, and Edification.

Praise

To commemorate the first anniversary of his conversion, Charles Wesley wrote the lyrics of "O' For A Thousand Tongues" in 1739. It is said his inspiration came from a statement made by Moravian leader Peter Bohler who said, "Had I a thousand tongues, I would praise Jesus Christ with all of them."

~~~~~~~~~~~~~~~~~~~~~~~~~~~~~~

"O' for a thousand tongues to sing
My great Redeemer's praise,
The glories of my God and King,
The triumphs of His grace."

~~~~~~~~~~~~~~~~~~~~~~~~~~~~~~

God has given you a wondrous instrument, your voice and the ability to communicate — to talk. Lift up your voice! Sanctify the use of your tongue by using your voice to worship God — magnify and give adoration to Him in praise. This is superlative God-talk. Psalm 96:2-3 instructs you to "sing to the LORD, bless His name; proclaim good tidings of His salvation from day to day. Tell of His glory among the nations, His wonderful deeds among all the peoples." Jesus, the Son of God, lifted His voice in praise to God, the Father: "I praise Thee, O' Father, Lord of heaven and earth" (Matthew 11:25).

So what is praise? Is praise a boisterous, hand-clapping, arm-waving demonstrative activity? Some churches are called "praise churches," and some churches have "praise services." What exactly is the God-talk of praise?

Praise is glorifying and worshiping God. It's taking time to express in words your appreciation, love, and respect of the Heavenly Father. Worship Him in word and song. In the first chapter of Ephesians, Paul verbally worships God "to the praise of His glory" (verse 12). He gives praise to God for "every spiritual blessing" (verse 3), for redemption and inheritance (verses 7, 11), and the sealing of the Holy Spirit (verse 13). Among many others, this passage gives the why and how of praise. Praise Him in prayer; Praise Him in song; Praise Him in all of life; Praise the Lord!

> "Give praise to our God... Hallelujah!
> For the LORD our God, the Almighty, reigns."
> (Revelation 19:5-6)

John MacArthur said that Jesus "saved us to serve Him and to **praise** Him. We are saved to be restored to the intended divine purpose of creation — to bear the image of God and bring Him greater glory."[iii]

Praise isn't for self-glory or to bring attention to yourself. Jesus recognized the deceptive prayers of the scribes and Pharisees. He said they sought the most prominent seats, did their benevolent deeds, wore brightly-colored tassels on their garments, and prayed on the street corners all for the praise of man (see Matthew 6:2, 5, 16).

Witness

"You shall receive power when the Holy Spirit has come upon you; and you shall be My witnesses" (Acts 1:8). Telling the good news of our Savior to an unsaved person is an obedient, appropriate talk. Remember, the Gospel came to you from someone who knew Christ—*pass it on.*

A Sign of Eternal Value
While talking to Al, a missionary to the deaf, I asked him to teach me to say in sign language, *Jesus Saves.* He instructed me to take the middle finger of one hand and point to the palm of the other, then repeat with the opposite hand. This signifies the nail prints in Jesus' hands and is the sign for "Jesus." Then he told me to cross my wrists in front of me, and then thrust them apart—making the symbol for broken bondage and the sign for "saves." Together, those motions comprise the sign for "Jesus saves!" It is also the most important message for life; it is God-talk.

Why Should I Witness?
The answer is simple. People are lost; they don't know the Savior and you've received the saving grace of the Lord Jesus Christ. The call of Jesus is: "Follow Me, and I will make you become fishers of men" (Mark 1:17). You can't truly follow Jesus without fishing— witnessing to unsaved people. Jesus is the message. Witness to the salvation that comes through faith in Jesus.

The Greek word *martus* (*witness*) in some form appears in the New Testament 167 times. A witness is limited to a person who has personal knowledge or experience of something. The root of *testimony* and *testify* is also the word *martus.* To testify is to make a public declaration or firsthand acknowledgement that something is true.

Be filled with the God-talk of witness—giving your witness (testimony) of Jesus Christ and the salvation you found in Him.

You are a witness (see Luke 24:48). Jesus said, "I chose you, and appointed you, that you should go and bear fruit" (John 15:16). Why having experienced saving grace would you choose not to share your God-talk of witness?

How Do I Witness?

It's important to recognize that Jesus said, "You shall be My witnesses" (Acts 1:8). He didn't say, "You *may* be," or "You *should* be." He said, "You *shall* be." Witness is *not* a gift to a chosen few. Others may be more experienced or may even be more effective — but you are a witness, just the same. The Holy Spirit will enable you; God equips you to fulfill His commands.

You ask, "How am I to witness, what am I to say?" You repented of your sins, asked Jesus to forgive you, and invited Him into your heart. He saved you! Your personal experience is the core of your testimony. "The one who believes in the Son of God has the witness in himself" (1 John 5:10). Go tell the Good News!

In addition to your verbal witness, your life and words are watched and heard. How to witness? Live a God-life. Let Jesus be seen in you. The attractiveness of your Christ-centered life will draw others to Him. *It's not you, but Christ in you.* Ministry in the name of Jesus is a compelling witness.

A Witness of Ministry

Our daughter Karen, and her husband Colin, were on their way to Gulf Shores, Alabama, for a few days of restful vacation. With no warning, they watched helplessly as a vehicle in front of them swerved, rocked violently, and veering out of control began rolling repeatedly in the grassy median. The SUV stopped on its side; it was a horrific wreck.

Traffic on both sides of the divided highway came to a screeching halt. The driver had been ejected and was severely injured; several men administered life-saving aid to him. The mother and two children, though injured, could be helped from the vehicle. The mother was hysterical and unable to attend to the two terrified children. Fearing the potential of an exploding gas tank, Karen and Colin walked the children to an area of safety and away from the horror of the situation. They began to have a witness of ministry to the traumatized boy and girl until paramedics arrived. They quoted Scripture, prayed with them, comforted, and reassured that they would receive excellent care. Through a loving witness of ministry, they manifested the love of Jesus.

Some of the most effective witnessing is that of ministering to someone in their time of need. Think of the many times Jesus taught us by his ministry to human needs in an effective witness.

To Whom Do I Witness?

In one of the churches I pastored, I was standing in front of a large area map considered our "church field." We were organizing members to witness to everyone in our community. The map was divided into zones, and the intention was to witness to everyone zone-by-zone, street-by-street, house-to-house.

One man trying to be practical said, "Pastor, the church field is too large, we can never do what you're asking."

"Perhaps you're right," I responded. Pointing to the map I suggested, "Let's eliminate this zone."

"Oh, no!" he exclaimed, "My brother lives in that zone and he is lost."

The Word of God is very plain: "*You* will be *a witness* for Him *to all men* of what you have seen and heard" (Acts 22:15, emphasis mine). As a witness, testify to what you have experienced and do so to all people (see Acts 9:15). Because God loves all of the people in the world; witness, give your personal testimony without restriction, profiling, elimination, or discretion. "He is able also to save forever those who draw near to God through Him" (Hebrews 7:25). A God-talk of witness will testify to *all* who are unsaved.

Divine Enablement

The Holy Spirit enables you to witness. God doesn't ask you to do the impossible, nor does He ask you to go alone. Jesus promised a Helper—the Holy Spirit. "When the Helper comes... the Spirit of truth... He will testify of Me, and you also will bear witness" (John 15:26-27, NKJV). The Holy Spirit enables you to effectively witness even under the most adverse circumstances. In fact, I call it God-talk because the Holy Spirit of God joins you in witnessing. "Our gospel did not come to you in word only, but also in power and in the Holy Spirit" (1 Thessalonians 1:5). Therefore, be reassured and empowered knowing that the Holy Spirit enables you when you share your faith and engage in the God-talk of witnessing.

An Unexpected Opportunity to Witness

It happened at a three-day statewide Evangelism Conference. One afternoon rather than a planned program with preaching and singing, the conference program was left open. Before we were dismissed from the morning meeting, the conference director announced that everyone would pair up for door-to-door witnessing in that community. The community was a sparsely populated rural area near a small southern town. Over 300 pastors divided up in over 100 teams and headed in different directions. Knocking on doors, standing in a field or barnyard, at the local filling station or corner grocery store, the teams shared their faith.

That evening, the program had to be extended as everyone was overflowing with joy recounting their afternoon. Dozens of meaningful experiences were shared. A number of professions of faith were reported. Two pastors said that at one home a woman answered the door in tears. They apologized saying it might not be an appropriate time to share with her. "No, please come in" she replied, "I've just received word of a family member's passing!" They were able to minister to her in her time of unexpected bereavement. Another pastor admitted, "This was the first time I have ever witnessed to someone and not encouraged them to attend my church. I just witnessed for Jesus!"

Edification

"Let us pursue the things... by which one may edify another."
(Romans 14:19, NKJV)

Do you realize that your Heavenly Father desires for you to let the glorified Christ live in you so your conversation (talk) will edify fellow Christians? The biblical word *edify* (*ŏikodomē*) means *to build up*. In biblical times, it was a term used in relation to construction or building. It's a word picture for building a strong, stable structure.

While God gave us apostles, prophets, evangelists, pastors, and teachers to equip and edify the body of Christ, the ministry of edification also includes you! You're aware of the importance of physical exercise and nutrition to achieve a strong, healthy body. Likewise, God wants you to build up, to exercise and feed the body of Christ through your conversation and lifestyle—your God-life.

As inconsequential as it may seem, your words and conversations are heard and evaluated by others—you have influence. Is your "talk" edifying the body of Christ?

An Overheard Conversation

Dean, a fellow staff member and close friend, and I boarded a plane in Anchorage and settled in for a long flight to Salt Lake City. It was not long before we were discussing Bible truths. A meal was served, and Dean prayed a prayer of thanksgiving. I recall we were concerned for one of the missionaries in Alaska who had a health issue and agreed to remember him in prayer. We acknowledged praises of the success of work in certain areas and discussed strategy to jumpstart other ministry work. Thus, the conversation went as the plane droned it's way south. At last, the plane landed and we were gathering our belongings to make a connecting flight to Atlanta. It was then that the eavesdropper interrupted.

"Excuse me," she said, "Are you preachers?"

"Yes," we responded.

"You'll never know how blessed I have been listening to your conversation," she acknowledged. Unknowingly, our conversation (talk) was used by God to edify a fellow believer.

Using your voice to edify is appropriate God-talk. What is the God-talk of your testimony? Is it all about your Savior, Jesus Christ? Do you witness to the lost and edify fellow believers?

Early in Paul's ministry, God's grace enriched him so that his message could edify—build up—the church at Jerusalem (see Acts 9:31). In addition to the grace shown to him, he was also grateful to God for the grace given to believers enriching their speech (see 1 Corinthians 1:4-5).

Edification is much more than conversation or lifestyle. It is the declared role of the church and ministers. "But [on the other hand], the one who prophesies—who interprets the divine will and purpose in inspired preaching and teaching—speaks to men for their upbuilding and constructive spiritual progress encouragement and consolation (1 Corinthians 14:3, AMP). Edification by the church is a divinely assigned task and responsibility. The proclamation of divine truth is for the enlightenment of believers, to edify them that they might be built-up to be Christ-like. This is the purpose and principle of effective bible-centered teaching—edification must always be a prime consideration of the ministries of the church.

Sadly, many Christians have not been built-up in the faith. Their description is seen in Hebrews, "Though by this time you ought to be teachers, you have need for some one to teach you the elementary principles of the oracles of God, and you have come to need milk and not [meat] solid food" (5:12). This condition is deplorable. Christians who are not new (babes) to the faith should be edifying others, not finding themselves in need of learning elementary truths of God's Word.

Unquestionably, there is an urgent need to edify the saints, to help them be built-up from stunted infancy to spiritual adulthood. Edification is the teaching or proclamation of biblical truths that increases or strengthens the spiritual life of believers. Edify, enlighten fellow believers so they can grasp the "strong meat" of God's Word, and incorporate life-giving truths into daily lifestyle.

- **Who in your life has edified or built you up?**

- **Take a moment and reflect on wise, helpful, inspiring words someone said to you that were directional hinge points in your life.**

Chapter Three

Prayer-Talk

"Prayer is the highest use to which speech can be put.
It is the highest meaning that can be put into words." [iv]

Prayer-talk is God-talk that returns to its source—directed to God. To talk effectively *for* God and *about* God, it's imperative that you talk *with* God. As you seek God-life, faithful prayer-talk is vital. Paul reminds you to "pray without ceasing" (1 Thessalonians 5:17). Do you live in a spirit of prayer, whispering to God, conscious of His presence throughout the day?

Charles Spurgeon reminded us, "Prayer is the slender nerve that moves the mighty muscle of God." Prayer is an intimate and personal opportunity for you to have one-on-one time with God. It is a cherished use of your voice; it is preeminently the supreme talk of mankind—prayer-talk!

Prayer is an opportunity for one-on-one time with God.

Marriage counselors agree that a common element in troubled marriages is lack of communication. It follows that insufficiency of communication with God through His Word and through prayer is indisputably a core reason for weak, ineffective Christians.

You'll find that you can't manifest God-life without effective prayer-talk. Churches will never be spiritually strong nor will the kingdom of God be advanced without Christians developing a mature prayer life. The affliction of spiritual weakness and carnality in the life of believers can be directly attributed to prayerlessness.

Have you considered the diminishing influence of Judeo-Christian principles in today's society? In a few short decades, we've stood by while agnostics, atheists, and morally liberal activists have forced laws to be changed that were written based on Christian values. They continue to bear pressure and great influence on our courts and with our political leaders. Public school systems often promote individual/social ethics and morality that are contrary to biblical teaching. In fact, prayer, the Bible and its' principles are less and less present in the public school room. For instance, while espousing the theory of evolution, biblical creationism cannot be mentioned.

Without question, prayerlessness has invited spiritual weakness that has resulted in a loss of influence by the Christian church. P.T. Forsyth calls prayerlessness the "sin behind sin."

Consider the diminished effectiveness and weakness of the Christian church. Why doesn't the church have a greater influence on community life and social order?

Andrew Murray raised this probing question:
"What is the reason that many thousands of Christian workers in the world have not a greater influence?... The prayerlessness of their service. In the midst of all their zeal in the study and in the work of the Church... their faithfulness in preaching... they lack that ceaseless prayer which has attached to it the sure promise of the Spirit and the power from on high. It is... the sin of prayerlessness which is the cause of the lack of a powerful spiritual life!" [v]

It is my observation that Christians have many priorities above an active, effective prayer life. Some immerse themselves in church work, Bible study, and various activities in lieu of a disciplined prayer life. For you to have read this far in this book indicates your sincere desire to have a day-to-day God-life. Are you committed to a prosperous prayer-talk, a fulfilling prayer life?

Let's explore how to have an effective Prayer-talk.

Pray in Agreement with the Will of God

"Nevertheless, Thy will be done." How often I have concluded a prayer with these words, and how frequently I've heard others summarily close their prayers with a similar phrase. "Nevertheless" isn't appropriate when you're praying in agreement with the will of God.

~~~~~~

"This is the *confidence* which we have before Him, that,
if we ask anything *according to His will*, He hears us.
And if we know that He hears us in whatever we ask,
we know that we have the requests
which we have asked from Him."
(1 John 5:14-15, emphasis mine)

~~~~~~

Biblical prayer—praying in the will of God—is with confidence. The word *confidence* (*parrhēsia*) implies *boldness* or even *outspokenness*—boldness in your prayer-talk with God.

Paul sets forth a simple formula for successfully praying with confidence.

Pray in agreement with the will of God.
Prayers in agreement with God's will are heard.
Prayers in agreement with God's will are answered.

Commenting on 1 John 5:14-15, John Stott, in his work *The Letters of John* wrote, "Prayer is not a convenient device for imposing our will upon God, or for bending His will to ours, but the prescribed way of subordinating our will to His."

Our Lord taught us in the "model prayer" that all prayers should be: "Thy will be done" (Matthew 6:10). When your prayer-talk is submissive to His will, He hears you. "If anyone is God-fearing, and does His will, He hears him" (John 9:31). At Gethsemane, Jesus prayed, "Not as I will, but as You will" (Matthew 26:39 HCSB). God has a plan, a destiny, a will, for you. Your heart's cry should be that of the disciples, "Lord, teach |me| to pray" (Luke 11:1).

How Do I Pray in Agreement with God?

Three biblical principles lead to a successful prayer life, or how to pray in agreement with God's will. Pray according to the Word of God; pray in agreement with the Holy Spirit; and pray in the name of Jesus.

Let's review these guidelines for praying in the will of God.

1. Pray According to the Word of God.

"Thy word I have treasured in my heart" (Psalm 119:11). Bible study is not primarily to discover the rich theoretic, linguistic, poetic, metaphysical, and philosophical truths of Scripture, but to learn more about God and His will and purpose for your life. It is not a collection of writings from antiquity—it is the God-breathed, living, powerful, and contemporary word from God. God spoke through His Word at the beginning of human existence, and He is still speaking through His Word today!

The Word of God gives clear instruction for living God-life and having effective prayer-talk. By faith, grasp the concept that there's no need to pray, "If it be Your will" when God's Word gives you a clear, straightforward promise. When you pray and claim God's promises in His Word, you have the assurance that you are praying in God's will. God reveals His will and extends His promises to you this very day (see Hebrews 3:7). All of His promises are *living* promises (Hebrews 4:12).

Claim God's promises... all are His Will.

Prayer for the unsaved:

"The Lord is not slack concerning His promise... but is... not willing that any should perish but that all should come to repentance" (2 Peter 3:9, NKJV).

Forgiveness of sins:

"If we confess our sins, He is faithful and righteous to forgive us our sins" (1 John 1:9).

Escape from temptation:

"God is faithful, who will not allow you to be tempted beyond what you are able, but with the temptation will provide the way of escape also, that you may be able to endure it" (1 Corinthians 10:13).

Fulfillment:

"He has satisfied the thirsty soul, and the hungry soul He has filled with what is good" (Psalm 107:9).

Freedom from worry:

"Casting all your anxiety upon Him, because He cares for you" (1 Peter 5:7).

Provision:

"God shall supply all your needs according to His riches in glory in Christ Jesus" (Philippians 4:19).

Encouragement:

"Let us not lose heart in doing good, for in due time we shall reap if we do not grow weary" (Galatians 6:9).

Companionship:

"I will not leave you as orphans; I will come to you" (John 14:18).

Fearful:

"Be strong and courageous, do not be afraid or tremble at them, for the LORD your God is the one who goes with you. He will not fail you or forsake you" (Deuteronomy 31:6).

Healing:

"I will restore health unto thee, and I will heal thee of thy wounds, saith the Lord" (Jeremiah 30:17, KJV).

God's Word can serve effectively as a bond of communication in prayer-talk between you and God. When reading the Bible, integrate your reading into a prayer. Make Scripture personal and let it express your deepest needs and feelings.

Pray Scripture.
Prayer for Forgiveness:
> O' Lord, Master, You are good, and ready to forgive my sins, sending them away—forgetting them forever; and You, Adonai, are abundant in mercy and loving-kindness, I come with thanksgiving, humbly calling upon You (see Psalm 86:5).

Prayer in Time of Trial or Stress:
> O' God, Elohim, You are the one true God, I have no delight or desire on earth beside You, my flesh and heart may weaken and fail, but You, O' God—Father, Son, and Holy Spirit—are my Rock and the strength of my heart and my portion forever (see Psalm 73:26).

Prayer in Times of Joy:
> My lips shall shout for joy when I sing praises to You, O' Holy One, from my inner being, which You have redeemed and purchased for Yourself, I praise You. My tongue also shall talk of Your righteousness all the day long (see Psalm 71:23-24).

Prayer for Assurance:
> O' God, Jehovah, eternal "I Am," it is so good and comforting for me to draw near to You, the one true God Yahweh for I know when I draw near to you, You will draw near to me. I have put my trust in You. My Lord God, that I may be cleansed, and have a pure heart; that I may declare all Your works (see Psalm 73:28 and James 4:8).

The Word of God is not inert, but operates and produces results—revealing the will of God. Allow God's Holy Word to be your guide.

2. Pray in Concert with the Holy Spirit.

Prayer is more than expressive words and beautiful phrases woven together to form a poetic soliloquy. In truth, we sometimes may not know how or what to pray. That's okay, because according to John Bunyan, "the best prayers have often been more groans than words."

"In the same way the Spirit also helps our weakness; for we do not know how to pray as we should, but the Spirit Himself intercedes for us with groanings too deep for words; and He who searches the hearts knows what the mind of the Spirit is, because He intercedes for the saints according to the will of God" (Romans 8:26-27). The Greek word translated *helps* (*sunantilambánomai*) in this verse is a long word composed of three Greek words. It is a word picture of a person coming to another's aid by getting under, taking hold, and sharing the load the burdened one is carrying.

P.T. Forsyth clearly expresses the Holy Spirit's aid in prayer. "Words fail us in prayer oftener than anywhere else; and the Spirit must come in aid of our infirmity, set out our case to God, and give to us an unspoken freedom in prayer." [vi]

Stop for a moment and think about this: When you pray *in the Spirit*, the Holy Spirit Himself intercedes on your behalf to know and to fulfill the will of God. Amazing! It is the indwelling Holy Spirit who prays. Remember, your prayer-helper, the Holy Spirit, is of one mind with the Godhead—He *wills* for you to achieve your divinely appointed destiny. When the Holy Spirit prays for you, it is in agreement with God's will. The Holy Spirit teaches you how to pray in God's will, and enables you to pray when words fail you.

- **Do you call upon your "Helper" in your God-talk of prayer?**

3. Pray in the Name of Jesus.

"If you ask Me anything in My name, I will do it" (John 14:14). Most prayers I hear conclude, "In the name of Jesus." I habitually end my prayers, "in Jesus name, Amen." What does it mean to pray "in the name of Jesus?"

To pray in the name of Jesus is not a magic formula or a spiritual key that will open a treasure chest of heaven's blessings. The mere using of "the name of Jesus" must not be used as an "abracadabra" magical power that will give you your heart's desire. The unfathomable proposition is that, human and frail, we can pray to EL SHADDAI, ALMIGHTY GOD, be heard, and receive a response.

But wait! Why are endless prayers offered, yet they go unanswered? Perhaps you pray in a selfish, self-centered attitude—for *your* sake, to fulfill *your* will—the petitions fall silent and answers never come. When you pray selfishly, you pray in your own name—not in Jesus' name—it is an ill-based prayer. You ask amiss, and your prayers are unheard. It is not a matter of God not answering your prayers—He never heard them.

The big question is: *How can I make this prayer in the name of Jesus?* Or, ask yourself, "Is this a prayer Jesus would pray?" How dare we casually or indiscriminately petition heaven tacking on, "in Jesus' name," as if He would pray the same.

In Jesus' name, we mortals can only know the forgiveness of sins and have the unfathomable privilege of prayer in the name of Jesus. "He is able to save forever those who draw near to God *through Him*, since He always lives *to make intercession* for them" (Hebrews 7:25, emphasis mine).

How can you pray in the name of Jesus? When your mind is His mind, when His will is your will, you can truly pray to the Father in the name of Jesus your Lord. When praying in the authority of Jesus' name, your prayers will be answered.

Think about it, when "Christ is completely *and* permanently formed (molded) within you" (Galatians 4:19, AMP, emphasis mine), the Father will always answer your prayer. *For me to live* [and pray] *is Christ.*

Successful prayer life is praying in concert with the mind, teachings, and priorities of Jesus—in His name. To pray "in the name of Jesus," you pray in the spirit of your Lord's humility and meekness, of His mercy and forgiveness, of His love and truth. Then, you will receive.

- **Is Christ formed (molded) within you?**

- **Are you living and praying like Christ? Are your prayers the prayers Jesus would pray?**

The Scope of Prayer-Talk

Not all prayers are alike. Early in my ministry, churches conducted *Schools of Prayer* scheduled for five nights—Monday through Friday. The services were unique in that each night focused on a different aspect of prayer—Adoration, Confession, Thanksgiving, Supplication, and Intercession. Teaching and all prayers were focused on the theme for the evening. These services purposed to enlighten and expand the scope of prayer-talk.

Adoration

"O come, let us adore Him, O come, let us adore Him,
O come, let us adore Him, Christ the Lord."
O Come, All Ye Faithful, translated by Frederick Oakeley

As I write this section, it is only a few days until Christmas. Songs and hymns of the celebratory season are nonstop on the radio. More than once, I've heard, "O come, let us adore Him... Adore Him!... Adore Him!... Adore Him!" Adore, worship, and honor God for His gift of Christmas—Jesus Christ, our Savior.

- **Take time now to verbalize your adoration and devotion to God for who He is—His majesty, His holiness, His love, and His caring heart.**

Jesus taught us to pray: "Our Father who art in heaven, *hallowed* be Thy name" (Matthew 6:9, emphasis mine). When praying, spend time worshipping God in reverential respect, devotion, and homage. Prayer is the means by which we give our Lord the adoration and glory due to Him. The more you learn about the EL SHADDAI, who is Almighty God of heaven and earth, the more you'll sense the need to prostrate yourself in adoration, worship, and submission.

Adoration is lovingly worshipping God, who is infinitely worthy, and esteeming Him with all humility. "Give unto the LORD the glory due unto His name... worship the LORD in the beauty of holiness!" (1 Chronicles 16:29 NKJV). Like Isaiah, when you recognize that you're in the presence of the Lord, you bow in awe, and with reverent wonder, you glorify, praise, and magnify Him (see Isaiah 6).

"A true love of God must begin with a delight in His holiness" (Jonathan Edwards). In *If Ye Shall Ask*, Oswald Chambers wrote, "O Lord this day my soul would stay upon Thee as Creator of the world, and upon our Lord Jesus Christ as Creator of His life in me. Oh for the power of thy Spirit to adore thee in fuller measure."

Confession

"I acknowledged my sin to Thee... I said,
'I will confess my transgressions to the LORD.'"
(Psalm 32:5)

When Isaiah saw the LORD, ADONAI who is the SOVEREIGN MASTER of all that exists, he recognized his own need for repentance and confession. Before the Sovereign Lord God, Isaiah recognized his lips (talk) were impure and unclean. Isaiah recognized that God who is holy knows the language, speech, and words of his mouth.

Page Kelley, in his commentary on Isaiah wrote: "Isaiah saw God and in the light of that vision he saw himself. Whenever one draws near to God, he not only has an increased awareness of God's holiness, but also of his own sinfulness. Isaiah had never realized the depth of his sin, and depravity until he saw the measure of God's holiness."[vii]

- **Like Isaiah, do you sense the need of confession before Adonai, Sovereign Master?**

The miracle of God's grace is the wondrous truth that He readily accepts the confession of a repentant soul. I want to be very clear— saying, "I'm sorry" to God is not sufficient. And, turning over a "new leaf" isn't adequate. Remember, earlier I said the common word used in the New Testament for *confess* (*homologēo*), means *to speak the same thing, to assent,* or *to agree with another.* When you confess your wrongs (thoughts, words, actions) to God, you agree with Him acknowledging your sins.

Thanksgiving

"Always giving thanks for all things in the name of our
Lord Jesus Christ to God, even the Father."
(Ephesians 5:20)

Prayer-talk of thanksgiving should be the easiest for all believers. If your prayer-talk has been in the sequence of adoration, then confession, by the time you get to thanksgiving, your heart should virtually explode with worshipful gratitude. God is so good! You have so many reasons to be thankful.

Rejoice… and Again, I Will Say Rejoice!
 I studied New Testament Greek under a godly man who during the Second World War was a pastor of a large church in Germany. Hitler, the merciless dictator, sought to purge ruthlessly all Christian leaders sending them to labor camps or annihilation centers.

 During this horrific time, in the middle of the night, a gun butting against their front door awoke this dear pastor and his wife with a heart-stopping terror that had gripped most of their country. Still in their nightclothes, they were ordered by heartless soldiers into the street. There, they watched his library ransacked and burned. Powerless, they were pried away from their three young daughters and forced onto a truck. The couple was taken to a labor camp. It was two long and difficult years before they heard their girls were safe, and three years before the family was reunited.

 It was a privilege to learn from him. In Germanic fashion, every morning when he came into the classroom we stood as he clicked his heels, and together we declared, "*Chaírete… palin erō chaírete.*" "Rejoice… again I will say, rejoice!" (Philippians 4:4). It was my professor's life verse, a verse of thanksgiving.

Melancholy, despondency, gloom, and doom are not evidence of God-life or the fullness of the Holy Spirit. Our admonition is to give thanks for *all* things! How can this be? My professor modeled how one could rejoice and give thanks for all things even when difficulty abounds.

When you're living God-life, prayer-talk will give thanks for *all things*. There are endless reasons to go to the throne of God with an offering of thanksgiving. Before bombarding heaven with requests for blessings, rejoice and give thanks for the many you've already received. Prayers of thanksgiving is God-talk of a believer who is living God-life.

Remember what you read in section two? With God-faith, believing is seeing. At the tomb of Lazarus, Jesus prayed, "Father, I thank Thee that Thou heardest Me" (John 11:41 HCSB). The raising of Lazarus *followed* Christ's prayer of thanksgiving for the raising of His friend. When your God-talk is praying with thanksgiving for blessings and victories *yet to come*, you manifest God-faith.

Before you ask anything in prayer, first, thank God for what He has done. "Rejoice always; pray without ceasing; in everything give thanks; for *this is God's will for you* in Christ Jesus" (1 Thessalonians 5:16-18, emphasis mine).

My day is always better when I pause in the morning and acknowledge to God how thankful I am for Jesus and the endless blessings and favors in my life. The Bible reminds us we should wake up "singing with *thankfulness* in [your] hearts to God. And whatever [you] do in word or deed, do all in the name of the Lord Jesus, *giving thanks* through Him to God the Father" (Colossians 3:16-17, emphasis mine).

Supplication

There are prayers, and then there is the intense prayer of supplication—making an impassioned petition to God with an urgent request. Supplication is asking with persistence; it is pleading with a deep sense of need. It's much more than simply praying, it is invoking God with insistent entreaty—diligently pressing, urging Him to act.

Hebrews 5:7 gives insight to the prayer life of Jesus. "In the days of His flesh, when He offered up both prayers and supplications or appeals, with vehement cries and tears to Him who was able to save Him from death, and was heard because of His godly fear (my translation)."

Hezekiah (King of Judah) was sick to the point of death. Isaiah, a prophet of God, delivered the word of the Lord to him, "set your house in order, for you shall die and not live." How would you have received this information? What would you have done in response to it? Hezekiah prayed with supplication beseeching God to spare his life. God heard his prayers, saw his tears, and added fifteen years to his life (see 2 Kings 20:1-6).

Praying Through

Old timers called supplication "praying through"—they prayed with importunity until the answer came. I was a new pastor when a member told me, "You need to get to know Mrs. Mayo, she can 'pray through.'" I made a priority to meet and get to know this godly woman; she was indeed a prayer warrior! When she "prayed through" and the assurance of answered prayer came, she would shout, "Whoopee! Whoopee! Whoopee!" Neighbors would know Mrs. Mayo had "prayed through" and had an answer to her prayer. She would open the back door and shout, "Whoopee!" I learned to have confidence in her supplications and it never failed. When she said a specific prayer was going to be answered, it happened. *Whoopee*!

When you pray with supplication, you're praying to JEHOVAH JIREH, (*Yahweh Yir'eh*), THE LORD WILL PROVIDE. God is all-powerful, and able to the uttermost. Bear in mind to whom you are praying and pray with faith. "Without faith it is impossible to please Him [God]" (Hebrews 11:6).

JEHOVAH JIREH, THE LORD WILL PROVIDE

The word *jireh* is the Hebrew word *to see*. With God, to see is to foresee; God is all-knowing. The Lord God will provide; *provision* means *to see ahead* or *foresee*. God is your Provider! He is never surprised or unaware of the provision needed to meet your supplication. Abraham understood this truth. On Mt. Moriah, Abraham and his son Isaac learned that God sees and provides. It was here that Abraham faced his greatest crisis, an unimaginable test of faith—sacrifice Isaac! No, God intervened and provided a ram for the sacrifice (see Genesis 22).

Pray with supplication, JEHOVAH JIREH has perfect foresight; He can meet your every need. "Call to Me, and I will answer you, and I will tell you great and mighty things, which you do not know" (Jeremiah 33:3).

- **Is your prayer-talk to JEHOVAH JIREH? Do you trust in the Lord to provide?**

Intercession

Standing in the doorway of the church following Sunday morning worship service, a small hand took mine, "You said last week you'd pray for my Mom and she is still sick. Please pray for her." I heard the young voice, but in my heart I cried, "Oh God, I forgot, I failed, I let an opportunity for intercession slip by." Since that day, I now take time to write down every prayer request as I receive them. I write on scrap paper or on bulletins and put them in my pocket to be reminded during my daily prayer time. I'm learning to be a faithful intercessor.

Intercession is always for others, their needs, their challenges, and their trials. You have the indescribable privilege of prayer and the priestly responsibility of interceding on behalf of others. You are a priest of the kingdom of our God (see Revelation 1:6; 5:10). It is part of your calling in Christ to make intercession for others. "Me, mine, and ours" are set aside, and others' burdens become yours.

You may ask: *How important is intercession?* One of the greatest prophets of Israel, Samuel, said, "Far be it from me that I should sin against the LORD by ceasing to pray for you" (1 Samuel 12:23).

Another prophet, Isaiah, was "astonished that there was no one to intercede" (Isaiah 59:16). When Nehemiah returned to the city of Jerusalem that had been mostly destroyed by invaders, he sat down and wept, mourned, fasted, and prayed for days. Then he lifted up his voice in intercession for the exiles. "Hear the prayer of Thy servant which I am praying before Thee now, day and night, on behalf of the sons of Israel" (Nehemiah 1:6). Do you remember when Peter was in jail? Intercession was made without ceasing for him, and he was delivered out of prison (see Acts 12:5).

- **Are there those in your acquaintance who have wondered why there was not an intercessor?**

- **Is there someone you need to stop and intercede for right now?**

There are no limits, no restrictions for whom you should intercede. Not all prayer is intercession; in fact, Paul distinguishes between prayer and intercession. "I exhort... first of all, supplications, prayers, intercessions, and giving of thanks, be made for all [people]" (1 Timothy 2:1, KJV). Intercession is an impassioned entreaty between you and your merciful, prayer-hearing God. Intercession is for a specific person with a specific need, and you position yourself between the needy party and the great Provider. Pray with specificity for needs of family, fellow believers, unsaved, those who use and persecute you, those in authority, and for laborers in the harvest for lost souls—*for all persons.*

Intercession is a prayer of passion; you recognize the seriousness of the need and the unlimited possibility of God's ability to answer. Moses found the people of Israel had committed a great sin by turning to idols and he interceded, "If You will forgive their sin— and if not, blot me, I pray You, out of Your book which You have written" (Exodus 32:32, AMP). His prayer was a heart-rendering, life-offering incisive petition to God.

It is not casual praying; rather, it is heart wrenching. Jesus is the consummate example of an intercessor. While enduring the incredulous cruelty of the crucifixion, He prayed for the insensitive, heartless executors: "Father forgive them; for they do not know what they are doing" (Luke 23:34).

Prior to Peter's denial, Jesus said to him, "Simon, Simon, behold, Satan has demanded permission to sift you like wheat; but I have *prayed* for you, that your faith may not fail" (Luke 22:31-32, emphasis mine). Realizing His earthly ministry was short, Jesus prayed to the Father to keep those who the Father gave Him. The unwavering security of the believer is that the living Lord even now is making intercession on your behalf.

"He is able to save forever those who draw near to God through Him, since He always lives to make *intercession* for them" (Hebrews 7:25, emphasis mine). Not only is Jesus interceding on your behalf, but also the Holy Spirit, your Comforter, is interceding. "The Spirit also helps our weakness... the Spirit Himself intercedes for us" (Romans 8:26). Victory in your prayer-talk is assured and supported by double intercession—that of the indwelling Holy Spirit and of the glorified Christ.

A Reflection

God-talk begins with the sacrifice of your lips (see Hosea 14:2), a cleansing, or purification of talk (speech) so Christ, the Anointed One, can fully live in you. The glory of His presence will bring appropriate God-talk to your lips, and you will effortlessly magnify EL SHADDAI, Almighty God with your voice. Mature grace and knowledge of your Lord will always empower you. When the Son of God is formed in you, it will be observable by your *God-talk*.

- **Does your talk portray the person you should be, the person God wants you to be?**

SECTION FIVE

GOD-REST

"We who have believed do enter into rest."
(Hebrews 4:3, KJV)

There were times in my childhood when we lived with my paternal grandparents in the beautiful mountains of East Tennessee. Life there was without some of today's conveniences—plumbing, central heat and air—that was life in the mountains. However, I have a storehouse of happy memories. I'm sure it was very different for my parents who had little rest. Coping with a wood-burning kitchen stove, coal grates, hand-drawn water, no washing machine or dryer, tending a summer garden, harvesting and canning for the winter left little time for rest. I remember hearing my mother saying, "I'll rest when I get to heaven." Of course, she meant God's *eternal* rest.

Yes, there is a Heaven's rest—a time when life's battles will be over. As God's children, through Jesus Christ, we will rest in the presence of God, our heavenly Father. In the New Jerusalem, "He shall wipe away every tear… there shall no longer be any death… mourning, or crying, or pain" (Revelation 21:4). There will be an eternal, everlasting rest in the fullness of the presence of God. Oh, what joyous rest from life's toils and trials—resting in our Father's house, prepared especially for you and for me.

My hope is for you to discover that there is another rest—*God-rest*—that you can enjoy in this life. A rest provided by a loving Heavenly Father that you can have *even in the midst of life's stresses, trials, and challenges.* Jesus promised, "I will not leave you as orphans" (John 14:18). Moreover, He will not leave you alone in times of testing or when facing life's difficulties. He promises you reprieve from the challenge of living a God-life in a godless world—*God-rest.*

You may think or even say: *That sounds great, but if you only knew what I have to face, how can I have rest?* Yes, you will face struggles, pressures, demands, and heartaches. However, remember, our God is an awesome God, and upon His own authority, He promises you God-rest in your time of need.

~~~~~~

God-rest, tranquility in the midst of life's storms.

~~~~~~

What is *God-rest*? It is tranquility in the midst of life's storms that the world cannot understand. Have you ever wondered, *is such a rest possible*? Do you need such a rest now? This section challenges you to discover a quality of God-life that can only be experienced when entering God-rest in times of stress and turmoil.

—Chapter One—

Seeking God-Rest

Take your Bible and look at the fourth chapter of Hebrews. It begins with a concern for believers who appear to be living without God-rest. "The promise of entering His [God's] rest still stands, let us be careful that none of you be found to have fallen short of it" (Hebrews 4:1, NIV). Are you forfeiting one of God's promised blessings—God-rest? Do you need to find God-rest?

God-rest is founded in faith, a God-faith that gives serenity and discovers "the peace of God, which surpasses all comprehension, shall guard your hearts and your minds in Christ Jesus" (Philippians 4:7). God-rest is sustained by the God-faith discussed in section two.

~~~~~~~~~~~~~~~~~~~~~~~~~~~~~~~~~~
God-rest is sustained by God-faith.
~~~~~~~~~~~~~~~~~~~~~~~~~~~~~~~~~~

A defining characteristic of God-faith is an active principle, a *faithing* that makes God-rest possible. Trouble is inevitable, and an active faith is the only way to have God-rest in times of your personal trials. Many Christians never have God-rest because they don't have a *life-changing faithing* of God's promises and assurances. They stop at reading and accepting God's Word intellectually without putting faithing principles into action.

At the Metropolitan Tabernacle in Newington, England, on the Lord's Day evening, July 6, 1873, Charles Spurgeon preached from Hebrews 4:3 and said: "We do enter into rest, even in this present life; all who are believers in the Lord Jesus Christ are already enjoying rest of heart; and in proportions as faith possesses their souls, in that proportion they enjoy peace."[i] I am encouraging you to let God speak to you through His Word and discover God-rest in the midst of your busy daily activities.

How Can I Find God-Rest?

God-rest, like so many things, does not happen without decisive action on your part. It must be appropriated by a living faith. When Joshua assumed leadership of the Israelites, he said, "Remember the word which Moses… commanded…'The Lord your God gives you rest'" (Joshua 1:13). Conquering the land was not without difficulties, but they acted upon the Word of God, and achieved victory — rest in the Promised Land. Their rest came when they chose to believe God's Word and acted on it.

Belief, Confidence, Obedience

Do you long for and desire God-rest in your daily struggles? Finding God-rest requires faithing in three basic Christian disciplines — *belief*, *confidence*, and *obedience*. They are much closer in meaning than may appear at first reading, and, at times, they are even interchangeable. The strength of confidence and obedience is found in your belief and trust, which is the ground of your understanding of God. Faith or trust is strengthened by confidence in, and obedience to God and His Word.

Merely acknowledging Jesus Christ as the Son of God is not enough. To enter into God-rest, you must have an unshakable confidence in His Word and be submissive to Him in obedience. You may then *enter into* God-rest while yet in the tumultuous world in which we all live.

~~~~~~~~~~~~~~~~~~~~~~~~~~~~~~~~~~~~~
God-rest requires confidence (belief)
and obedience (trust) in God's Word.
~~~~~~~~~~~~~~~~~~~~~~~~~~~~~~~~~~~~~

A Bumpy Ride

It was a dark night, with no moon above and no visible lights below as we flew over western Colorado on our way to Denver. The plane bumped and then bumped again. With no warning, it dropped, tilted sharply to one side, then to the other. A calm, steady voice came over the intercom, "We are encountering turbulence, please fasten your seatbelts. Beverage service will be discontinued and cabin crew should be seated immediately."

Suddenly, jagged lightning flashes illuminated the sky from each side of the plane. By the sound of the powerful jet engines, we knew the pilot was taking the plane to a higher altitude trying to avoid the horrendous western storm. Repeatedly, that calm voice spoke steadily over the intercom quieting and reassuring everyone. Bump, bump, up and down with quick movements tilting to the right and then the left. Overhead storage doors sprang open and luggage fell, beverages spilled, and the cabin was in utter confusion. On we flew through the turbulent night.

Eventually, we safely taxied to our gate at the Denver airport. Everyone felt relief and inexpressible gratitude. As we exited the plane, the pilot with the reassuring voice stood by the door. One of our travelers asked him, "How did you stay so calm in that storm?" The pilot smiled and replied, "I was talking to an Air Traffic Controller the entire time. He had us on his scope, and I was confident if I followed his instructions, he would bring us through safely."

Did you appreciate what he said? He was confident in and obedient to the controller's word—and he was at rest through the storm.

What is the Benefit of God-Rest?

God-rest will give you inner strength because you acknowledge the management and control of your life is in God's hands. While human nature compels you to rush through each day, the Word of God admonishes, "Rest in the LORD and wait patiently for Him; do not fret" (Psalm 37:7). Remember, God said that on the journey of life, you will pass through valleys, even the shadow of death, but He will give you rest in green pastures, by quiet waters, and along paths of righteousness (see Psalm 23).

God-rest is a heavenly renewal in an earthly environment. It is enduring peace imparting refreshment and strength to your soul. When in the toil of the day's challenges, you have that special reserve with God—God-rest—and you are blessed with a heavenly moment.

Such times remind me of a chorus written by John Patterson. "O what a wonderful, wonderful day, a day I will never forget... Heaven came down and glory filled my soul."

F. B. Meyer, eminent mentor of the deeper life, commented on, "made us alive... raised us up... seated us... in heavenly places, in Christ Jesus," (Ephesians 2:5-6). He gives us this beautiful interpretation: "We have been raised up together with Him in the mind and purpose of God, and have been made to sit with Him in the heavenlies; so that in Jesus we have already entered into the rest of God, and have simply to appropriate it by a living faith."[ii]

~~~~~~~~~~~~~~~~~~~~~~~~~~~~~~~~~~

God-rest is a heavenly experience
in an earthly environment

~~~~~~~~~~~~~~~~~~~~~~~~~~~~~~~~~~

Entering into God-rest is possible for you, but it is not automatic. God is willing; are you seeking His promised God-rest? "Seek peace, and pursue it" (Psalm 34:14). *Peace (sālom)* has various meanings. When seeking God-rest, sālom is *completeness* or a *sense of tranquility*. *Seek* and *pursue* are both active, persistent and aggressive words. God-rest *is* available to you for today's challenges. Jesus said, "Ask, and it shall be given to you; seek, and you shall find; knock, and it shall be opened to you" (Matthew 7:7).

What a blessing when we receive God-rest for today's stress. Your testimony can be like David's, "I sought the Lord, and He answered me, and delivered me from all my fears" (Psalm 34:4). Yesterday's God-rest will not suffice for today's hardships. It requires a daily walk of faith to enter into His rest for today. God-rest, a heavenly rest in an earthly environment.

In the following pages, we'll look at potential obstacles on the way to God-rest. Some barriers are heavy and at the time may seem unmovable or insurmountable. Your God is able to give what He promised. His faithfulness and loving kindness will bless you with God-rest.

- **Will you pray, "God I believe, I want to have God-rest in today's challenge?"**

- **In the midst of today's storm, is your faith strong enough to have God-rest?**

—Chapter Two—

Trusting in the Faithfulness of God

"The LORD's loving-kindnesses indeed never cease,
for His compassions never fail.
They are new every morning; great is Thy faithfulness."
(Lamentations 3:22-23)

There are numerous roadblocks to God-rest. We all have encountered one or more of them and they prohibit any form of peaceful, tranquil life. The absence of God-rest in our life does not make you different; it places you with the rest of us.

Look at three strong biblical men who at times were void of God-rest:
Jeremiah: "I am weary with my groaning and have found no rest"
  (Jeremiah 45:3).
David: "Oh, that I had wings like a dove! I would fly away and be
  at rest" (Psalm 55:6).
Job: "I am seething within, and cannot relax; days of affliction
  confront me" (Job 30:27).

God-rest is peace and composure in the midst of trials, stress, and disorders. If *for* |you| *to live is Christ*, then you can have His peace, a God-rest when circumstances would normally dictate otherwise.

Remember, God-rest is *not* a cessation from ministry, work, or service. Rather, during life's demands and pressures, you experience tranquility. God-rest makes it possible for you to abide in the presence of the Lord, and to nourish your soul with His peace, even when encumbered with pressing responsibilities.

Roadblocks Can Be Negotiated

Roadblocks can be negotiated and don't have to spoil your day. Eleanor and I enjoy vacationing in Jackson Hole, Wyoming, and have spent many memorable retreats there over the years. From time to time, roadblocks could have prevented us from enjoying the spectacular beauty of that area. One particular summer, roads were closed for construction. A hard winter resulted in rockslides and familiar trails washed out. Roadblocks to our peaceful serenity. Some years, there were wildfires, torrential rain, and even roaming bears. Did any of these challenges keep us from rest and recuperation? No! We negotiated the roadblocks and discovered new trails to spectacular views we had not seen before. There are no boulders, deep valleys, high mountains, treacherous rivers, threatening storms, or other perils on life's road that can destroy God-rest. All obstacles can be negotiated.

God has made available the gospel (Good News) of rest to every believer; yet, few live from day-to-day with the peace of God-rest. Why? There are some common and formidable roadblocks—some are real, others contrived or imagined. Yet, any roadblock is capable of inhibiting you from God-rest.

Blessings of God's Faithfulness

It is unimaginable the utter turmoil that would occur if God were to vacillate—becoming uncertain or inconsistent. God and the Word of God are dependable and reliable. Praise His name! He is consistent and true! His faithfulness is dependable!

Let's identify six blessings of God's faithfulness to help you negotiate roadblocks to God-rest.

1. God Is Faithful, He Comforts!

"Blessed be the… God of all comfort; who comforts us in all our affliction… our comfort is abundant through Christ" (2 Corinthians 1:3-5).

Physical, mental, or emotional problems can be roadblocks. Everyone knows about pain and suffering, and we struggle to answer *why*. Christians are not exempt from suffering, or from questioning God. *Who is to blame? Am I to blame?* Understandably, some suffering comes from inappropriate and ill-advised actions or bad habits. But, not all. Thankfully, Jesus gave some insight to the questions of *why* and *who*: "Neither hath this man sinned, nor his parents, but that the works of God should be made manifest in him" (John 9:3, KJV).

No one is exempt from illness; it is part of our human imperfection. So, how can you cope with pain or illness, or watch a loved one suffer? Where is God-rest during these hardships?

Perhaps you struggle with unmanageable emotions. Emotions can be ignited or energized by a variety of life situations and when uncontrolled, cause pain and suffering for you and those around you. When your physical/mental body is suffering, it can damage/destroy your career, marriage, or other meaningful relationships. You can lose hope and optimism for your future.

Common physical, mental, or emotional roadblocks:
- ➤ Health Issues
- ➤ Anxiety Disorder
- ➤ Mental Illness
- ➤ Terminal Illness
- ➤ Physical Disability
- ➤ Eating Disorder
- ➤ Intentional Self-harm
- ➤ Depression

God comforts you during your trying times. "Therefore draw near with confidence to the throne of grace, that [you] may receive mercy and may find grace to help in time of need" (Hebrews 4:16). So go boldly to God's throne, obtain mercy, and find help in your time of need. You may never understand why you had to endure the trial, but you can depend upon the fact that God is in control, and He can use every situation to bring you closer to Him. He can give you comfort, God-rest.

An Uncommon Rest

Bob was my friend and fellow staff member. He had an emergency operation for an embolism on a major artery near his spine. "There is a five to ten percent chance the surgery will paralyze you," warned the doctor. Sadly, the surgery paralyzed him from the waist down. He handled it magnificently. In the years that followed, in a motorized chair and an adapted van, he remained active and continued his ministry. He inspired everyone.

When a serious heart problem took him back to the hospital, Bob, still full of life, made his illness into a ministry opportunity. His joyful, outgoing witness brought hospital staff to his room day and night. Bob witnessed, laughed, told jokes and humorous stories, and from his hospital bed won several to a saving faith.

Bob never left the hospital. A memorial service held at the hospital was overflowing with hospital staff gathered in memory of one who in the face of eternity had an uncommon God-rest.

Why was Bob paralyzed? Why was he hospitalized? Why did he die? No one knows the answer to these questions. As Bob said during a visit with him, "I am now fully in God's hands, and that's okay." He had God-rest.

The Lord is our faithful prayer-hearing and prayer-answering God. We are encouraged to pray for the sick. "Call for the elders of the church, let them pray... prayer offered in faith will restore the one who is sick, and the Lord will raise him up" (James 5:14-15). Our God is "JEHOVAH-ROPHE, THE LORD WHO HEALS" (Exodus 15:26, interpretation mine). God miraculously blesses and heals through physicians, surgeons, and medications. (see Isaiah 38:21; Mark 6:13).

JEHOVAH-ROPHE, THE LORD WHO HEALS

When Paul and Luke the physician were shipwrecked on Malta, they found the father of Publius very sick. Paul prayed, "laid his hands on him and healed him" (Acts 28:8). The word translated *healed* (*iáomai*) describes a miraculous healing. "After this had happened, the rest of the people on the island who had diseases were coming to him and getting cured" (Acts 28:9). The word translated *cured* (*therapeuo*) is clearly the practice of medicine by Luke. This word is the root of the English word therapeutics—treating disorders and diseases by remedial agents and methods. Our God works miracles—all things are possible through Him. Even in the time of sickness, God can give you peace and God-rest.

2.   God Is Faithful, He Sustains!

"Cast your burden upon the LORD, and He will sustain [provide for] you; He will never allow the righteous to be shaken [to slip, totter or fail]" (Psalm 55:22).

Negative thoughts and attitudes can be roadblocks.

God will sustain you when negative thoughts and attitudes well up within you and threaten to take away your peace. These often originate from an incorrect image of yourself or opinion about God. The influence of attitudes, positive or negative, will have a direct bearing on your behavior. While optimism can give added zest to life, pessimism can disrupt good judgment and gain mastery of your will causing you great distress.

Moods and dispositions evolve through various conditions and accumulated feelings over time. Sometimes unpleasant situations are created by your personal sensitivity—being too quick to take offense at other's insults, or their failure to consider your feelings. To allow unpleasant incidents to dominate you is your personal failure. An acute sensitivity can develop into a mental complex that interprets every action by others as personal attacks or conspiracies. Some people go so far as to develop a persecution complex.

Some hindering negative roadblocks:
➢ Boredom
➢ Self-pity
➢ Doubt
➢ Jealousy
➢ Worry
➢ Impatience
➢ Pessimism

Many take an emotional elevator to a lower level due to boredom or self-pity. They live in a "woe-is-me" or paranoid existence. However, they need to wake up. Praise the Lord! Rejoice in His Word! The King of Glory is your Father, and Jesus is your Lord. Rejoice in the day God has given!

Socrates said, "If all misfortunes were laid in one common heap, whence everyone must take an equal portion, most people would be content to take their own and depart." Even the eminent prophet Elijah went into the wilderness, sat under a juniper tree, and had a "pity-party" (see 1 Kings 19:4). Be careful, don't wallow in your sorrows, or feel sorry for yourself—it can have a long-term negative or defeatist effect on your life. God created you, filled you with the Holy Spirit, and blessed you with His favor.

"Happy Pappy"
The shift superintendent was showing me through a large machine shop. It was a noisy, unpleasant, and dangerous place. Over the loud clanging, banging, and screeching machines, the "super" said, "Up ahead is a machinist you've got to meet."

I shall never forget Bill; a man who at first glance you might think had a boring job. For eight hours, non-stop, day after day, he stood on his feet operating a machine, never moving, doing the same thing repeatedly. Boring? Not for Bill! He sang, praised God, and quoted favorite Scripture verses. Oh, he was harassed, was the brunt of jokes, and was called "Holy Joe," "Preacher," and "Happy Pappy," to name a few. But, Bill had uncommon peace, a God-rest in the midst of it all. His witness was strong, and quietly, co-worker after co-worker would come to him requesting prayer, counsel, or wanting to know more about his Lord. To Bill, every day was the day the Lord made and he rejoiced and was glad in it (see Psalm 118:24).

Daily worry or anxiety is disruptive to peace. A physician said that anxiety is the silent killer of our generation. Anxiety and apprehension are byproducts of a lack of faith and confidence in God. You must acknowledge that God is in control and that He can make all things work together for good.

So therefore, "be anxious for nothing, but in everything by prayer and supplication with thanksgiving let your requests be made known to God" (Philippians 4:6). I like the interpretation of that verse attributed to D.L. Moody, "Worry about nothing, pray for everything, and thank God for anything."

Immediately following the admonition of verse 6 is Philippians 4:7: "The peace of God, which surpasses all comprehension [understanding], shall guard your hearts and your minds in [through] Christ Jesus." A surpassing God-rest awaits those who resist negative impulses.

3. God is Faithful, He Assures!

"Let us all come forward and draw near with true (honest and sincere) hearts in unqualified assurance and absolute conviction engendered by faith" (Hebrews 10:22, AMP).

Deep-seated, dark emotions and behavioral dysfunctions are roadblocks.
The good news is that God gives assurance that He, all He is, and all He can do, will faithfully come to the aid of those who seek Him. In your dark and murky emotion, He can and will sustain when you feel overwhelmed.

There are abnormal, even psychopathic, emotions that are out of tune with reality. Brooding and deeply buried feelings sometimes erupt in unacceptable actions, and dysfunctional emotions can lead to personal harm or even criminal behavior.

Emotional and behavioral roadblocks:
➢ Guilt
➢ Anger
➢ Fear
➢ Grief
➢ Suicidal Thoughts
➢ Hatred
➢ Road-rage
➢ Violent Inclination

Believers still do sin, the Holy Spirit convicts us, and guilt is the consequence. Guilt is disabling and often separates believers from church, friends, and even family. Guilt is a heavy burden. But wait; there is hope! "If we confess our sins, He is faithful and righteous to forgive us our sins and to cleanse us from all unrighteousness [remove the guilt]" (1 John 1:9). Your hope of forgiveness and removal of guilt is God's pledge to you.

We are surrounded by angry people. One news analyst was being interviewed on television and was asked, "Can you describe the world in a word?" Thinking for a moment the analyst said, "Yes, fear and anger, our world is full of fear and anger." Anger leads to behavioral extremes and can be devastating.

Some people seem ready to be angry at the least provocation, with little or no cause. Christians should manifest a godly spirit, "do not be eager in your heart to be angry, for anger resides in the bosom of fools" (Ecclesiastes 7:9). Wisdom teaches "to be angry is to revenge the faults of others upon ourselves." (Alexander Pope, 1688-1744). There are those who become easily enraged and vindictive toward others for simple and relatively innocent actions. Jesus warned Christians to not be angry without cause (see Matthew 5:22). Uncontrolled anger toward family and others can result in generations of regret. Some even become angry with God for numerous reasons. "An angry man stirs up strife, and a hot-tempered man abounds in transgression" (Proverbs 29:22).

If you desire to live God-life when faced with disruptive and challenging situations, you must control sinful anger. There is an old saying worth hearing, "Two things a man should never be angry at; what he can help, and what he cannot help." And, Thomas Jefferson said, "When angry, count to ten before you speak; if very angry, one hundred." This reminds me of what Jesus said, forgive seventy times seven, or until you have lost count.

However, there is justifiable anger. God gets angry. He gets angry with persons, nations, and wrongful acts (see Psalm 80:4). When the prophet Zechariah gave a call of repentance to Judah, he said, "The LORD was very angry with your fathers" (Zechariah 1:2). Yet, God did not sin in His anger—it was justifiable.

Christians are told, "be angry, and yet do not sin" (Ephesians 4:26). Christians have ample reason to have a righteous anger in today's world—an anger that should enlist action, but not sin. When prayer is prohibited in schools and public places, when Nativity scenes and the Ten Commandments cannot be displayed in public, when the Bible is prohibited to be read or displayed in business establishments, when the theory of Darwinism is taught but biblical creation cannot be mentioned, when our national abortion rate exceeds 1.3 million per year, Christians should justifiably become angry.

Fear is the direct opposite, the antithesis of faith. Faith cannot survive in the presence of fear. It's a strong emotion caused by anxious concern, anticipation of failure, impending danger, or lack of provision.

Fear is an emotion that intimidates, terrorizes, destroys peace and tranquility, and causes avoidance. When Adam and Eve heard the voice of God, they were fearful and fled from the presence of the Lord God. The fear of God's presence was due to their sin of disobedience to God's command (see Genesis 3). Fear is rooted in a lack of overcoming faith. The infectious emotion of fear will destroy your witness and spiritual growth.

Throughout the Bible, God urges believers to not fear:

To Isaac: "Do not fear, for I am with you" (Genesis 26:24).

To the nation Israel: "Do not fear or be discouraged" (Deuteronomy 1:21, NKJV).

To Isaiah: "To those who are fearful-hearted, be strong, do not fear" (Isaiah 35:4, NKJV).

When you harbor fear, it infects your thinking and permeates your personality. Fear conditions you to expect what you most dread; it establishes a relationship to that which is feared. Conversely, faith conditions for what is *faithed*—it acknowledges the presence and power of God.

4.   God Is Faithful, He Forgives!

"He [Christ] was manifested to take away [lift up and carry away] our sins [transgressions]" (1 John 3:5, KJV).

Self-inflicted wounds can be roadblocks.

We are often our own worst enemy. Self-centeredness, moral failures, mistakes, and bad judgments often inflict pain and regret. Foolish decisions and indiscretion invariably result in some form of suffering for you or for others.

Doctors tell us that a lack of self-discipline is the root cause of many physical problems. Lack of self-control has a devastating consequence and causes great personal suffering.

Common Self-inflicted Wounds:
➢   Credit Card Debt
➢   Substance Abuse
➢   Dishonesty
➢   Envy
➢   Obesity
➢   Loss of Self-Control
➢   Cheating
➢   Lawbreaking

Early in the history of mankind, Adam and Eve failed to take God at His word. They failed to obey Him. This failure led to three telling mistakes recorded in the third chapter of Genesis: they questioned God (verse 1), they contradicted God (verse 6), and they disobeyed God (verse 6). Even though they forfeited their God-rest, God did not forsake them; rather, He faithfully protected, provided, and forgave them even after they were cast out of the Garden of Eden.

There are several words in both the Old and New Testaments defining sin. The basic idea is transgression, or missing the mark. *Transgression* means *disobeying God, breaking His law*, and *willfully choosing to defy His word*. The choice to sin is an act of lawlessness. Whatever you call your shortcomings, bad habits, wrongful acts, or addictions—they are rebellion, or sin against God and alienate you from Him. Like the prodigal son, you choose lawlessness and travel away from God. Just as the prodigal son alienated himself from his father, you commit the same rebellious act of hostility (see Luke 15:11-32). You may ask: *Will God truly forgive my transgressions?*

Let the following Scripture verses speak to your heart:
Isaiah 43:25: "I, even I, am the one who wipes out your transgressions."
Psalm 103:12: "As far as the east is from the west, so far has He removed our transgressions from us."
Hebrews 10:17: "Their sins and their lawless deeds I will remember no more."

The good news is that God is faithful to forgive. Guilt can be removed. If you have trespassed or crossed a defined fence, you can cross back over. The prodigal son returned, confessed his failures, mistakes, and poor judgment, and his loving father forgave and accepted him. Are you living with the certainty of forgiveness?

5. God is Faithful, He Delivers!
"God is faithful, "He will show you how to escape temptation's power" (1 Corinthians 10:13, Tay).

Temptations that overpower and lead you astray are roadblocks.

Temptations are common; they affect all humanity. While the nature of temptations varies, all ages, genders, and status of people have temptations. Your temptation reveals your inner nature. In other words, what tempts you is unique to your own weakness. We each are tempted in different ways. Learn from your enticements, it is always an accurate indicator of your inner weakness.

Temptation itself is not sin, but when you yield to temptation, it becomes sin. The good news is that God always provides a way out of temptation, look for it.

"Way Out"

Road signs in England are well done and appropriately posted, but different than that in the United States. After a long day of challenging driving, Eleanor and I stopped at a busy supermarket before returning to our room. When leaving the rather complicated, congested "car park" and anxiously searching for an exit, I was relieved to see a sign posted "Way Out." It was my escape and a welcome relief.

Claim deliverance and victory in the faithfulness of God. He will provide an escape, an exit, a "way out." Your God-rest will be challenged by temptations, but with God's help, every one is manageable. The assurance of God's faithfulness makes it possible for God-rest in your times of trials.

Some temptations that hinder God-rest are:
➢ Gossip
➢ Cheating
➢ Gambling
➢ Infidelity
➢ Pornography Addiction
➢ Chemical Substance Abuse
➢ Alcoholism
➢ Lying
➢ Computing, Gaming, or Texting Obsession

Don't ever forget, "your adversary, the devil, prowls about like a roaring lion, seeking someone to devour" (1 Peter 5:8). How does Satan defeat, decimate, and debilitate believers? He perverts Scripture (see Matthew 4:6). He opposes God's work (see Zechariah 3:1). He hinders the gospel (see Matthew 13:19). He works in those who are disobedient to the Word of God (see Genesis 3). Satan is a real, active, cunning, and powerfully wicked being who is engaged in warfare to defeat God's plans and seduce believers.

6. God Is Faithful, He Rescues!

"The Lord knows how to rescue [deliver] the godly" (2 Peter 2:9).

Life situations or predicaments out of your control can be roadblocks.

God will rescue you from challenging or difficult life situations that are out of your control. There will always be personal, family, and vocational difficulties. If you wait for perplexing problems to be settled before you have God-rest, it will never happen.

You may be in a circumstance such as single parenting that is not of your choosing and feel overwhelmed. Or, your retirement portfolio is in jeopardy because of the stock market. You may have lost your job, or filed bankruptcy or even lost your home. What about the loss of a loved one? Many of your vexing circumstances are not a result of your actions and are out of your control to "fix them."

There is no promise that life will always be fair. It's not. There is a lot of suffering and hurt in our world. You may have known unspeakable and tremendous hardships — great disappointments that either left you bitter and resentful or weakened your self-esteem. God can rescue you and give you God-rest.

Difficult situations that can become roadblocks are:
➢ Raising a Family
➢ Divorce
➢ Work Issues
➢ Single Parenting
➢ Marital Stresses

- ➢ Business Failure
- ➢ Legal Issues
- ➢ Job Loss
- ➢ Loss of a Loved One
- ➢ Home Foreclosure
- ➢ Stock Market Fluctuations
- ➢ Retirement
- ➢ Aging
- ➢ Persecution or Prejudice

Ruth and Naomi

Remember the story of Ruth, the heathen girl from Moab? Ruth married a son of Naomi, but her marital happiness was short-lived when her husband died. Ruth, who now embraced Jehovah God, decided to return to the Holy Land with Naomi. Faithfully caring for her mother-in-law, Ruth labored as a scavenger, salvaging the grain left by the reapers. God rescued Naomi and Ruth, and blessed Ruth with a happy marriage to Boaz. And, she became the great-grandmother to King David.

Take heart, God is faithful to rescue you and give you God-rest. Trust God to deliver you—to do great and mighty things on your behalf and guide you in His will. Therefore, "humble yourselves… under the mighty hand of God, that He may exalt you at the proper time" (1 Peter 5:6).

> **Two things you can do for delivery from hurt and pain:**
> **Let go of the past**. Let your wounds heal. You can't let past problems or heartaches dominate your life. Release the pain and hurt. Ruth let the pain of bereavement go and looked toward a new and promising life.
>
> **Forgive those who hurt, mistreated, or maligned you**. It's Scriptural, don't wait for an apology. Forgive and get the heavy burden off your back. Do it for your own good and for the sake of the Gospel.

The principles sound simplistic, but they are not. Look again: let go of hurtful things, and forgive others. It isn't easy, but it is what you are called to do in God-life. It's sound biblical principle. As you've learned, God is present to help. He will sustain you through your dark days and nights of difficulties. Roadblocks can be negotiated with God's help. You can have God-rest.

—Chapter Three—

Resting in God's Goodness

"Taste and see that the Lord is good;
blessed is the man who trusteth in Him."
(Psalm 34:8 KJV)

In the midst of a sermon, I said rather emphatically, "God is good!" As a chorus, the congregation resounded, "All the time!" Someone had taught them an appropriate response. "God is good, all the time!" This is compatible with the biblical revelation of God; He is a God of goodness. The repeated emphasis on the *goodness* of God is a distinctive feature of the "I Am" of Scripture.

There is tranquility of God-rest enveloping you when you have unwavering trust, God-faith, in the goodness of God.

God Is Absolutely Good

No one who ever walked among men on this planet knew the goodness of God more conclusively than did Jesus Christ. Jesus identified God as the criterion of goodness. "No one is good except God alone" (Mark 10:18). A core belief in Jewish teaching is the supreme [absolute] goodness of God. "O give thanks to the Lord, for He is good; for His lovingkindness is everlasting" (1 Chronicles 16:34).

God is good to all mankind. The agrarian and often nomadic herdsmen of Bible times understood the goodness of God to all people. Remember, Jesus reminded them of the goodness of God in causing the sun to rise, and the rain to fall on the righteous and unrighteous (see Matthew 5:45). God's goodness is not a reciprocal act in return for our goodness. It is grace. His goodness is a reflection of His character. As W. T. Connor explains, "He does not wait for men to deserve His blessings before bestowing them. He showers underserved blessings on all men, not simply the good." [iii]

God is good to His children. He supplies a providential care for you before your need is recognized or expressed. Jesus assured the believer that the Father knows all of your needs before you ask Him (See Matthew 6:8). God has intimate knowledge and compassionate concern about the smallest detail of your life. God considers no concern you may have inconsequential. Jesus said that not one sparrow, the most common bird, falls to the ground without God's notice; further, God knows the very number of hairs on your head (see Matthew 10:29-30).

A New Pair of Gloves

It was an unusually cold winter. Snow and ice were exceptionally heavy for middle Tennessee. Charles, a fellow student, asked me to speak to the youth of the church he pastored. The occasion was an out-of-doors youth rally in a State Park.

At the park, when Charles noticed my red hands, he asked, "Did you forget your gloves?"

"No, I don't have any gloves," I responded.

"Here," he said while taking off his soft new leather gloves, "take mine." I was touched by his kindness to loan me his gloves while I was speaking before the group.

Afterwards, when I tried to return them, he insisted, "No, they are yours, I have another pair." I was overwhelmed by his generosity.

A week or so later, we were coming out of afternoon classes together, it was cold and beginning to snow. As I put on my prized new leather gloves, Charles was putting on his well-worn, scuffed gloves. I tried to trade with him, but he wouldn't agree to do so. He insisted I keep the new ones. I was deeply moved by his extraordinary goodness, he gave me his very best gloves. It was a lesson never to be forgotten; these years later, I still remember his selfless act. Likewise, God always gives His best to you.

~~~~~~~~~~~~~~~~~~~~~~~~~~~~~~
God always gives His best to you.
~~~~~~~~~~~~~~~~~~~~~~~~~~~~~~

God's goodness made you special, and He wants you to have a successful life. He will ensure a meaningful life if you submit yourself to Him. Think about it, "Was Christ, the Anointed One, triumphant in His life?" "Yes, without question," you respond. I don't want you to forget that living a God-life is *no longer [you] who lives, but Christ lives in [you]* (Galatians 2:20, adaptation mine).

God's goodness has blessed (prospered) you with every spiritual blessing (see Ephesians 1:3). How good is God? What are the benefits of His blessings? "The blessing [goodness] of the Lord makes one [prosperous] rich" (Proverbs 10:22, NKJV).

I want you to think about God's goodness and your prosperity. The Greek word *prosper (euodoō)* means to *help along the way, succeed.* Does it have to do with finances? Yes, but not exclusively. God's goodness is for you to "have a prosperous [successful] journey by the will of God" (Romans 1:10, KJV). The tense implies that it is God's will for you to have ongoing happiness, achievements, and well-being—the goodness of His blessing.

God's favor for you is to "prosper and be in health, even as thy soul prospereth [spiritual health]" (3 John 2, KJV). Perhaps the key to God's goodness is 2 Chronicles 26:5, "As long as he sought the LORD, God prospered him." Never forget for one moment that God is compassionate and gracious, abounding in loving-kindness (see Exodus 34:6). God loves you and wants to give His best to you along the way; His will is for you to succeed and to flourish as a Christian.

~~~~~~
"Do not fear; you are of more value than many sparrows."
(Matthew 10:31)
~~~~~~

God Is Compassionate Toward Sinners
"The goodness of God leadeth thee to repentance"
(Romans 2:4, KJV).

God does not overlook sin or the rejection of His Son as one's personal Savior. The wrath of God is the inevitable punishment of sin. However, the forbearance of God does not mean you can continue sinning carte blanche, banking on the love of God. God's patience gives the sinner an opportunity for forgiveness, but it is eternally important that the window of opportunity not be allowed to pass.

During a lifetime of choices, there is only one decision that is of eternal consequence, the decision to accept the mercy and forgiveness of God by receiving Jesus Christ as your personal Lord and Savior. Yet, the masses of unrepentant humanity go on living, rejecting the grace of God, ignoring His goodness, and thereby sentencing themselves to an everlasting death. The wealth of God's grace is not to be treated contemptuously. You should never disdain the riches of God's goodness, forbearance, and long-suffering.

How good is God? Jesus said, "God loved the world in this way: He gave His one and only Son, so that everyone who believes in Him will not perish but have eternal life" (John 3:16, HCSB). The goodness of God went beyond any expectation in the gift of His Son as mankind's Savior.

In 1 John, God's inherent goodness is seen in His compassion toward sinners:

"The love of God was manifested in us, that *God has sent His only begotten Son*... that we might live through Him" (1 John 4:9, emphasis mine).
"He loved us and *sent His Son* to be the propitiation for our sins" (1 John 4:10, emphasis mine).
"The Father has *sent the Son* to be the Savior of the world" (1 John 4:14, emphasis mine).

A few years ago, a popular solo in churches emphasized changes that occur when Jesus comes into a life. I love a line from that song, "For all is changed when Jesus comes to stay."[iv] God's goodness and kindness appeared to lost mankind in the person of Jesus Christ; and when you accept Jesus as Lord and Savior, *all is changed.*

"When the kindness of God our Savior and His love
for mankind appeared, He saved us, not on the basis of deeds
which we have done in righteousness, but according to His mercy."
(Titus 3:4-5)

Two descriptive words in Titus accompany the appearance of Jesus to redeem mankind. They enable your God-rest. The first is *kindness (chrēstótēs)*; which may also be translated *goodness.* This speaks of God's generosity and sincere benevolence to mankind. The Spirit of God is so kind and good that He is anxious to give whatever is necessary for the benefit of mankind.

The second is *love to man.* When looking at the root words for the Greek word translated *love to man (philanthrōpia)*, two words come together. One is *philéō, friend, to be fond of;* and *anthrōpos, man* or *mankind.* When these words are combined, the resulting meaning is God's fondness and love for mankind—His creation. From this compound Greek word, we have the English word *philanthropy, to promote welfare* or *goodwill to fellow man.* God's goodness and love is manifested to lost mankind in the person of His Son, Jesus Christ.

God's Goodness Is an Inspiration for Believers
"So rid yourselves of all wickedness, all deceit,
hypocrisy, envy, and all slander.
Like newborn infants, desire the unadulterated spiritual milk, so
that you may grow by it in (your) salvation,
since you have tasted that the Lord is good."
(1 Peter 2:1-3, HCSB)

The salvation God provides for you is not only the initial and culminating occurrence of receiving eternal life, or God-birth; but also the process of growing or maturing in God-life. Through a study of the Word of God, you will be able to put off, discard, and overcome virtueless ways of the heathen world. The goodness of God, seen in every book of the Bible, is the motivation and stimulus for you *to live as Christ*, a God-life.

Bless His name, "O taste and see that the LORD is good" (Psalm 34:8). The Word of God is an agent of God to cleanse believers so they can manifest God's goodness and kindness in their lives. "To make her [church, you] holy, cleansing her [you] in the washing of water by the Word" (Ephesians 5:26, HCSB).

When you have a deep and abiding understanding of the goodness of God, that it is perpetual and reliable, you are enabled for God-rest.

—Chapter Four—

"Come... and Rest a While"
(Mark 6:31)

Terry and his wife came directly from seminary to be director of a mission center in downtown Atlanta. It was located in a large, crime-ridden apartment complex. Daily there were dangerous, life-threatening situations occurring. Addicts, drunks, gangs, and criminals were all settled comfortably in that area. Terry gave himself to the challenge—caring, loving, ministering, and serving. Easy? No. Without obstacles? No. At times, frustrating? Yes! All of this and more. But they remained committed, giving themselves to the ministry. This couple's ministry began to have a positive effect. Fewer calls for police, children were playing safely, and the nighttime was more peaceful in the area. Of course, there were challenges—a lot of them. All kinds of challenges. "Preacher" Terry and his wife lovingly, faithfully, gave special care to each "opportunity."

When being interviewed, Terry was asked, "Are you safe serving there?"

He quickly responded, "I have perfect peace (rest), I'm in the hands of God." The whole community slowly began to respond with care, appreciation, and love for "preacher" Terry. They spent their entire ministry at the center and when they retired, the center was renamed in honor of them.

Jesus commissioned His disciples to go, proclaim the gospel, and call for repentance. In their ministry, they experienced threats, lack of response, prejudice, persecution, and other stress. Recognizing their need, Jesus called for them to "come away privately to a separate, solitary place and rest a while" (Mark 6:31, translation mine). It was time for the disciples to have God-rest. Jesus invited them to a *rest* (*anapausis*) where they would be refreshed, or *rejuvenated* in their spirit. The rest offered was not a rest of inactivity, but one of reinvigoration. God-rest is a refreshing recovery of your spiritual strength, a revival of your spirit.

The apostles needed a time of renewal because almost immediately they faced the crisis of feeding a crowd of 5,000 without food, a storm so severe their lives were threatened, and the challenge of the wild man of Gennesaret.

Remember, in the midst of life's pressures and stresses, you must come aside, find God-rest, and be refreshed of body and soul in order to have an effective ministry.

Don't Miss Your Rest!
"Let us… be diligent to enter that rest."
(Hebrews 4:11)

- **There is a promised God-rest for you in your daily life. Take your Bible and read Hebrews 3:7- 4:11. This insightful passage emphatically announces the good news of a promised rest that is available for you.**

The writer of Hebrews uses the Jews of the exodus as an appropriate illustration of how an entire generation failed to enter God's promised rest because of their unbelief. Canaan was the Land of Promise and rest, a celebrated land of milk and honey. This was to be the homeland for Israel—here they would *settle down*, colonize the territory, and find promised rest. But, they missed it. A whole generation missed the promised rest!

While the book of Hebrews is written from heaven's perspective, where Jesus is the High Priest, the passage before us addresses life here and now. There is a rest, a heavenly rest, a God-rest for you today. "We which have believed *do enter* into rest… they shall enter into *my rest*" (Hebrews 4:3, KJV, emphasis mine). The word most frequently translated *rest* (*katápausis*) in Hebrews 3:7-4:11 means *to settle down*.

~~~~~~

"We who have believed enter that rest."
(Hebrews 4:3)

~~~~~~

How did the Jews of the exodus miss the promised rest? The tragedy for the Jews of the exodus is that they heard the promise of God's rest, a land of plenty, where they could settle down and enjoy the Lord's promises, but they hardened their hearts in unbelief and missed the promised rest (see Psalm 95:8-11; Hebrews 3:8). For a generation they wandered aimlessly in an arid desert, complaining and questioning God. They even turned to idolatrous worship rejecting the Lord God.

No Calls Please

When serving at the national mission agency, my days were non-stop scheduled with meetings, appointments, staff, etc. By mid-afternoon, I would sense a need for a break, a rest. I would ask my administrative assistant, "Please, no calls or interruptions for 15 to 20 minutes." It was my oasis of recuperation, a time to settle down, a God-rest in the midst of my busy day. A word with the Lord, a few deep breaths, some quiet moments, and I was rejuvenated.

God-rest is based on an unwavering faith in the promises of God, an unfaltering faith in God's ability to provide God-rest in the midst of the demands of this life. The life-profile of today's citizenry is one of nervous disorders, physical exhaustion, two wage-earner families, and a myriad of illnesses caused by worry and anxiety. And Christians are not exempt. Finding God-rest in your day is an urgent spiritual necessity for you. We are to be "zealous and exert ourselves and strive diligently to enter into that rest [of God]—to know and experience it for ourselves" (Hebrews 4:11, AMP).

Learn From Jesus
"Take My yoke upon you, and learn of Me, for I am gentle
and humble in heart; and you shall find rest for your souls."
(Matthew 11:29)

This invitation from Jesus is two-fold. He offers you the refreshment and renewal of God-rest in daily living, and He assures you that He will be your co-laborer. It is a personal invitation, "Come to Me… I will give you rest… take My yoke… learn from Me… you shall find rest" (Matthew 11:28-29).

"Weary and heavy-laden." Does this sound familiar? Can you identify? It is the call of our Savior when you are tired and have a weariness of the body, or even more incapacitating, when you have emotional stress, mental tiredness, or spiritual fatigue. Jesus calls you to rest, to have God-rest. You need spiritual refreshment, rejuvenation, and a renewal of your inner soul. Jesus said, "I will give, impart, supply a God-rest for you (my translation)."

The Savior offers to yoke with you. The yoke is not deliverance from work, but a shared instrument in work. God-rest is not *from* work, but *in* work. Jesus says, "learn from Me," a personal invitation to you. When you yoke with Jesus, your load becomes light. Understand that *your* burden becomes *our* burden with Jesus. The yoke, the load, now is a shared load. He provides relief in the very time of your need. When you yoke with Jesus, the promised rest, God-rest, is already present in Him.

- **Have you engaged in a daily quiet time and asked Jesus to share your load?**

- **Have you accepted Jesus' yoke—His word and faithing His promises?**

Tell it to Jesus

While serving as Director of Missions for the state of Georgia, I was planning a retreat agenda for missionaries. When meeting with the program committee, we discussed music selections for the conference. Someone said we should have a theme song for the conference.

"What should it be?" I asked.

One of the missionaries quickly recited the words of an old hymn—"Are you weary, are you heavy hearted? Tell it to Jesus, tell it to Jesus; are you grieving over joys departed? Tell it to Jesus."

We laughed, but I realized they were weary, weary in well-doing. They needed God-rest. We used the requested song and they found renewal, refreshment during the conference.

"You shall find rest for your souls."
(Matthew 11:29)

Jesus did not escape difficulties, trials, hardships, or burdens in His earthly life. Yet, in the midst of it all, He could know the rest of spiritual refreshment and renewal, God-rest. The reality is that your life will also have weariness and burdens. With a compassionate voice, Jesus calls you to God-rest.

A New and Living Way
"A new and living way which He inaugurated for us [you]."
(Hebrews 10:20)

Jesus calls you to what He made possible for you. There is a new and living way—or a new way of living. When the gales of life are buffeting you, and rest for your soul is elusive, there is a new way of living. There is a God-rest; a privilege Christ secured for you through His death on Calvary's cross. You can have God-rest because His death has obtained for you access to the very presence of God. This new and living way is not a one-time happening, but from now on, in your every time of need, you can have the blessing of God-rest.

- Have you responded to the call of Jesus: "Come and rest a while?" Do you recognize when you need to "settle down" and spend some time with Jesus in God-rest?

SECTION SIX

GOD-WALK

"Walk in My instruction."
(Exodus 16:4)

Tom was an honest, hard-working farmer in our community, who had little or no regard for religion. Occasionally, he would attend the funeral of a fellow farmer, but even then, he would slip into church late and sit near the back of the sanctuary.

Our congregation had prayed for him through the years; pastors and evangelists had witnessed to him—all to no avail. He was never rude, nor did he offer any excuses for his disinterest in church or becoming a Christian. As if he didn't hear a word you said, he'd politely thank you for coming by and then go his way. Then, one day, everything changed.

Words cannot describe the shock and disbelief when Tom came to church one Sunday morning with his neighbor. During the altar call, the entire congregation was overwhelmed with unspeakable joy when Tom came forward to profess Christ as his personal Savior.

Church custom was to ask those who came forward to give their testimony. When I asked Tom what influenced him to accept Christ as his Savior, Tom pointed to his neighbor and said, "Him. He walked the talk every day."

~~~~~~

God-walk is making the Lord visible
in your daily activities and interactions with others.

~~~~~~

When words from many who had shared their testimony and witness had failed, a neighbor's "path" or *walk* led Tom to the Lord.

A *God-walk* means living a transparent life—manifesting, or making the Lord visible, in your daily activities and interactions with others.

—Chapter One—

Walk of Faith and Love

> "For I am not ashamed of the gospel of Christ:
> for it is the power of God unto salvation
> to every one that believeth."
> (Romans 1:16, KJV)

Let's begin this section with an overview of what a God-walk is. The empirical evidences of a God-walk are *faith* and *love*. All other graces in the Christian's life are rooted in these two biblical imperatives. You might say these are the vertical (faith) and horizontal (love) aspects of the Christian life and are fundamental to God-walk. Think about it: Faith and love—vertical and horizontal— together they form a cross. God-walk is lived out in the shadow of the cross; you are crucified with Christ.

Walk of Faith

The walk of faith is your response to the divine revelation of God in His Word that commences, continues, and culminates with a personal commitment to and relationship with the crucified and risen Christ (see Romans 1:16, my life verse). It is the discovery of how you can honor our infinitely holy God with your life.

The Lord is righteous in His every thought and action, without exception. "In it [the gospel] the righteousness of God is revealed from faith to faith" (Romans 1:17). The cardinal virtuousness of God is one of His indisputable attributes. In Christ, God declares you righteous, which means you have a right standing before Him. That right standing—or relationship with God—expresses itself in a walk of faith. "The righteous will live [walk] by his faith" (Habakkuk 2:4). This walk is from faith to faith; it is a growing, developing, maturing life of faith. The faith principle declares you righteous by faith, and you are to live and grow in faith.

I don't do well on tall ladders or in high places. I don't enjoy looking out windows from tall buildings. When viewing astronauts taking space walks, I sit in disbelief. How can anyone don a space suit, exit the spacecraft, and float thousands of miles from earth? In a television interview, an astronaut was asked virtually the same question. He responded that he had faith in his suit and equipment. You see, he was not so much doing a space walk, but a faith walk.

~~~~~~~~~~~~~~~~~~~~~~~~~~~~~~~~~~~

"We walk by faith not by sight."
(2 Corinthians 5:7)

~~~~~~~~~~~~~~~~~~~~~~~~~~~~~~~

The 32ⁿᵈ Floor

The 32nd Floor

Our daughter, Susan, was living in Hawaii when I was there on a ministry assignment. She invited me to see her apartment and off we went, not realizing that I would face a height challenge. Her apartment was on the 32nd floor and that was bad enough. However, when we exited the elevator, I faced a personal test.

The walkway was a narrow, open breezeway on the outside of the building with what appeared to my acrophobic state, only a knee-high railing. I took two steps backwards and stood still. Susan, oblivious to my struggle, was waving her arms, and excitedly pointing out Waikiki's landmarks. When she realized I wasn't following her she turned and asked, "Dad, why aren't you coming?"

"Is that how to get to your apartment?" I asked. She confirmed that it was.

Hoping for a different answer, I asked, "Is that the *only way* to get there?"

Puzzled she replied, "Yes, Dad, what's wrong?"

"I don't think that I can do it!"

"Come on, Dad! You can do it!"

After a few moments, I struggled forward with eyes cast down, focusing only on the walkway and hugging the wall, I followed her steps to the door. I totally missed her beloved view.

After we arrived safely inside her apartment, I collapsed on her sofa in relief and announced, "Susan, show me everything you want me to see because I won't be coming back again!" I was not making a second visit. She enjoys teasing me to this day. Yes, I had a reluctant faith walk; I should have released any dependency on myself and trusted God.

~~~~~~

Faith walk releases any dependency on self and trusts God.

~~~~~~

Faith is mandatory for a God-walk; in fact, the two are almost synonymous. We must accept the Word of God as divine revelation, trust His every promise, and manifest faith by obeying Him (see Romans 16:19). Accepting the Lord Jesus Christ as your Savior enables you to say, *It is no longer I who live, but Christ lives in me; and the life which I now live... I live by faith in the Son of God* (Galatians 2:20).

The miracle of God's grace brings Christ to live within you through the presence of the Holy Spirit. "Inconceivable, how could this be?" The Holy Spirit dwells in you because you are declared to be "the righteousness of God in Him" (2 Corinthians 5:21). Astounding! Unimaginable! But true. God has, by His grace, made you righteous in His sight. Now, you can walk in His holy company because you have been brought into right relation with Him. This gives you the opportunity and potential for God-walk.

Walk in Love

God is Love

The evangelist's sermon was based on the familiar text John 3:16. The service was in a tent located in an area populated with homeless, addicts, and society's dropouts. A disheveled man approached the evangelist at the close of the service and said, "God doesn't love me."

"Yes He does," responded the evangelist, "He can't help Himself, for God *is* love." He loves the whole of humanity. You and I do not earn or deserve God's love, but He loves us because that's who He is.

~~~~~~~~~~~~
"God is love."
(1 John 4:8)
~~~~~~~~~~~~

God is the fountainhead, the wellspring of love. He personifies love. He does not selectively choose to love, for He who has no beginning or ending *is* love—the embodiment of love. The evangelist was right; God can't help but love, for He is love. Love is the essence of God, His very nature.

In response to God's love for us, the only adequate and acceptable action is to walk in love. In Judaism, a foundational text is, "Hear, O Israel! The LORD is our God, the LORD is One! And you shall love the LORD your God with all your heart and with all your soul and with all your might" (Deuteronomy 6:4-5). The Jewish culture calls this the *Shema*, after the first Hebrew word in verse four, the imperative verb (*sama*), *to hear*. To hear the Word of God and not obey is not to hear Him at all.

Jesus was asked, "Which is the great commandment in the Law?" He referred to the Shema as the great commandment to be followed. "Love the Lord your God with all your heart... soul... mind" (Matthew 22:36-37). You are to walk in love.

How can I, a finite, mortal human, love the Lord God of heaven and earth? Loving God begins by accepting His gift of love—salvation through Jesus Christ, who took upon Himself our sins and was crucified that we might have eternal life.

Your God-birth was a miraculous event that not only gave you eternal, everlasting life, but also the potential of living a God-life with a God-walk in this present world. God-birth gives you "everything pertaining to life and godliness... in order that... you might become partakers of the divine nature" (2 Peter 1:3-4). Through a God-birth you receive the Holy Spirit, who abides within you and enables you to manifest God's love in a daily walk of love.

After accepting Christ, the way you show your devotion to God is through obedience. Have you considered that the basis of keeping the Ten Commandments (Exodus 20:3-17) is to walk in a biblically-based love of God?

Read the Ten Commandments in light of love.
> Love worships only Jehovah.
> Love does not make graven images.
> Love does not take God's name in vain.
> Love worships on the Lord's Day.
> Love honors parents.
> Love does not murder.
> Love does not commit adultery.
> Love does not steal.
> Love does not lie.
> Love does not covet.

God-walk obeys His commandments.

God-walk is exemplified in your daily life when you obey the Lord's commandments. Let's discover steps to achieving your God-walk.

- **Think about how God's love has been visible in your walk.**

- **By faith, are you walking with the Lord? List some of the places you have walked together.**

—Chapter Two—

Walk In or By the Spirit

W alking in the Spirit is often erroneously interpreted to mean emotional or physical activities such as dancing, laughing, crying, running around, and demonstrating erratic behavior. However, this is a distortion of biblical truth. An emotional high expressed through such behaviors is a momentary experience that soon ends; while walking in the Spirit is the daily lifestyle adventure of God-walk.

A believer is born again through a personal faith in the sacrificial death of Jesus. In this exercise of faith, the believer is indwelt by the Holy Spirit (see Romans 8:9). The word *spirit* intrinsically means *one's very self* or *essential nature*. A believer is inhabited by the Spirit of God, and thus shares in God's nature. God-walk is permitting the Holy Spirit to manage your daily life and to magnify Christ in all you do. In other words, your God-life will be apparent in your God-walk.

~~~~~~

God-walk permits the Holy Spirit to manage your daily life.

~~~~~~

A Journeyer with the Holy Spirit

Paul emphasized the vitality of a Spirit-filled God-walk, becoming a journeyer with the Holy Spirit. In the fifth chapter of Galatians he depicts the difference between life as a carnal, or flesh-centered believer, and a Spirit-filled believer. The "works" or life of the flesh-centered believer is given in verses 19-21. The "fruit" of the Spirit-filled believer is seen in verses 22-23. Although some may see the flesh-centered and Spirit-filled to be a comparison between the unsaved and saved, it is not. Rather, it defines the struggle between the flesh and Spirit in every believer's life.

Paul uses four descriptive verbs to guide you in pursuing a God-walk.

"Walk by the Spirit"
"*Walk by the Spirit*, and you will not carry out the desire of the flesh" (Galatians 5:16, emphasis mine). *Walk (peripatéō)* is to live daily with the conscious presence of the Holy Spirit in all of your activities. A Christian is to have a general life-style of a Spirit-led life. The believer is to exalt the Lord Jesus Christ by living in a newness of life, a spirit-led life.

"Led by the Spirit"
"If you are *led by the Spirit*, you are not under the Law" (Galatians 5:18, emphasis mine). *Led (ágō)* is directed or guided by the Spirit.

"Live by the Spirit"
"If we *live by the Spirit*... (Galatians 5:25, emphasis mine). *Live (zaō)* is to come alive in a Spirit-filled life.

"Walk by the Spirit"
"...let us also *walk by the Spirit*" (Galatians 5:25, emphasis mine).
Walk (stoicheō) means to keep in step with the Holy Spirit. Note: this is a different word with a very different meaning from "walk" in verse 16. The first "walk" is inclusive of all of

life. This "walk" is specific; every step, thought, and action must be in line with the Holy Spirit. As a soldier marches in cadence, the believer must walk in line, in step, in submission to the Holy Spirit.

What joy! We can live a life that is synchronized with the Holy Spirit! Is this your daily walk? Are you walking in the Spirit, sensitive to His guidance in every area of your life? You have been invited on an exciting lifetime journey with the Holy Spirit, from faith to faith.

A journey is never without decisions, opposition, and unexpected challenges. This is surely true in the journey of life. In the midst of Paul's admonition to walk in the Spirit, we are reminded: "the flesh sets its desire against the Spirit, and the Spirit against the flesh; for these are in opposition to one another" (Galatians 5:17).

Paul reasoned, if you are saved—made alive by the Spirit—you ought to walk in accordance with direction of the Spirit. In fact, to Paul, it would be absurd to be alive in Christ and not walk by the Spirit. Look again with me at Galatians 5:25, "If by the (Holy) Spirit we have our life [in God] let us go forward walking in line, our conduct controlled by the Spirit" (AMP). Another translation says, "Keep in step with the Spirit" (NIV). You are to order your steps (lifestyle) by the Holy Spirit—who assists and disciplines you in your God-walk.

Boot Camp

In the grey light of a new morning, the sound of crisp, authoritative commands could be heard across the grounds, "Chin down, chest out, stomach in!" The day had begun for the new U.S. Marine recruits at boot camp.

The drill sergeant barked, "If you are going to be a Marine, you are going to look like a Marine! Foh-woad, ho!"

The disciplined walk of a Marine distinguishes who he is, defined by a lifestyle of discipline and fidelity until death. In fact, the Marines have a saying: "Once a Marine, always a Marine." They are always faithful—*Semper Fidelis*—to their colleagues, their calling, and their country.

How much more should a believer demonstrate a God-walk of discipline and fidelity? Literally, Christians should strive to keep in step with the Holy Spirit.

The admonition of Scripture is that the Holy Spirit is to direct your every step, attitude, and action. Like a well-trained member of a drill team, you march with the Holy Spirit as one—every realm of life synchronized together, under the authority of the Commanding Officer.

You and the Holy Spirit march as one.

The Word of God, Our Guide

I want to focus on a key passage that will enlighten your understanding about walking in the Spirit. Jesus said, "It is the Spirit who gives life; the flesh profits nothing; the words that I have spoken to you are spirit and are life" (John 6:63). The evidence of walking in or by the Spirit is not seen in physical or emotional exertions, but by discovering and obeying the Word of God. It is your road map. The Holy Spirit enables you to live a God-life when you use His inspired word as a guide for your God-walk.

The Holy Spirit is the Divine Agent.
The Word of God is the Divine Guide.

The Word Is Living

Jesus said the words He spoke are life. Paul said, "The word of God is *living*" (Hebrews 4:12, emphasis mine). The word of God is much more than history, poetry, and biographies. It is God's living, active word, and He is speaking to you today through His Word (see Hebrews 3:7). The Bible is a "today" book; it is a living, contemporary, relevant, real-time guide for today's world.

The Word Is Energizing

The word of God is not only living, but also energizing. "The word of God is... *active*" (Hebrews 4:12, emphasis mine). The word translated *active* (*energéo*) means *effectual, fervent*; it is full of vibrant vigor. It is from this root word we get the English word *energy*. The Word of God invigorates and rejuvenates. It is full of living power that enables your God-walk.

The Word of God energizes.

The Word Is to Be Obeyed

"The words (truths) that I have been speaking to you are spirit and life" (John 6:63 AMP). Every word Jesus uttered is truth and the embodiment of His own divine Spirit. The Spirit of God dwells in the words of Jesus and operates through them by communicating a God-walk to you. In fact, the entire Bible is the infallible Word of God and is to be obeyed. The Bible is our faultless guide for God-walk.

Second Timothy 3:16 explains, "All Scripture is inspired by God and profitable." The phrase *inspired of God* in Greek is a single word (*theópneustos*). It is formed by combining two Greek words, *théo* (*God*) and *pneúma* (*breath* or *spirit*), God-breathed. The suffix (*tos*) of the Greek word (*theópneustos*) indicates a passive voice; the subject is acted upon, breathed out by God. It is important to reemphasize this principle truth.

This important understanding is reiterated in 2 Peter 1:21: "No prophecy ever originated because some man willed it [to do so]... it never came by human impulse... but as men spoke from God who were borne along (moved and impelled) by the Holy Spirit" (AMP). The entire Word of God is Spirit breathed and is to be obeyed. It is the appropriate guide for you.

Walking in the Spirit is walking in the Word of God;
Walking in the Word of God enables your God-walk.

Achieving God-walk is possible! As we noted in chapter one, "His divine power has granted to us everything pertaining to life and godliness, through the true knowledge of Him who called us by His own glory and excellence. For by these He has granted to us His precious and magnificent promises, in order that by them you might become partakers of the divine nature" (2 Peter 1:3-4). Walking in the Spirit is walking in the Word of God, and walking in the Word of God (His precious and magnificent promises) will energize your God-walk.

— Chapter Three —

A Crucified Walk

"I have been crucified with Christ."
(Galatians 2:20)

He was a young, well-trained, successful pastor of a growing church. He sat across from me—head bowed, shoulders drooped, voice barely audible mumbling, "I'm only human. Everybody makes mistakes."

A promising ministry and a marriage were now in jeopardy. Why? This young pastor had walked in the flesh, giving in to his carnal appetites and failing miserably in his God-walk.

What must you do in order to control the desires of the flesh, your humanness? Sin must die, not simply be restrained, suppressed, or controlled, but be crucified completely.

A crucified walk denies self;
it is no longer you, it is Christ.

Ego-centric vs. Christo-centric

Galatians 5:24 tells us "those who belong to Christ Jesus have crucified the flesh with its passions and desires." The word *flesh* means we live and make choices under the influence of our senses. The fundamental sin of a believer who is walking in the flesh is that he or she lives an egocentric life, rather than a Christo-centric life. Clearly, a crucified walk requires you to deny any claim you have to yourself. It can no longer be you who decides the course of your life, it must be Christ.

Walking in the flesh refers to a self-centered life that is perversely focused on fulfilling your desires and fleshly passions—living in carnality. Bear in mind, when Paul was writing to believers in the Church of Galatia, he was not writing theoretically, he had experienced the battle between his mind-body desires and the Spirit. "I know that nothing good dwells in me, that is, in my flesh; for the wishing is present in me, but the doing of the good is not" (Romans 7:18). Within the believer, there will always be an ongoing conflict between living a God-life with a consistent God-walk and living an undisciplined life driven by sin-nature.

Wasn't the young pastor right? We are all only human; everybody makes mistakes. Yes, we all live in a body that will be driven by passions and desires unless it is kept under control. Paul wrote, "I discipline my body [flesh] and bring it under strict control" (1 Corinthians 9:27, HCSB). He literally was saying, "I strive and contend (give myself a knock-out blow) with my natural, fleshly body." He was not willing to be mastered by his body. You are admonished to "present your bodies a living sacrifice, holy, acceptable unto God" (Romans 12:1, KJV). A sacrifice? Yes! A crucified walk? Yes!

Two Crucifixions

Many believers think once you have accepted the atonement of Jesus at Calvary, the sin account is settled and life goes on. True, the sin account is settled, but what about your life? Most preaching focuses on being saved by the crucifixion of Christ, not living by crucifixion of self. The first crucifixion is *for* you, the second is *by* you. Both crucifixions are found in Scripture. Of course, this concept of two crucifixions is new to many Christians. Let's take a moment to explore this important principle.

- **Before we continue, turn to Galatians 2:20 and 5:24 and read them carefully. Ask God to guide you in understanding the two crucifixions.**

The First Crucifixion [Jesus] Was for You.
The first crucifixion was at Calvary, and it was *for* you. By faith, your old self was crucified with Christ, the penalty of your sin was done away with, and through His grace, you were set free from your enslavement to sin (see Romans 6:6). A God-walk begins at Calvary, at the crucifixion of Jesus Christ.

God-walk begins at Calvary.

The gospel message is redemptive; God demonstrated His love to you through Christ's death while you were yet a sinner (see Romans 5:8). When you accepted the love of God as manifested in the crucifixion of Jesus, and prayed for forgiveness of your sin, your sin debt was pardoned and taken away. God nailed it to the cross of His Son, Christ Jesus (see Colossians 2:13-14) and provided you with salvation, a deliverance.

"It was the Father's good pleasure for all the fulness to dwell in Him [Jesus], and through Him to reconcile [thoroughly change]... having made peace through the blood of His cross (Colossians 1:19-20).

Through a personal faith in the crucified Christ, you can say, "I have been crucified with Christ," and my sins are forgiven (Galatians 2:20). The crucifixion of Christ Jesus was *for* you—a free gift that you could not earn and cannot lose. The transaction is complete, settled, and eternally recorded in heaven in the Lamb's book of life (see Revelations 3:5).

The Second Crucifixion is by You.

You must crucify your fleshly nature, sensual appetites, and selfish practices. This is something that must be done *by* you—it cannot be done *for* you. You bring your sins to be crucified and put to death (see Romans 6:11).

Do you recall when Peter's mind was set on earthly things and he rebuked Jesus for talking about His future suffering and death (see Mark 8:31-33)? Peter was thinking about his own interests, not of God's concerns. He and the other disciples were obviously enjoying the fellowship and teaching of Jesus. They had witnessed miracles and observed the thousands of people who drew near to hear the carpenter's son. And they wanted it all to continue. They had no desire for talk of suffering, death, or Jesus being separated from them.

Yet, Jesus reminded them that God's will was not always the fulfilling of your desires and wishes. The life of the believer is not a life of ease; rather, it is one of obedience. He said: "If anyone wishes to come after Me, let him deny himself, and take up his cross, and follow Me" (Mark 8:34).

"Take up your cross." That means that your fleshly desires must be crucified. In a figure of speech, your flesh nature must daily be executed, nailed to the cross of self-denial. Paul emphasized that your body is the Lord's, and must be committed to Him. "I will not be mastered by anything... the body is not for immorality, but for the Lord... flee immorality... your body is a temple of the Holy Spirit" (1 Corinthians 6:12-13, 18-19). As you choose to worship, choose also to honor, and care for your body as the sanctuary (temple) of God. *Christ in you.*

~~~~~~~~~~~~~~~~~~~~~~~~~~~~~~~~~~

Your body is a sanctuary of God.

~~~~~~~~~~~~~~~~~~~~~~~~~~~~~~~~~~

The Super Bowl, the World Series, the heavyweight battle, the championship match of a God-walk is described in the fifth chapter of Galatians. This chapter could be entitled "The Clash of the Titans," the gladiatorial contest between the flesh and Spirit. This gigantic ongoing struggle is real, and it's a battle to the death. "The flesh sets its desire against the Spirit, and the Spirit against the flesh; for these are in opposition to one another" (Galatians 5:17). The flesh and Spirit are opposing combatants that confront each other daily in your life. The Spirit must be victorious in your life because it is vital to your God-walk.

Paul's use of flesh (fleshly appetites and emotions) also addresses the mind and will. You do not yield to the flesh until the battle is lost in your mind and will. A God-walk is not a simple physical thing, it is a victorious battle of your mind and will (see Romans 7:15-25). Sadly, some (even in Christian leadership) think of themselves as being beyond the temptation of the flesh. I can only imagine the shouts of victory by Satan and his demons when a believer thinks himself impenetrable to the fiery darts of the enemy and loses the battle.

The insightful Timothy George explains, "No Christians are so spiritually strong or mature that they need not heed his [Paul's] warning, but neither are any so weak nor vacillating that they cannot be free from the tyranny of the flesh through the power of the Spirit."[i] I don't believe it could be better worded. Therefore, become alert and vigilant to your adversary, Satan, who skillfully uses your flesh and its desires. And remember, He who is in us is greater than he who is in the world.

A Memorable Visit

Ed, a preacher friend, said, "I want you to go with me to visit one of the godliest men I know." We pulled into the driveway of a modest home, and getting out, Ed said, "We'll go past the garden to his study."

It was probably once a tool shed, now filled with books, a home-made work desk, and one chair. Meeting this wonderfully dedicated, openly sincere, and gracious man was a cherished blessing.

The point of my remembering him was the note cards he had thumb-tacked to the doorframe. Curious, I began reading the few tacked there.

"I had ill-will towards... today."

"I spoke in haste... today."

"I did not... today."

"I did... today."

"I'm crucifying them," the kindly host explained. "Every time I go in and out, all day long, I stop and read them, and at the close of the day, I tear them up and throw them away—I rid myself of them." He was crucifying the deeds of his flesh.

Martin Luther (1483–1546) wrote, "Although the flesh be yet alive, yet can it not perform that which it would do, forasmuch as it is bound both hand and foot, and fast nailed to the cross."[ii] In other words, the crucified God-walk is one of vigilance and action. A God-walk is never accomplished in a passive mode.

To portray the crucified life, Paul uses three action-packed verbs.

"Lay aside the old self." (Ephesians 4:22)
A decisive act of rejection, a putting away by you.

"Be renewed in the spirit of your mind." (Ephesians 4:23)
Continually revisiting, renovating, and conforming your mind to Christ.

"Put on the new self." (Ephesians 4:24)
Accepting the reality of God-birth by the assumption of a new life—a brand new lifestyle in the image of Christ (see Romans 8:29).

When you're renewed in the spirit of your mind, you continually crucify sin. "Consider the members of your earthly body as dead" (Colossians 3:5). Bring them under control, treat them as dead, crucified. Mortify—put to death—subdue your fleshly impulses. This spiritual campaign is between your flesh and Spirit.

- **Remember the note cards on the door frame? Have you identified and written out your deeds or thoughts that need to be crucified?**

The Spirit of God enables you to mortify sin. Yet it is your volitional act that brings your fleshly deeds to the cross to be crucified and put to death. No one else can crucify your sin.

- **"Lord Jesus, help me to identify with Your death and crucifixion until my sin is crucified and dead to me."**

In summary, "Our old self was crucified" (Romans 6:6). In Greek, the grammar of *crucified* is in the aorist imperative passive, which means that the sin debt was settled punctually and promptly in the past when you as a repentant sinner accepted the crucified Christ as your Savior. It is a finished act. Also, Galatians 2:20 tells us, "I have been crucified with Christ." In Greek, *crucified* is in the perfect indicative passive, which is the strong assertion that salvation is a completed act in the past. You have been to Calvary, and the precious shed blood of Jesus has settled the sin question. Salvation is perfectly secured and you are justified. *The first crucifixion was for you.*

There is a marked difference in Galatians 5:24, "Those who belong to Christ Jesus have crucified the flesh." In Greek, *crucified* is in the aorist active indicative, which means that you as a believer, in an objective act, have taken your fleshly passions, desires, and appetites and have crucified them. This is a definite decision that you make. You must resign any claim you have to yourself, your flesh-centered desires, and confess, *It is no longer I, but Christ who lives in me!* Your confessed deeds are to be discarded, nailed, and crucified. The writer of Hebrews included himself in Hebrews 12:1, "Let us also lay aside every encumbrance, and the sin which so easily entangles us." You must allow the Holy Spirit to speak through the Bible and identify those impulses that must be crucified. *The second crucifixion is by you.*

- **Have you experienced the glorious self-denial of being crucified with Christ?**

- **Are your sins daily being taken by you to the cross of self-denial?**

Two Wills

Darkness was descending and we were in an open boat, fishing off the coast of Florida. I asked the deacon who had taken his pastor and me fishing, "How will we find the inlet and miss the rocks in the dark?" My concern was the jagged, exposed boulders he had pointed out to be dangerous when we left the harbor a few hours earlier.

"That's easy," was his casual reply, as we headed to the shore in pitch darkness. "See those two blinking lights? We are going to line them up so there will only be one. Then, we can go safely into the harbor."

~~~~~~~~~~~~~~~~~~~~~~~~~~~~~~~~~~~
Two lights become one.
God's will and my will become one.
~~~~~~~~~~~~~~~~~~~~~~~~~~~~~~~~~~~

Have you ever thought about Jesus the Son of God, and God the heavenly Father both having wills? Well, they did. And to accomplish God's plan of redemption, both the Father's and the Son's wills had to become one.

Jesus spoke of the will of His Father who is in heaven (see Matthew 7:21). The eternal struggle is to place divine will above self-will. Jesus is the Son of God—God Himself. He is the Christ, the Anointed One, the Messiah. As one of the Godhead, His nature and every attribute are the same as the Trinity—God the Father and God the Holy Spirit. They are one (see John 10:30).

Jesus, the sinless Christ, who is holy in every way, must now become sin, take upon Himself your sin and mine. The purest became defiled, "O' God is there any other way?" Jesus was the Son of man—fully human. The excruciating death by crucifixion was only hours away when in the garden of Gethsemane we hear Jesus aligning two wills, "Father, if it is Your will, take this cup [the suffering He would undergo] from Me: nevertheless not My will, but Yours, be done" (Luke 22:42, NKJV). Jesus, through self-denial, aligned His human will with the will of the heavenly Father.

God-walk is journeying in the will of God. A crucified walk will not be a reality until the two wills—yours and God's—become one. "Be careful how you walk, not as unwise men, but as wise... do not be foolish, but understand what the will of the Lord is" (Ephesians 5:15, 17). Remember the model prayer? Jesus taught us to pray, "Thy will be done" (Matthew 6:10).

Results for doing God's will are many. Two of the most rewarding are:
Doing the will of God, pleases God (see Philippians 2:13).
Doing the will of God, Jesus will claim you as His brother or sister (see Matthew 12:50).

What indescribable blessings await when you crucify your flesh nature and faithfully seek to walk in the will of God!

~~~~~~

God-walk is journeying in the will of God.

~~~~~~

Two Results

Your Choice: Carnal Walk vs. God-Walk

The result of walking in the flesh is a carnal life. The evidence of a crucified walk is a spiritual life, or God-walk. Remember, Galatians was written to "all the brethren... to the churches of Galatia" (Galatians 1:2). Some were carnal; some were spiritual. A carnal Christian is governed by the appetites of his human flesh. The word *carnal* (*sarkikos*) means *worldly, human, flesh nature*. Carnal Christians are saved, but as a result of their lifestyle, they don't receive or enjoy a fullness of the spiritual blessings of God in their lives.

Paul identifies the deeds of the flesh in the Galatian churches (see Galatians 5:19-21). He emphatically states that Christians who engage in these sins, "shall not inherit the kingdom of God" (Galatians 5:21). What? Inherit the kingdom by morality, or lose the kingdom by immorality? Is Paul saying that by living a moral life you inherit eternal life? No! Salvation is by faith, not by works (see Galatians 3:11). Then, what does Paul mean when he writes "shall not inherit the kingdom of God"?

Two understandings are important. First, *the kingdom of God* means *the rule of God within the believer.* Second, *inherit (klēronomeō)* is to *receive as one's own,* or to *possess.*

If Paul is addressing carnal Christians in the churches of Galatia, he is saying that they have not submitted to the rule of God in their lives. When God's rule of grace is established in the heart, the catalog of immoral improprieties listed by Paul will not be evidenced in the life of a kingdom citizen. When believers are unable to live above the lecherous deeds of the flesh—they are carnal.

On the other hand, if Paul is addressing unbelieving members in the churches of Galatia, he is saying those who *habitually practice* the deeds of the flesh are without a transforming, saving faith. Those who are continually doing such things show themselves not to possess the kingdom of God. They have not received the redemption of their souls, a God-birth.

It is my opinion that Paul was addressing carnal believers in the church at Galatia. This is the predominant theme of the epistle.

~~~~~~~~~~~~~~~~~~~~~~~~~~~~

You are the King's domain.

~~~~~~~~~~~~~~~~~~~~~~~~~~~~

When Jesus was asked when the kingdom of God would come, He answered them, "the Kingdom of God is within you" (Luke 17:21 NKJV). He did not come to establish a religion or earthly empire, but His eternal Kingdom—a government of divine origin. "The government will rest upon His shoulders" (Isaiah 9:6).

The kingdom of God today is the presence of Christ in you through the person of the Holy Spirit. It is the rule of God within you. Therefore, you must accept the authority of God—His Kingship—in your life. It is His Kingdom and you are the King's domain.

- **You are the King's domain, is He pleased with your walk? Is it a God-walk?**

—Chapter Four—

Walk Before God

"I shall walk before the LORD in the land of the living."
(Psalms 116:9)

Davin made a holy resolution to live a sanctified life as a king, father, and husband, and to be holy in his every day activities. Look at Psalms 116:9 and consider the affirmation of David, "In my daily life, I will walk before the Lord." In Hebrew, the word *walk* (*hālak*) means *to go on habitually, up and down, back and forth.* The word *before* means *in the face of,* or *presence of.* Herein is a good understanding of God-walk. In your daily life, you habitually live in the very presence of God.

"Let's Get Real"

In the midst of a recent series of sermons on *Covenant Promises,* I brought a message on "Abraham, Father of Nations." Following the service, a young man came to me and said, "I smiled when I realized that you were affirming that the story of Abraham and Sarah was literal." He smirked in unbelief.

I restated the fact that God established a covenant of faith with Abraham. When Abraham was 99 years of age and Sarah was 90, Isaac was born naturally to the couple. Looking at the young man who believed the Scripture was fiction, I said, "Are you asking, how in the world such a thing could happen?"

"That's right," he responded. "Let's get real!"

"Would you be surprised," I asked, "if you were to learn that Abraham and Sarah asked the same question?"

"Did they?" he questioned.

"Yes, but God had a word of encouragement for them. Listen to what He said: 'I am God Almighty; walk before Me, and be blameless. And I will establish My covenant between Me and you'" (Genesis 17:1-2).

The young man who questioned the literal truth of Scripture did not grasp the truth of EL SHADDAI [GOD ALMIGHTY]. Not so with Abraham, he grasped that the One who appeared to him was the all-powerful LORD GOD. He was the Mighty One—*EL, THE STRONG ONE WITH INFINITE POWER* (omnipotent), and *SHADDAI, ALMIGHTY* and *ALL-SUFFICIENT*. Abraham trusted in the incomparable Lord God and accepted His promises as already accomplished (see Romans 4:16-22). He knew that God was with him and would not forsake him. You must trust and believe as well.

EL SHADDAI, THE MIGHTY, ALL-SUFFICENT GOD

Knowing God's trustworthy, able character and His command to walk before Him in obedience, enable you to have a God-walk— an active life of accountability in His presence (see 2 Corinthians 5:10). You respond to His call with an awareness of His almighty power and wisdom, and a deep desire to walk before Him in obedience to His Word and conformity to His will. A mature God-walk is a lifestyle that characterizes a God-life, of living habitually in the conscious presence of the Lord, and conducting your life in every place and at all times as though you were in the Holy of Holies before God Almighty.

Conduct your life in every place and at all times as though
you are in the Holy of Holies before God Almighty.

The Laughter of Faith

Returning to the story in Genesis, when God told Abraham that
his wife Sarah would be a mother of nations and that kings would
descend from her, Abraham laughed (Genesis 17:17). His was a
joyful laughter of wonder, hope, and anticipation. His faith had been
renewed, his hope had been rekindled, and the blessed prospect was
impossible for him to express with words. So, Abraham laughed.

Following God's revelation of His promise to Abraham, three
visitors appeared as men (one was identified as the Lord) and foretold the miraculous birth of Isaac. Sarah was nearby in the tent, and
when she heard the startling prophecy, she laughed within herself
(Genesis 18:12). Hers was a laugh of incredulity. She was thinking,
after I have become old, ha! The promise was so far beyond prob-
ability that she laughed a chortle of unbelief.

Like Sarah, the young man who approached me after my sermon
was laughing with skepticism at God and His Word. The Lord questioned Sarah's laugh of scoffing unbelief. "Why did Sarah laugh,
saying, 'Shall I indeed bear a child, when I am so old?'" (v. 13).

Then the unbelievable happened. In about a year following the
visit of the three men to Abraham's tent, "The LORD did for Sarah
as He had promised" (Genesis 21:1). Sarah bore a son and she said,
"God has made laughter for me; everyone who hears will laugh with
me" (Genesis 21:6). Sarah laughed with rapturous delight, but this
time she laughed *with* God. The psalmist proclaimed, "Our mouth
was filled with laughter… the Lord has done great things" (Psalms
126:2). When you walk before God in everyday life, you will have
many occasions to laugh with God because of the wondrous blessings He will give. Perhaps some blessings will be beyond your
expectation or belief.

Chapter Five

Walk With God

Many of today's churches have virtually replaced the timeless old hymns with choruses. The intent is to offer easy to learn, catchy songs that magnify, glorify, and exalt God in an exuberant, contemporary act of worship. However, many choruses are poorly written and are sung to predictable tunes. Recently, a chorus in the morning worship service addressed God and said, "Come, walk beside me." God is not to be summoned to walk beside us—*we join Him!* We are to die to self, and walk with God, a God-walk.

~~~~~~

God is not summoned to walk beside us—we join Him!

~~~~~~

Enoch's God-walk

The Bible records that Enoch walked with God. After the birth of Methuselah, Enoch "walked with God three hundred years" (Genesis 5:22). The rhythmic biblical obituaries in Genesis read, "he lived so many years and died." But in the account of Enoch, the seventh generation from Adam, the wording changes. "Enoch walked with God; and he was not, for God took him" (Genesis 5:24). Enoch's most important accomplishment in life was that he walked with God. He lived a devout life, in close communion with his Lord. Enoch "obtained the witness that before his being taken up he was pleasing to God" (Hebrews 11:5). Enoch walked with God in his daily living. He was the father of a family, a prophet, and a preacher of righteousness (see Jude 14-15). All these responsibilities and accomplishments were important, but were secondary to his walking with God—achieving God-walk.

God wants you to walk with Him in your daily life—work, recreational, social, and home life. God-walk is not withdrawing to a cloistered or protected environment, but walking with the Lord in every aspect of your world.

A Word from Amos

"Can two walk together, except they be agreed?" (Amos 3:3, KJV). Amos asks a rhetorical question, the answer is obvious and unmistakable—two must agree on the time and place to begin—and then the direction to go if they are to walk together.

A walk with God begins at Calvary. It must begin with the acknowledgment of sin, and of God's forgiveness. Having settled the sin debt, you can pursue the blessing of living the life for which you were created.

Walking with God involves companionship, direction, and movement. It is not an isolated, occasional event; rather, it is a determined, dynamic lifestyle—a daily, personal commitment. When you share your testimony, do you tell of a distant past experience you had with God? Or, is it recent events? Walking with God is to be today's venture.

~~~~~~
Make walking with God today's venture.
~~~~~~

When You Walk with God, Walk in Righteousness.

When you walk with God, you walk in righteousness, and when you walk in righteousness, you are a blessing to God. "The Lord loves the righteous" (Psalm 146:8).

Walk Uprightly.

Walking uprightly is to be morally scrupulous, firmly maintaining a code of right behavior. You may ask, "How can I know the way to walk uprightly?" You must "give earnest heed to the voice of the LORD your God, and do what is right in His sight, and give ear to His commandments, and keep all His statutes" (Exodus 15:26).

Walk Circumspectly.

Walking circumspectly means defining and marking off carefully the boundaries of your behavior. "See, then, that ye walk circumspectly" (Ephesians 5:15, KJV). There are some do's that are inside those boundaries, and some don'ts on the outside. "Therefore be careful [look carefully] how you walk, not as unwise... but as wise, making the most of your time [life]" (Ephesians 5:15-17).

Walk a Straight Path.

Walking a straight path means providing a faithful testimony for those who watch you. "Strengthen the hands that are weak and the knees that are feeble, and make straight paths for your feet" (Hebrews 12:12-13). When you walk with God in righteousness, you live in such a way that your course of conduct leaves a straight path for others to follow (see James 2:18).

When You Walk with God, Walk with Integrity.

Integrity is the unremitting union of your values and behavior.

Walk in Honesty.

"O LORD, who may abide [sojourn] in Thy tent?... He who walks with integrity... and speaks truth [honest] in his heart (Psalm 15:1-2). You must live honestly before others if you desire to walk honestly before God. This may sound obvious; but sadly, some who are prominent in church on Sunday cannot be trusted or believed on Monday.

This concerned Paul, "We take thought beforehand and aim to be honest and absolutely above suspicion not only in the sight of the Lord but also in the sight of men" (2 Corinthians 8:21, AMP).

Temptations abound—to stretch the truth, embellish a report, obscure or deny a fact, omit incriminating evidence, or to simply invent falsehoods. The root of these and other like temptations is for the defense and preservation of your ego.

But wait! If you have been crucified with Christ, then *Christ lives in you.* You have no ego. He is your reputation and confidence! The Bible asserts that Christ is truth, and that He is honest. "Let us walk honestly, as in the day [open to be seen by all]... put ye on the Lord Jesus Christ" (Romans 13:13-14, KJV).

Walk in Humility.

You are a child of God, and He has given you an incomparable invitation to walk with Him. "What does the Lord require of you... to walk humbly with your God" (Micah 6:8). This reminds me of a quotation attributed to John Bunyan, "He that is humble, ever shall have God to be his guide."

Walking humbly with God means living in an unpretentious manner, submissive to His will. When you walk humbly, you are not proud, haughty, or arrogant. It is not difficult to walk humbly with God when you realize the truth of who you are in Christ. You are crucified with Christ, and are only alive in Christ.

Can you embrace a humility that says, "All I have or ever hope to be is in Christ?" Having received reconciliation as God's gift through Christ, you should ever after walk humbly with God with rejoicing and gratitude.

Walk in Good Works.

Portray the goodness of God through acts of benevolence, and without concern for compensation or recognition. Paul gave an extensive list of good deeds for the believer to exhibit.

"Love must be without *hypocrisy. Detest evil*; *cling to* what is *good. Show family affection* to one another with *brotherly love.* Outdo one another in *showing honor.* Do not lack diligence; be *fervent in spirit*; serve the Lord.

Rejoice in hope; *be patient* in affliction; *be persistent* in prayer. *Share* with the saints in their needs; *pursue* hospitality. *Bless* those who persecute you; bless and do not curse. *Rejoice* with those who rejoice; *weep* with those who weep. *Be in agreement* with one another.

Do not be proud; instead, *associate* with the humble. Do not be wise in your own estimation. Do not repay anyone evil for evil. Try to do what is honorable in everyone's eyes.

If possible, on your part, *live at peace* with everyone. Friends, *do not avenge yourselves*; instead, leave room for His wrath" (Romans 12:9-19, HCSB, emphasis mine).

A Pastor Who Walked with God

It was an unpretentious engagement. I was to preach for two weeks in a revival at a rescue mission in an unseemly area of Nashville, Tennessee. As a college student who was anxious to preach, I said yes to the invitation. The pastor told me that in addition to a morning Vacation Bible School and the evening evangelistic service, I was to go with him all day, every day. I've forgotten much of what I learned in college classes, but the two weeks at the mission remain fresh to this day.

Spending at least 12 hours every day with the pastor who walked with God, I learned many lasting lessons. Pastor Ralph was always ready to help and to do something good for everyone. There were drunks, street kids, battered women, prostitutes, petty criminals, the hungry, the abandoned, and the list goes on. The pastor sought to help them all. I learned the imperative to be ready and responsive — to do good works and to meet the needs of others in the name of Jesus. I learned that the God of the Bible is indisputably good (see Matthew 19:17). God is consummately kind and compassionate, and when you walk with Him, that walk is permeated by His goodness.

Think about it, God has given you an invitation to join Him in a life journey, to learn about Him and participate with Him in doing good deeds. Learn to walk with God from spending time and observing mature Christians. They can show how—together with the Lord—you too can be "zealous for good deeds" (Titus 2:14).

Are You God's Poem?

When a poet forms his work of art, he is careful to choose each word and is attentive to maintain balance in his composition. Poems have a specific meter, the words are arranged in a measured rhythm, and they repeat a basic pattern. In Ephesians 2:10, we are told that "we are His workmanship." The word translated *workmanship* is the Greek word *poiēma*, the word from which we get *poem*. You are God's poem, carefully made and chosen by God, composed for a specific purpose, and with a meter, that repeats a basic pattern. The pattern is the image of God, His goodness, and excellent deeds.

~~~~~~

What God bids you to do, He prepares you to do.

~~~~~~

What God calls you to do, He will bring it to pass (see 1 Thessalonians 5:24). On your walk with God, He has particular good works for you to perform, and has gifted you through His grace to perform the good works He has purposed for you.

God asks for your submission, He will perform all these actions through you. "God is able to make all grace abound to you, that always having all sufficiency in everything, you may have an abundance for every good deed" (2 Corinthians 9:8).

To walk with God and not be involved in good works is inconceivable. "I was hungry... I was thirsty... I was a stranger... naked... I was sick... I was in prison." Jesus said the good deeds you did to one of these, even the least, "you did it to Me" (Matthew 25:35–36, 40). Walking with God in integrity is to perform the good works He has created you to do. Stay alert for unexpected opportunities to help, to give a word of encouragement, or to aid someone along your walk today.

When You Walk With God, Walk in Holiness.

God is holy. The seraphim of heaven introduced Isaiah to God with a heavenly anthem, "Holy, Holy, Holy is the LORD of hosts" (Isaiah 6:3). God is holy in His moral purity and divine perfection. To Hosea, God said, "I am God... the Holy One" (Hosea 11:9). The holiness of God is emphasized throughout the Bible.

Holiness and sanctification have the same root (*hagios*), and it indicates being set apart. Walking in holiness is being separated to God (see 1 Peter 1:16), and means that you have a lifestyle appropriate to one who is separated (see 1 Thessalonians 4:3, 7). Holiness is a "what would Jesus do?" attitude about daily living. It is allowing the Holy Spirit to live out Christ's purpose and character in your life, to be Christ-like. One of the ways we can imitate (follow) God is by walking with Him daily in a separated life.

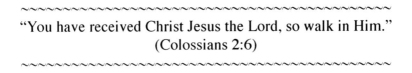

"You have received Christ Jesus the Lord, so walk in Him."
(Colossians 2:6)

When You Walk With God, Walk in the Lordship of Christ.

In your God-birth, you received a person—the living Lord Jesus Christ. Being born again is not memorizing a summary of religious teachings, or conforming to a set of ideals. It is not identifying with a religion, a denomination, or even a local church. It's not submitting to one or more church ordinances, decrees, or practices. All of this is perfunctory, inadequate, and deficient for being born again. Being born again is confessing your sins, and accepting Jesus Christ as Lord of your life.

He is the Lord Christ. Occasionally a minister will give a dualistic invitation at the close of his sermon. "You have received Jesus as your Savior, now come and make Christ Lord of your life." Can a person be saved and not receive Jesus as Lord?

Believers do not make Jesus Christ Lord—HE IS LORD. "God has made Him both Lord and Christ... this Jesus whom you crucified"

(Acts 2:36). Thomas declared "My Lord and My God" (John 20:28). In the home of Cornelius, Peter proclaimed, "He [Jesus] is Lord of all" (Acts 10:36). Jesus Himself accepted the title "Lord" (see Mark 5:19).

Lord (*kúrios*) in Greek means *one having power, authority,* and *dominion.* Jesus Christ, our Savior, is Lord of Lords and King of Kings. He is your Lord, the King of your life. You are in His Kingdom and He is to rule and reign in your life.

How can you accept Jesus, whom God has made Lord and Christ, and not accept His Lordship? Salvation is much more than receiving Jesus as a Savior from the eternal punishment of sins; it is joining Thomas when he said to Jesus, "My Lord and my God!" (John 20:28).

The Lord God has exclusive ownership—and thus sovereignty—over you (see Deuteronomy 3:24). You are not your own, you were "bought at a price; therefore glorify God in your body and in your Spirit, which are God's" (1 Corinthians 6:20, NKJV). Your body (walk) is not your own, you are to glorify God with your life (walk).

~~~~~~~~~~~~~~~~~~~~~~~~~~~~~~~~~~~
Lord, I choose to walk with You,
to do what You say,
to strive to do Your will.
~~~~~~~~~~~~~~~~~~~~~~~~~~~~~~~~~~~

Jesus is addressed as Lord (*kúrios*) more than 700 times in the New Testament.

The Lordship of Christ is the governing dynamic reality of the Christian faith—He is the living Lord, the Owner, and Master of your being. Walking with God is only possible when a believer acknowledges God's right to govern in His Kingdom and His authority and sovereignty over kingdom citizens. The declaration of one who desires to walk with God is, "Not my will, but Yours, ADONAÍ, KÚRIOS, Lord."

- **Have you acknowledged the Lordship of Christ in your life?**

Therefore, walk with God who "sends rain on the righteous and the unrighteous" (Matthew 5:45), who shows mercy (see Romans 9:16), and who is a refuge for the oppressed (see Psalm 9:9).

- **Are you consciously walking with God in your life?**

—Chapter Six—

Walk After God

"You shall walk after the LORD your God and fear Him,
and keep His commandments and obey His voice"
(Deuteronomy 13:4, NKJV).

The quietness of a cool Egyptian evening was disturbed when God called Moses and Aaron to follow Him and take the children of Israel from the land of captivity (see Exodus 12:31). God called the Israelites to walk after Him. "The LORD went before them by day in a pillar of cloud to lead the way, and by night in a pillar of fire to give them light" (Exodus 13:21, NKJV). These pillars were the manifestation of the presence of God. He promised to go before His people—to show them the way and to keep them from stumbling.

Does God lead His children today? Yes! He provides "pillars" of His presence for you today. There are revelations in the Word of God, in godly counsel from friends, through open and closed doors, through inner peace, by way of prayer, and the affirmation in your spirit by the Holy Spirit. When you walk after God, others may not understand you. Remember, Abraham was not understood when he left Ur. Noah was not understood when he built the ark. Hosea was not understood when he reconciled with Gomer. Job was not understood when in spite of his great loss he praised God. Moses and Aaron were not understood by the Israelites.

What is necessary for you to fortify your soul and to walk after God? The Word of God is the divinely anointed guidebook for following God, for God-walk. "The sheep hear his voice, and He calls his own sheep by name and leads them out... He goes before them, and the sheep follow Him because they know His voice" (John 10:3-4). The shepherd and his flock are never separated; he is with them day and night. This is a beautiful and reassuring understanding of the relationship of Jesus (the Good Shepherd) and believers (lambs and sheep).

Before going further, it is important to understand that these lambs and sheep have declared, "the Lord is my Shepherd" (Psalm 23:1).

There are five inherent truths in the illustration of the shepherd and His sheep that are indispensable to walking after God.

1. Sheep listen for the Shepherd's voice (see verse 3). Our days are inundated with voices, sounds, noise, and clamor. Sometimes you may think it is impossible to hear and understand anything or anyone, even God. But wait, the voice of God is recorded in His Word. Take time to read His Word, to pray, have a quiet time, meditate, and you will recognize His voice.

2. The Shepherd, our Lord, knows you by name (verse 3). Names are important, especially your name. You are not a number, part of a group, or a nameless "hey you." You are a unique creation with a name, you're special, your name is your individual identification. Our Lord knows our name, calls us, and speaks to each of us by name.

- **Pause a moment and recognize the remarkable truth that God does not order you; He calls you. He respects your will.**

3.   The shepherd goes before the sheep (see verse 4). The logistics of walking after God are important. I enjoy watching the old western movies and television shows, it's a great escape to a different time and life. Occasionally, there is a cattle drive when cowboys herd the cattle and drive them to market. How different it is with the shepherd and the sheep. The Shepherd, our Lord, goes before the believer. He never drives you; He is the Shepherd-leader. His tender voice is "come follow Me." He knows the road ahead, dangerous curves, rocky precipices, lurking dangers, and even route changes. He goes before you, follow and walk after Him.

4.   Sheep follow the Shepherd (see verse 4). They know His voice, trust Him, and willingly follow Him. Once again, God does not drive the believer. He invites believers to follow Him, to do His will. The decision is yours.

5.   Sheep never follow strangers (see verse 5). A last look at the shepherd/sheep relationship is important. There are all kinds and varieties of voices. False teachers and spurious doctrine abound. God's Word is a true and reliable guide to keep you on the right path. Be vigilant to not listen to or follow strangers with false teaching. Walk after God with His Word as your roadmap. The voice of God is the Word of God, hold to that assurance with confidence. Remind and teach other believers—the lambs and sheep of God's flock.

You need never to be anxious in following after God. The Word of God is nourishment for your soul. It is the living, powerful, and focused guide for the inner man. Reject every influence that would draw you away from the Word of God and listen to His voice.

Again and again, Jesus gave the invitation for believers to follow Him. "Follow Me, and I will make you fishers of men" (Matthew 4:19). "If anyone [you] wishes to come after Me… deny himself [yourself], and take up his [your] cross, and follow me" (Mark 8:34). The call for discipleship remains true today.

God-walk means that you follow close behind the Savior and embrace the self-denial necessary for God-life. "Lay aside the old self… be renewed in the spirit of your mind… put on the new self…

the likeness of God" (Ephesians 4:22-24). Walk after God. Let Him go before you and show you the way.

—Chapter Seven—

Walk in Newness of Life

"We have been buried with Him through baptism into death, in order that as Christ was raised from the dead through the glory of the Father, so we too might walk in newness of life." (Romans 6:4)

It has always been a joyous occasion for me to administer the ordinance of baptism. What a privilege to say to a new believer, "Upon a public profession of your faith, and in obedience to His divine command, I baptize you in the name of the Father, Son, and Holy Spirit." Then, immersing the new Christian in the water—a symbol of the grave—as a public testimony, I raise them up and say, "You have been raised to *walk in newness of life with Christ.*" As Christ was raised from the dead, so we should also walk in newness of life (see Romans 6:4).

What does it mean for us to walk in a new life? What does this promise mean to you? Reading Romans 6:4 one day, for the first time I focused on the fact that it says we *might* walk in newness of life. This compound word is sometimes translated *should, could,* or *might.* It carries dual meanings. But, it does mean the decision is up to you.

You are dead to sin, and have the potential to live with a God-life, the new life He gives you. "We shall live in the power of

God" (2 Corinthians 13:4). The new birth gives the immeasurable, surpassing power of God's presence to you; the potential of living in a way that you've never had before (see Ephesians 1:19-20). Setting your affections on things above, you live for righteousness—in the newness of life He has provided for you.

Walking in newness of life. The word *newness* (*kainós*) means *new in form, quality*, or *of a different nature, as contrasted to the old*. When Jesus was raised from the dead, the separation between God and man was removed; and believers were enabled to have a new quality and new form of life.

When you by repentance and faith, are crucified with Christ, *you no longer live*, but *Christ lives in you*. Christ living in you should be a revolutionary experience. When your life is folded into Christ, Christ is folded into your life.

Paul asserts a radical change will take place in a believer's life when he is in Christ. "If any person is (ingrafted) in Christ, the Messiah, he is (a new creature altogether), a new creation, the old (previous moral and spiritual condition) has passed away. Behold, the fresh and new has come" (2 Corinthians 5:17, AMP).

A New Creation in Christ

You are dead to sin, and alive in Christ. Behold! A new life! A new creation! A newly birthed intimate relationship with the Savior has been established. The old things of the flesh that once dominated you have passed away—they are dead. The Scripture is emphatic, old things have not become new—they have *passed away*. A new person with a new lifestyle, a new value system, new desires, and new ambitions has been created. In Christ, you become transformed into a new creation.

"Beholding... the glory of the Lord, are being transformed into the same image from glory to glory... by the Spirit of the Lord" (2 Corinthians 3:18, NKJV). You are being *transformed* (*metamorphóō*). Remember, a metamorphosis is to change into another form; a complete change that will show forth in character and conduct.

When you have a God-walk (newness of life), you discard your conformity to the world, and commence to have a form and manner of Christ. Your transformation continues "until Christ is completely and permanently formed (molded) within you" (Galatians 4:19 AMP). You embark on a wonderful walk with God, a God-life.

- **Your transformation is ongoing, what of Christ has been formed in you lately? In the last month? In the last year?**

SECTION SEVEN

GOD-MIND

"I will put My laws into their minds,
and I will write them upon their hearts.
And I will be their God,
and they shall be My people."
(Hebrews 8:10)

Everything you do evolves from what you think. Living a God-life must be built on thoughts with a *God-mind*. If you love God *with all of your mind*, you will allow God to put His laws (words) into your thoughts. You do this so that you might know His mind. You cannot change the way you act until you change the way you think. Thinking with a God-mind will change your behavior to that of a God-life—living with godly characteristics. A God-mind enables you to have godly perspectives based on His word.

This section will seek to answer the question: *How do I achieve a God-mind?*

Let's begin with three important initiatives: Recollection, Consciousness, and Disposition—all necessary to live with a God-mind.

Recollection is retrieving God's Word from your mental storehouse, reviewing, and meditating upon it. Memory is a mirror of the mind. The Holy Spirit is your Helper in recalling the truth of God's Word, so you can put its principles into practice. "The memory of the righteous is blessed" (Proverbs 10:7).

Consciousness is always being aware of the principles of God's Word. You must be alert to life situations and apply the appropriate biblical truths (God's thoughts) to each of them.

Disposition reveals your prevailing mood, temperament, and personality relating to biblical truths. Your fleshly disposition must be crucified, enabling you live by God's principles. Your inclination should always be a commitment to let Christ live in you.

Living with a God-mind is not otherworldly. Rather, it means denying self and letting God live in you, thinking His thoughts. It is impossible to live a God-life without a God-mind.

Spirit of Life vs. Sin and Death

Living a God-life with a God-mind is God's glorious promised gift to you as a believer. The Holy Spirit is the divine commission in Christ to free you from the old law and enable you to live a new life with a God-mind. "The law of the Spirit of life in Christ Jesus has set you free [liberated you] from the law of sin and of death" (Romans 8:2).

The law of the Spirit of life, the Holy Spirit, has freed or liberated you from the law of sin, which is death. The word *liberated* (*eleutheroō*) means *to deliver* or *to make free*. The law of the Spirit of life is stronger and dominant; however, the law of sin and death still contends to control you.

Listen to the apostle Paul's struggle: "So then, on the one hand I myself with my mind am serving the law of God [God-mind], but on the other, with my flesh the law of sin" (Romans 7:25). Paul's desire was to manifest a God-mind and defeat the law of sin and death in his body.

It's a battle of your mind. The Holy Spirit has made you alive in Christ, therefore you are to "present yourselves to God as those alive from the dead, and your members [body parts that relate to fleshly senses] as instruments of righteousness to God" (Romans 6:13). You are in Christ, and *Christ is in you*, your inner person must be controlled by a God-mind.

You must be vigilant, for the law of sin and death remains active in your flesh. Remember, it's a battle, and Satan is always seeking someone he can prey upon. His passion is to make you believe you are a prisoner of the law of sin and death, taking away your God-mind focus in your decisions of life (see Romans 7:23).

This section explores the remarkable function of the mind. You will progress from veiled minds, various obstructions to living with a God-mind. Discover how to live and prevail with a God-mind.

- **Do you think, make decisions, reason by a conscious recollection of God's Word, and a disposition to live by it's principles?**

—Chapter One—

Speaking of the Mind

T he mind is that intangible function of mankind that distinguishes him from all else. The mind refers to and is manifested by intellect, insight, understanding, judgment, memory, and will. Mankind is set apart from all other creatures by being created in the image and likeness of God (see Genesis 1:26). This miraculous event has nothing to do with man's physical nature, but speaks of his rational and moral disposition.

The regenerated moral consciousness of the mind determines the will to live a God-life with a God-mind. "The Son of God has come, and has given us understanding, in order that we might know Him" (1 John 5:20). Paul's mind wanted to obey the law of God in order to perform acceptably before God. "Thanks be to God through Jesus Christ our Lord! So then… I myself with my mind am serving the law of God" (Romans 7:25). With the indwelling Holy Spirit, he was keenly sensitive to growing in grace—or a maturing, progressive sanctification. Paul's delight in the *law of God* is evidence that he was regenerated—that he had experienced a God-birth. His desire was to live a Christ-like life.

In the next pages, we will consider comparative functions related to the mind. The mind is a miraculous gift from God to you.

The Mind and the Brain

Your mind and brain are intrinsically and fundamentally different—the terms are not interchangeable. The brain is physical matter. The mind is incorporeal—it has no physical form.

The *brain* is an organ of the body that receives impressions derived from your senses. After receiving these communicative messages from the sensory and nervous systems, the assimilated raw data is interpreted and managed by the brain, which evaluates and forms ideas, judgments, understandings, and thoughts. This processed data is then communicated to the will (volition), which forms your choices, consents, and actions.

Your *mind* is the control center for all of your actions and has the power of judgments, opinions, and conceptions. It has the ability to reflect, plan, design, and control your whole body. It is stronger than any one or all physical appetites of the flesh. It forms the will and has qualities that rise above the physical—it generates your power of choice.

The function of the brain is to collect data. The strength of the mind is its ability to think. Thought is evidenced in judgments (see Romans 14:12-23) and in the resolve of the will (see Philippians 3:14). You are capable of changing the composition, structure, form, and character of your lifestyle. The call is for you to be transformed—functioning with an operative God-mind.

The Mind and the Heart

The heart is an essential body organ. In literature and daily conversation, the identity of the mind and heart often blend together. The heart may refer to moral or mental, emotional, or rational activities. The merging of the mind and heart is certainly true in Scripture. The Greek translation of the Old Testament (Septuagint) translates the Hebrew word *heart* (*lēb*) both *mind* (*nous*) and *heart* (*kardia*).

While the heart is the organ that supplies blood to the body, it is also seen to be the true ego—the inner or "hidden person" (1 Peter 3:4). The heart can be impure (see Romans 1:24). It can receive the love of God (see Romans 5:5). And, salvation is a matter of the heart (see Romans 10:9). It can express wisdom (see Psalm 90:12), because the Holy Spirit is given to the believer's heart (see 2 Corinthians 1:22). The heart also can have secrets (see 1 Corinthians 14:25). David's charge to his son Solomon was to know God and "serve Him with a whole heart and a willing mind; for the LORD searches all hearts, and understands every intent of the thoughts [mind]" (1 Chronicles 28:9).

The heart represents the seat of emotions, feelings, affections, and desires. Your emotions are somewhere between the intellect and the will on one hand, and the body and it's passions on the other. While Scripture frequently interchanges mind and heart, a God-mind controls and manages the center of your emotions. In Deuteronomy 6:4-5 (the Jewish *Shema*), the mind and heart—the intellect and emotions—are closely related. You are commanded (mental) to love the Lord God with all your heart (desires) and keep God's words (intellect) in your heart (thoughts).

Love the Lord God with all of your heart
and keep His words in your mind.

The Mind and the Conscience

God has endowed all mankind with a conscience—an active principle within you that determines right from wrong, what to do, and what to avoid. Observably, across the face of humanity, individual consciences vary. Enormous differences exist in the interpretation of what is right and wrong.

The conscience is the inner activity or faculty that shapes your conduct and character; it empowers your moral discrimination and ethical judgment. Your morality is determined by the measure of your developed conscience, and thus right and wrong choices will vary from person to person.

Moral actions are decided by *intellect* (mental analysis), *sensibility* (ethical judgment), and *will* (determination). Conscience is the individual's *ego-arena*, in which these three operatives function. Look with me more closely, at how these faculties form the conscience in all mankind.

Your Intellect

The intellect, the capacity of knowing, is the gatekeeper for the judicial aptness of the conscience. By this, I mean that the conscience is not a law book; rather, it is discriminating in its function—deciding what is right or wrong by the law it receives from intellect, whether that be the law of the street or the law of God. Paul acknowledged both the law of God in the inner man, and the law of flesh (Adamic nature) in this life (see Romans 7:22-23). Good illustrations of the conscience challenged by conflicting laws can be seen in Cain and Abel or Jacob and Esau.

In the study of civilizations and the varied cultures and people groups—or even varied behaviors within a community or family—you discover individual consciences differ greatly as to what is right or wrong. Not everyone operates from the same law book. However, conscience is always "infallible," in that it decides right and wrong from the law provided by the intellect.

Remember Saul, the persecutor of Christians who became Paul, a missionary and evangelist for Christ? In both instances, he was operating from his conscience. His value system (conscience) had radically changed because of his knowledge (intellect) of Christ. "I count all things to be loss in view of the surpassing value of knowing Christ Jesus my Lord" (Philippians 3:8).

The conscience is not God—it is the ego-arena of the individual, the sphere of discrimination that judicially interprets whatever law is received from the intellect. When the input of the intellect (mind) is flawed, then the conscience of what is right and wrong results in a flawed morality (see Titus 1:15-16).

The conscience is not an original authority, it operates on the knowledge or data received via the intellect. When God's Word cultivates the conscience, you can function with a God-mind. We do follow our conscience, thus it is paramount we have a God-based conscience to follow.

Your Sensibility

Sensibility is awareness of and responsiveness to your culture. It is a code of ethics on how you respect, treat, respond, and interact with others. Your cultural environment nurtures your ethical judgment, your conscience.

Everyone's conscience is affected by cultural environment. Your law book of right and wrong is influenced by where, with whom, and in what culture you live. Some actions that would be considered right in a primitive culture may be considered offensive to a more civilized society. The prevailing culture is a teacher of acceptable norms within your community.

Culturally accepted moral principles contribute to the formation of the sensibility of your conscience. It is not only essential that your intellect receive the Word of God, but also that your chosen culture be that of the body of faith. The believers in the early Jerusalem church "were continually devoting themselves to the apostles' teaching and to fellowship, to the breaking of bread and to prayer" (Acts 2:42). In a fellowship of believers, the teaching and proclamation of God's Word, intercessory prayer, testimonies, discussions, and the Christian community of interests all contribute to a God-mind conscience.

The Bible urges believers to "give attentive, continuous care to watching over one another, studying how we may stir up (stimulate and incite) to love and helpful deeds and noble activities; not forsaking or neglecting to assemble together [as believers]... admonishing—warning, urging, and encouraging—one another" (Hebrews 10:24-25, AMP). The church is an autonomous culture within the civic-social structure of the community where godly fellowship is enjoyed.

Your Will

Your will is the navigator of your intellect (acquired knowledge) and sensibility (ethical judgments). The will is your power to choose between alternatives and to decide the actions required to accomplish your objectives—it chooses both the *goal* and the *means by which to achieve that goal.*

A Christian's will should function in the sphere of biblical rationality—ideas, thoughts, commands, judgments, and actions. A biblically-based will is dynamic; it is marked by productive activity, energy, and change. It deliberately chooses the course of action that best reflects the acquired God-mind. The model prayer teaches us to pray to our heavenly Father regarding our will.

Our present day pluralistic society is congested with a perplexing spectacle of values, goals, and lifestyles. It is not a godless society—but one teeming with idols, all pleading for your attention and commitment. Your challenge is to determine God's will, and resolutely pursue God's ordained plan. Joshua stood before the Israelites and challenged them to have a Yahweh-centered will—to be obedient to God. His appeal to the Israelites is appropriate for all believers: "Choose for yourselves today whom you will serve." His own commitment was manifestly clear: "as for me and my house, we will serve the LORD" (Joshua 24:15).

Your challenge is to determine God's will
and resolutely pursue God's ordained plan.

Think About It

Whenever your mind is disturbed, distracted, or doubts, there is a corresponding effect on your conscience—your intellect, ethical judgment, and will. The effect of a cluttered, uncertain, and doubting mind is especially devastating when attempting to fulfill the will of God, to achieve your destiny. However, the opposite is also true: "Thou wilt keep him in perfect peace, whose mind is stayed on thee: because he trusteth in thee" (Isaiah 26:3, KJV).

When your will is uncertain or undefined, your creativity, imagination, and physical system are all adversely affected. Remember the drama in the Garden of Gethsemane just before Jesus was arrested? Having resolved His will to fulfill the Father's plan, Jesus was the calmest one during the spectacle of His arrest. Because Peter did not intellectually conform to God's will, he was physically upset.

In frustration, he drew his sword and struck out (see John 18:10). While Jesus was calm and collected, Peter was a bundle of nerves.

- **Is your inner being calm and collected? Or is it unfocused, distracted, and uncertain?**

—Chapter Two—

Veiled Minds

W hy do some choose not to have a God-birth? Why do others never comprehend God-mind? The resolution to both of these questions is fundamentally important for God-life. Both have to do with the mind. Isaiah said eyes have been blinded and hearts hardened. Paul said the god of this age has blinded unbelievers. Their minds have been veiled from the truth of God's Word. The Bible reveals a number of veils that obscure the life-changing truth of God's Word and effectively precludes having God-mind.

Think about this, when you analyze statistics for those who accept Jesus Christ as their Savior, there are significantly fewer conversions as people grow older. Why? It is not God's fault, the gospel is a *whosoever* gospel (see John 3:15-16). Jesus Christ is "able to save to the uttermost those who come to God through Him" (Hebrews 7:25, NKJV). The word *uttermost* (*panteles*) means the gospel is inclusive of not only anyone and everyone; but also saves completely, perfectly, and forever those who trust Him.

The Veil of a Hardened Mind

Let's begin with what may be the most common veil to God-mind. There are numerous accounts in the Bible of the veil of a hardened heart and mind. In referring to the Jews, Paul wrote, "Their minds were hardened; for until this very day at the reading of the old covenant the same veil remains unlifted, because it is removed in Christ. But to this day... a veil lies over their heart" (2 Corinthians 3:14-15).

Their minds or thoughts were *hardened* (*epōrōtha*), they were *calloused*. Hardened is used metaphorically of both the heart and mind. Paul said that Jews who refused the truth of the gospel as revealed in the Messiah had toughened hearts—a veil was over their minds, and they could not understand the truth because of their cynicism.

God called Isaiah to speak for Him to a calloused people (see Isaiah 6:9-10). Jesus also faced those who had veils of hardened minds, "Seeing they do not see, and while hearing they do not hear" (Matthew 13:13).

A hardened heart is the consequence of a veiled or closed mind. The problem is not intellectual inadequacy, but spiritual unbelief. Paul addressed the veiled minds of Israel as "stiff-necked and uncircumcised in heart and ears! You always resist the Holy Spirit; as your fathers did, so do you" (Acts 7:51, NKJV). They were spiritually stubborn. They mentally blocked out the truth of the Gospel and refused to turn to Christ—only He can lift the veil of the hardened heart.

A hardened heart is the consequence of a veiled mind.
Only in Christ can it be lifted.

Let's return to the age factor of conversion—and the consequence of repeatedly rejecting the Gospel, the good news of the Savior, Jesus Christ. The veil of a hardened mind is self-imposed. It is not societal, circumstantial, or inherited; it is a conscious choice. There are many testimonies of those who have overcome extremely difficult life situations, and have lived brilliant Christian lives of faith.

The *New American Standard* Bible states: "Who has defied [stiffened his neck against] Him without harm" (Job 9:4)? A hardened mind is a mind that actively spurns the Lord and rejects His Word. A veiled mind obscures His truth and therefore denies the very strength and source of a God-life.

An open mind accepts God and believes Him to be without limits in magnitude. He is able to do all things! A resolute faith of a believer can move any mountain of life when the veil of the mind is removed (see Mark 11:22-24).

God warns you not to harden your heart. "Do not harden your hearts, as at Meribah" (Psalm 95:8). After the Lord had miraculously delivered the Israelites from slavery in Egypt, they hardened their hearts in the wilderness. God had faithfully provided food and water; however, on an occasion when there appeared to be a dearth of water, the people grumbled, bitterly dissented, and contended with Moses and God (see Exodus 17:1-3). The people had a dark shroud over their minds, their memory, and their faith. Moses named the location *Meribah*—a place of *complaining*, *dispute*, and *contention*. Do these human responses sound familiar? They are the sounds of veiled minds. Minds become veiled and hearts calloused to the revelation of God because of unbelief.

The Veil of a Carnal Mind

"Get off the fence! Get on one side or the other!" the radio voice blared. While driving one day, I was listening to a religious station on the radio, and a preacher was expounding a message that was simply wrong. He was stressing an incorrect theology that once you are saved, you are completely delivered from any and all ways of the natural or fleshly life. To him, it was solely a matter of one side of a fence or the other—never both Spirit *and* flesh.

The book of Romans was written from the perspective of a believer who had experienced saving grace. Paul stressed that the Christian life was a battleground between the Spirit and the flesh. Paul was not a fence-straddler; he openly recognized that he continued to live in a sinful body: "I am of flesh" (Romans 7:14).

Paul was living a regenerated life, and yet struggling with a carnal, natural body.

Two truths are evident. In Christ, we are absolutely saved and delivered from the *penalty* of sin; however, we must still seek to be liberated from the *power* of our canceled sin. Paul's self-analysis in Romans 7:15-16 is insightful. He was keenly aware of an inner battle raging between the Spirit and his flesh. Your old nature must be conquered after conversion—it has nothing to do with salvation; it has everything to do with God-life. It is important to observe that Paul had no veil of carnality. He recognized his sin problem, confessed it, and had victory over it. How? What did Paul do to live a God-life with a God-mind?

Remember the three elements of living with a God-mind: recollection, consciousness, and disposition? Listen to Paul: "Who will set me free from the body of this death? Thanks be to God through Jesus Christ our Lord! So then… I myself with my mind am serving the law of God" (Romans 7:24-25). Paul is an excellent example of how these three elements contribute to a God-mind.

The tragic reality is that there is little difference between many professed believers and those who do not know the Lord. Believers who are carnal (fleshly) are governed by their senses—they walk and live under their influence; they are "babes in Christ." They are not spiritual, they have not grown in Christ, and the fleshly veil of carnality has obscured their understanding of how to live with a God-mind. They live with "envying, and strife, and divisions… carnal, and walk as men" (1 Corinthians 3:3, KJV). In no way can a mind veiled with carnality manifest a God-mind.

A veiled, carnal mind cannot manifest a God-mind.

A veiled, carnal mind cannot please God—in fact, it is hostile towards Him. Yet, through the overcoming presence of the indwelling Holy Spirit, you can overcome carnality and have a life controlled by a God-mind (see Romans 8:6-9).

The Veil of a Depraved Mind

In promoting a national missions offering, I was speaking to a church in another state. The pastor met me at the airport and while driving to the hotel where I would spend the night, he startled me with his request.

"Our church is a church of love, we accept anyone who attends, and we are never controversial." Then turning to me, he said, "We don't want you to preach on denominational exclusiveness, or harsh, argumentative, and fractious themes."

Not fully understanding, I asked for an explanation.

"Simply put," the pastor responded, "we don't preach or teach on such themes as the cross, death, judgment, or hell in our church." In a determined effort not to offend anyone, they lost their message, their purpose of being.

Romans 1:28 teaches, "They did not see fit to acknowledge God any longer, God gave them over to a depraved mind." How sobering! Few passages of Scripture more clearly and insightfully disclose what happens when an individual—or even a church—doesn't acknowledge God, and recognize the Word of God as inerrant and inspired. The first steps of repudiating God and His Word may be no more than what a student asked me during a college question and answer session.

"Sir, how can you be sure that the Bible is the word of God? Or at best, does it just contain the word of God?"

Continuing, he asked, "Is it not like other religious books, the work of biased men?"

What is a *depraved* mind? It is the mind that does not acknowledge God—spurns any knowledge of Him, and chooses to reject any evidence that He exists (see Romans 1:19-20). With this veil, this eclipse of understanding, it is impossible to have a God-mind.

The depraved mind does not *see fit* to acknowledge God, or think of God as worth knowing. As opposed to the hardened mind that is calloused to the truth or the carnal mind that is focused on the flesh; the depraved mind puts God to the test, judges Him, and deems Him unbeneficial to keep in mind.

Unanswered Prayer

A successful entrepreneur said he once believed in God, but no longer. The reason? He had prayed (put the Lord to the test) for God to heal his seriously ill family member. Sadly, in time, the loved one died. To him, God failed the test and he no longer saw fit to acknowledge Him—the Lord was no longer worth knowing because He did not perform as requested. How sad, the man now had the veil of a distorted or depraved mind.

What happens when someone leaves God out, no longer has Him in their mind, and decides that He is not worth knowing? God gives that person over to a "reprobate mind." Look again at Romans 1:28, there is an interesting play on words. "They *did not approve* [*ouk dokimazō*] of retaining God in their knowledge [mind], God gave them up to *unapproved mind* [*adŏkimŏs nous*] to do unacceptable things" (my translation). Kenneth Wuest explains, "They did not think it fit… to keep God in their knowledge, God gave them up to a mind which cannot stand trial." [i]

Theirs was a depraved mind. They declared Almighty God *disapproved*, they wanted nothing to do with Him. God in turn *disapproved* their depraved mind. "God delivered them over to a worthless mind to do what is morally wrong" (Romans 1:28, HCSB).

Apostle Paul gives a severe profile of the depraved mind—a defiled mind—one stained with sin. The root word for *defiled* (*miainō*) means to *stain*, or *dye with another color*. [ii]

~~~~~~

To the pure, all things are pure;
but to those who are defiled and unbelieving,
nothing is pure, but both their mind
and their conscience are defiled.
They profess to know God, but by their deeds they deny Him,
being detestable and disobedient,
and worthless for any good deed."
(Titus 1:15-16)

~~~~~~

Paul concludes (verse 16) with three strong words to describe the defiled mind.

A depraved mind is *detestable* *(bdeluktoi)* **in the sight of God.**
The charge is that they profess to know God, but their judgments and works deny Him. Their veiled, depraved mind is abominable and is loathed by God.

A depraved mind is *disobedient* *(apeitheis)* **before God.**
They not only confess to know God and profess to know the Bible, but defy the very Word of God. They confess and deny at the same time—nothing can be more lamentable to God.

A depraved mind is *worthless* *(adókimoi)*.
They failed the test of usefulness and are rejected or disapproved of by God. They are like counterfeit money, having failed the test of genuineness, and are found of no worth.

Accepting the Word of God as inspired and inerrant, and Almighty God (*El Shaddai*) as the Most High God (*El Elyon*) with an unwavering faith, is essential to avoiding the veil of a depraved mind. A real, vital knowledge of the Lord accepts the understanding that mortal man can never fully comprehend Him and His ways.

The Veil of a Rejecting Mind

We live in a day when God's Holy Word is vehemently despised by what seems to be a growing number of people. I've already mentioned in this book that there are restrictions barring the Ten Commandments, public prayer, reading God's Word, or displaying Scripture in government buildings or public places. Those are just a few examples of how God's Word and the Christian faith upon which our country was founded are being eradicated from daily life. To justify their anti-Christian campaigns, it's called "political correctness" or "separation of church and state."

It is vaguely reminiscent of the tyrannical and godless rule of Adolf Hitler. His mind was so veiled with contempt for God that he mandated the elimination of God's Word from the entire country, in both public and private places. Millions of Bibles and Christian books were burned in huge public bonfires. Remember my professor's wartime experience?

~~~~~~

The veil of a rejecting mind excludes God and His Holy Word.

~~~~~~

When a Nation Rejects

Historically, despising God's Word has always brought serious and disastrous consequences. In approximately 760 B.C., Amos' prophecy to Judah spoke to the rejection of God's Word: "I will not revoke its [Judah's] punishment, Because they rejected the law of the LORD And have not kept His statutes" (Amos 2:4). Judah's specific sins were rejecting the Torah, despising the Lord's instructions, and being led astray by lies.

The Torah (law) refers to the Ten Commandments, and more broadly to the Pentateuch (first five books of the Bible). [iii] The rejection of God's Word in Amos' day resulted in some very contemporary sounding consequences—rampant greed, sexual immorality, open idolatry (secularism), and drunkenness (addiction). Renouncing God's Word and disregarding His commandments always brings solemn and grave results.

In Numbers 15:30-36, there is an account of one who had the veil of a rejecting mind. He did not keep God's commandment: "Remember the sabbath day, to keep it holy" (Exodus 20:8). This particular man's infraction may seem small—he gathered some sticks for a fire, probably to cook a meal. However, the indictment for his disregard of the commandment was indeed grave—he had blasphemed YAHWEH, was irreverent towards God's Word, and had rejected the Lord's commandment. In essence, his mind was veiled, and by his actions he stated that God's eternal truth is not worthy of belief or practice. To him, the Lord of all was not to be revered or obeyed, and God's Word was not to be taken seriously. This is a portrait of the malevolent, willful sin of disobedience. This "stick collector" suffered an extreme punishment—death.

A veiled mind that rejects or disrespects the Word of God does not always result in an activist who carries signs and marches around courthouses, denying and repudiating the validity and authority of the inspired Word of God. A veiled mind of rejection may be by simply omitting the Word of God from your life. It has always been a fundamental misjudgment to despise, reject, or set aside the Word of God and His commandments. Again and again, Jesus stressed for believers to keep the commandments of God.

- **Why do today's believers treat God's Word and His commandments so casually? Why is it acceptable to minimize the straight-forward commandments of God?**

- **Are there veils on your mind? What are they? Are you asking God to remove them?**

—Chapter Three—

The Mind of God

T he view Paul had from Mars (Ares) Hill must have been breath-taking. Mars Hill, or the Areopagus (hill of Ares), was located on a neck of land on the western end of the Aeropolis—a steep hill rising in the center of the city of Athens. The Acropolis, once a military citadel, now had temples and statues on the sides and summit of this landmark. Archeologists believe no city has ever had such a display of sculptured artwork as Athens.

With the distant sparkling blue sea to his back, Paul looked down on an array of glistening white statues and colonnades that lined the streets and walkways. He could see clearly the Agora—the Athenian marketplace—where for days he had reasoned with whoever would listen (see Acts 17:17).

Now, Paul was standing on a stone bleacher, in an open-air assembly where the Council of Areopagus met. Statues dedicated to every known god were everywhere. In clear view, he could see the Parthenon that housed the gold and ivory statue of Athena. Paul observed that the Athenians were very religious and were anxious to learn of the God Paul had been proclaiming.

One of the idols Paul observed along the way was consecrated to the *unknown god*, because the Athenians did not want to offend any deity. Paul chose this statue and said, "The One whom you worship without knowing, Him I proclaim to you" (Acts 17:23, NKJV). Paul knew the mind of God. He knew God wants to be known.

The Lord wants you to know Him. Consider the numerous efforts God has made to be known to mankind. He walked in the garden and talked with the first family; He anointed kings, prophets, and priests. He sent angelic messengers and performed miracles. The ark of the covenant and the tabernacle revealed His holiness and His approachability. He breathed out His message—His mind, plans, and thoughts—and they became our Scripture. He sent His Son to identify with mankind and bear their sins so that they may be forgiven and spend eternity with Him.

You may ask: *How do I learn more about the Lord and understand His mind?* Consider God's proposition: "Know therefore that the LORD your God, He is God, the faithful God, who keeps His covenant and His lovingkindness" (Deuteronomy 7:9). He was saying, Know Me. Understand My mind. I am faithful and trustworthy. I am true to My Word. I am kind and merciful. The Lord God of heaven and earth is not a silent, inscrutable God. He wants to be known—He has made every effort to reveal His mind, thoughts, and will.

~~~~~~~~~~~~~~~~~~~~~~~~~~

God wants you to know Him.

~~~~~~~~~~~~~~~~~~~~~~~~~~

"Majesty, worship His majesty!" As these beautiful words were lifted in praise by the congregation, my mind began to think of the splendor and greatness of His majesty. "Majesty, Kingdom authority—flow from His throne, unto His own, His anthem raise."

I cannot think of any word more fitting to describe God than *majesty*. The Lord so desired that we know Him, His thoughts, His mind that He revealed Himself "in many and various ways" (Hebrews 1:1, RSV).

Consider three major revelations of God: the Sacred Scripture, the Holy Spirit, and the Living Word, Jesus Christ.

The Sacred Scripture

The mind of God is clearly revealed and illuminated through His inspired Word. The Bible is not merely a collection of sixty-six books. It is the incredible product of the mind of His Majesty, the Lord God. It is the supreme and ultimate written source of the knowledge of God, His inspired, infallible, inerrant Word.

William E. Gladstone (1809–1898) was arguably one of Britain's most renowned statesman and a significantly prominent Christian in public life in the last half of the nineteenth century. Eleanor and I have been privileged to visit his library in Hawarden, Wales. It houses over 250,000 books and periodicals, and it is said that Gladstone read 20,000 in his lifetime. This voracious reader said, "The Bible is stamped with a specialty of origin, and an immeasurable distance separates it from all competitors." [iv] Gladstone recognized that the Bible is distinguishably different from all other writings, because it reveals the mind and thoughts of the one true God.

God's Word expresses His thoughts and
His thoughts reveal His mind, the God-mind.

The Word of God, (Old and New Testaments), came by revelation of God and is completely trustworthy. "All Scripture is *inspired* by God and profitable for teaching, for reproof, for correction, for training in righteousness" (2 Timothy 3:16, emphasis mine). The Holy Spirit *breathed* all Scripture. Scripture is an inspired revelation as God unveils Himself to you. God does not only inspire Scripture, He inspires you through it as He unveils Himself to you. The Word of God is vitally necessary in understanding the mind of God.

When God utters His word, His thoughts become action. This principle is introduced in Genesis 1:3 when "God said" out of nothing, substance was formed. "By the word of the LORD the heavens were made, and by the breath of His mouth all their hosts… For He spoke, and it was done" (Psalm 33:6, 9).

In Exodus 20:1-2, "God spoke all these words, saying, 'I am the LORD your God.'" He was saying, "Here is My mind, I am giving you some of My thoughts in the form of commandments."

It was reported that during an evangelical crusade in Germany, an elderly man came to an event staff member with a crumpled page from a book. When told it was from the Bible, the man replied, "I knew that it was something special, for nothing I have ever read has affected me so." He was blessed by reading the words, mind, and thoughts of God.

God's Holy Word is your manual for living with a God-mind. Psalm 119 is the longest psalm and chapter in the Bible; it is a hymn of praise exalting the Word of God. And it proclaims that the Word of God is a "Lamp to [your] feet, and a light to [your] path" (verse 105). The Bible provides your path for living a God-life with the mind of God.

The Bible is the living, contemporary revelation of God. It is a *today book*, preserved and empowered by Almighty God. "Today… hear His voice" (Hebrews 3:15). Hear His voice—His words, His thoughts, His mind. The Bible, the inspired Word of God, is of inestimable value. It is reliably effective and spiritually nourishing for discovering and understanding the mind of God. Moses "received living oracles to pass on to you" (Acts 7:38). The Bible is not just a chronicle of the past—the history of a race, the fulfillment of prophecy, and the account of the life and times of the Messiah. It is a living guide for your discovery of God and His mind.

The Holy Spirit

The Holy Spirit's ministry is to guide you to an understanding of a whole sphere of heavenly truth. Jesus assured, "He [the Holy Spirit] will guide you into all the truth" (John 16:13). He will educate you about life and instruct you in living a God-life. Jesus knew there would be much to learn concerning living a God-life after He ascended to the Father. To calm and reassure the disciples, He promised a Helper who would guide them in the discovery of all truth (see John 16:7, 10, 13). Even now, two millenniums later, we do not fully comprehend the magnitude of all God wants us to know.

Look again at the Gospel of John, chapters 16 and 17, and understand that God—Father, Son, and Holy Spirit—wants you to comprehend how to live God-life. The Triune God desires you to discover His mind and live a God-life. Jesus was sent by the Father with the words (thoughts and mind) of God. The Holy Spirit was sent to communicate the message of Jesus (God's mind and will) to believers.

The Holy Spirit communicates God's mind and will.

The mind of the Father, Son, and Holy Spirit is one. The Holy Spirit gives illumination, revelation, and spiritual understanding of the Word of God in order to enable you to grasp the mind of God. "Behold, I have put My words in your mouth" (Jeremiah 1:9). The Holy Spirit breathes Scripture into existence, so, the Bible is literally the Word of God (mind of God), and like God, it is infallible.

A living guide—the Bible not only *was* inspired (breathed) by the Holy Spirit, but the Holy Spirit breathes within it. It is not only authoritative, but also life-giving, "you have been born again... through the living and abiding Word of God" (1 Peter 1:23). The Holy Spirit speaks the thoughts, mind of God through the Word.

The only difference between thinking and speaking are words. What the Holy Spirit *saith*, you are able to find in the *words* of the Scripture. The Word can penetrate your innermost soul with the thoughts (mind) of God. "The word of God is living and active" (Hebrews 4:12). The Bible is the *living* book of the living God, and it is manifestly *active* (*energēs*). It is operational, powerful, and full of living energy to those who believe. The Bible enlightens you about God's thoughts (mind), so that you can follow His will. When the Word of God is accepted as authoritative—when it is demonstrated in your life—you evidence a God-mind.

As we discussed earlier, the conscience is the life-active principle that determines right from wrong. Remember the three elements that shape our conscience—intellect, sensibility and will? The Word of God (His mind) instructs your intellect. The Word of God (His lifestyle) models your ethical judgment. The Word of God (His desire) nurtures your determination. Accepting the Holy Spirit's Word as authoritative—discovering God's thoughts and His mind—your conduct will magnify the Lord with God-mind.

The Living Word, Jesus Christ

Before we look at how to have the mind of Christ, a word needs to be said here about the revelation of the mind of God, the Lord Jesus Christ. God's thoughts (mind) are disclosed in the incarnation of Christ. "God... in these last days has spoken to us in His Son" (Hebrews 1:1-2). The personification of the Word of God is masterfully given in John 1:1-5, 14. Jesus came to express the mind of God. "No man has seen God at any time; the only begotten God, who is in the bosom of the Father, He has explained Him" (John 1:18). In Christ, through His words and teachings, you discover the thoughts (mind and will) of God.

~~~~~~

The mind of God is perfectly revealed in Jesus Christ,
the living Word.

~~~~~~

The Christ event reveals the mind of God as nothing else could. Jesus Christ is the God-man—fully man and entirely God. He is God's word, God's thoughts, God's mind. "In the beginning was the Word, and the Word was with God, and the Word was God" (John 1:1). The mind of God is revealed perfectly in the person of Christ—the living Word. He is none other than God Himself—He not only brought the Word of God, He incorporated it in His own person. God "has spoken to us in His Son" (Hebrews 1:2). If you want to hear God, listen to His Son: "He is the radiance of His glory and the exact representation of His nature" (Hebrews 1:3).

In the next chapter, you will learn about the inspiring challenge to live with the mind of Christ.

- **Will you commit to learning more about the mind of God through disciplined Bible Study?**

- **Will you seek and listen to the prompting and teaching of the Holy Spirit?**

The Mind of Christ

> "Who has known or understood the mind
> [the counsels and purposes]
> of the Lord so as to guide and instruct Him
> and give Him knowledge?
> But we have the mind of Christ, [the Messiah], and do hold
> the thoughts (feelings and purposes) of His heart."
> (1 Corinthians 2:16, AMP)

Let's begin with the first man, Adam—he was created with a mind. The tragic failure in the Garden of Eden was a mind failure. It was a mind failure when Eve listened to Satan, a mind failure when the "fruit" was picked, and a mind failure when Adam and Eve ate the forbidden fruit (see Genesis 3).

After the fall, the biblical emphasis is on the difference between God and mankind. "'My thoughts [mind] are not your thoughts [mind], Neither are your ways [lifestyle] My ways [God-life],' declares the LORD" (Isaiah 55:8).

Reformation will not remedy the enmity between God and mankind—a God-mind requires nothing less than regeneration, a God-birth. To have the mind of Christ, you must "be renewed in the spirit of your mind" (Ephesians 4:23). When you have been redeemed, your mortal mind has the opportunity to function with an understanding of the mind of Christ, a God-mind.

This brings us to a solemn thought, your mind is fundamentally more important to God than your outward actions; however, God does hold you responsible for your every thought and action (see Romans 14:12). Your acts are symptomatic of your mind; for when a thought pattern formulates, it dictates your outward behavior. There is a biblical principle that the greater includes the lesser. The greater was when David lusted for Bathsheba; then shamelessly committed adultery and murder. The greater was when Peter had water-walking faith; then he miraculously walked on water.

This principle is seen when Jesus shared His mind in the Sermon on the Mount (see Matthew 5). He taught that the law says to not commit adultery; however, the greater Christ-mind would say, do not lust in your mind. Likewise, the law instructed them to not murder; yet, the greater Christ-mind would say, do not have malice, hate, and anger dominating your mind. While to most people the greater would be adultery or murder, Jesus taught the greater Christ-mind does not harbor lust or anger. This truth is the first step in discovering the mind of Christ.

Peace, Perfect Peace

An incomparable benefit of having the mind of Christ is peace. "Perfect peace, whose mind is stayed on you [the Lord]" (Isaiah 26:3, NKJV). The Hebrew text says *abundant, abounding peace.* I always enjoy hearing George Beverly Shea sing, "Peace, peace, God's peace, coming down from heaven above." Perfect peace comes from the Lord—from a God-life with the mind of Christ where judgment never weakens to feeling; nor does the will yield to desire.

Remember the three Hebrew men cast into a burning fiery furnace as recorded in the third chapter of Daniel? In steadfast faith they said, "Our God whom we serve is able to deliver us" (verse 17). They could speak without fear because they trusted God completely. They had an unshakable faith. And God proved their confidence in Him was reliable. When the king looked into the furnace, he said, "I see four men loose, walking in the midst of the fire; and they are not hurt, and the form of the fourth is like the Son of God" (verse 25, NKJV). The Son of God is the Prince of Peace—and He joined them in the furnace to preserve their tranquility. He is our peace, and with the mind of Christ, we can have peace, peace, perfect peace in every situation.

A Call to Like-Mindedness

There is a synergistic fellowship among believers who are like-minded and have the mind of Christ. "May the God who gives perseverance and encouragement grant you to be of the same mind with one another according to Christ Jesus" (Romans 15:5). The translation *same mind* or *like minded* (KJV) literally means *to mind the same thing among one another.* Apostle Paul prayed that the believers in Rome would have the mind of Christ—a God-mind. To be like-minded with Christ would be manifested by unity or oneness in the fellowship. When believers have the mind of Christ, their values, priorities, and perspectives are in agreement. When you have the mind of Christ, you think like Jesus, and your decorum and lifestyle will resemble that of Christ's. Like-mindedness in Christ will bring genuine unity to the fellowship of believers.

The battle for the mind of a believer rages on. The devil relentlessly seeks whom he may devour (see 1 Peter 5:8). Forget the creature with horns, wearing a red suit and carrying a pitchfork; the devil is far too cunning to dress up in Halloween garb. He skillfully assaults the mind.

When Jesus was in the desert, Satan craftily and subtly tempted our Lord's mind, His thoughts. That's the devil's strategic battle plan. The last thing he wants is for you to have the mind of Christ. Paul understood this and was alarmed—even to the point of being fearful—that believers at Corinth would be led astray. "I am afraid that as the serpent deceived Eve by his cunning, your thoughts [minds] will be led astray from a sincere and pure devotion to Christ [His mind]" (2 Corinthians 11:3, RSV).

The danger of deception is so substantial in magnitude that Paul compared it to Satan's beguiling Eve in the Garden of Eden—when sin entered the world and defiled all of Adam's descendants (see

Romans 5:12). Satan brought doubt to Eve's mind by denying the truth of God's command (see Genesis 3:1-7); there is the frightful and real danger that he will do the same to Christians today.

The alarming potential is that your mind will be distracted from Christ; that your mind "may be corrupted from the simplicity that is in Christ" (2 Corinthians 11:3, NKJV). The word translated *simplicity* (*haplotēs*) means *singleness*, or *without dissimulation*. The peril is that the devil would cunningly deceive you, and your thoughts would "be led astray from their single-hearted fidelity to Christ" (2 Corinthians 11:3, Goodspeed).

This biblical principle teaches us that the mind is the critical control factor for the believer. The mind—not activities and actions—is primary in living a God-life with the mind of Christ, and is the fundamental target for the cunning dissuasion of the devil (see 2 Corinthians 11:14). When you maintain a "single-hearted fidelity to Christ," do's and don'ts are governed by Christ-centered thoughts. Take "every thought captive to the obedience of Christ" (2 Corinthians 10:5).

Hear the words of Christ, understand His thoughts, discover His mind, and live in obedience to Him. Rejoice in an overcoming victory. The mind of Christ can destroy the strongholds of those who wage war in the flesh. The believer who has the mind of Christ can defeat the arguments that oppose God—that debate the truth of the gospel, and every other thing raised up against the Kingdom of Heaven.

You can triumph and take every thought captive for Christ. Don't have duplicity of thoughts because Satan has ensnared your mind and implanted falsehoods. The successful battle plan is to seize those thoughts and place them under the Lordship of Christ—examining them and testing them with His mind.

- *To live Christ* **is to live with His mind. Are you actively developing the mind of Christ?**

—Chapter Five—

Renewing the Mind

"Do not be conformed to this world,
but be transformed by the renewing of your mind."
(Romans 12:2)

While visiting a Celtic chapel in Wales, I read this prayer from a devotional guide:

I'm ready Lord; I'll go if you send me.
I'm listening Lord, tell me what You would have me know.

Some time later, sitting in my study, I read this Celtic prayer more closely. The focus of the prayer is the mind—the mind listens and knows with words; the mind is the storehouse of knowledge. Understanding that my mortal mind is inadequate and insufficient to know the will and ways of God, it is paramount that my mind be renewed—I need a God-mind. The words of the Celtic prayer became mine, "I'm ready Lord... tell me what You would have me know." I encourage you to make this prayer yours.

How can your mind be renewed? Look with me at this command: "Gird up the loins of your mind, be sober [thoughtful and wise], and rest your hope fully upon the grace that is to be brought to you at the revelation of Jesus Christ" (1 Peter 1:13, NKJV). The Greek aorist middle participle translated *gird up* (*anazōmnumi*) literally means *prepare your mind for action*. You must discipline yourself. This metaphor visualizes the girding up of loose eastern robes preparatory to running or other exertion.[v]

What are you doing to renew your mind? Get ready and "concentrate your minds, with the strictest self-control, and fix your hopes on the blessing that is coming for you" (1 Peter 1:13, TCNT).

The initiative of disciplining the mind for life's challenges is much like rolling up your sleeves as you face a task—it is an energetic, punctual, and self-imposed exercise. Jesus told the disciples, "be dressed in readiness, and keep your lamps alight" (Luke 12:35). It requires a disciplined mind, one that has essential steadiness and is not intoxicated with worldly, human thoughts and the latest "in thing." Be proactive in renewing your mind and understanding things with a God-mind.

~~~~~~

A renewed mind processes information in a new way.

~~~~~~

Renewing the mind is an act of *thoroughness*. A renewed mind is not a refurbished mind—but a reconstructed mind that is regenerated in its way of processing information.

A Classic Car

A good friend invited me to see his collection of vintage cars. When he opened his garage door and turned on the lights, in front of me was a shining 1957 Chevrolet. I asked him if he had refurbished it himself. He corrected me, it had been completely rebuilt—it was a *re-NEW-ed* car. He pointed out the pristine AM/FM stereo radio, leather seats, new wheels and hubcaps, even a different motor that was covered with chrome, and many other details. It wasn't just painted or refurbished; it was renewed and rebuilt. Metamorphoses had taken place, not just a new surface appearance.

In Romans 12:2, "Do not be conformed... but be transformed by the renewing of your mind," the Holy Spirit uses the words *conformed* and *transformed*, yet they are poles apart. The Word of God gives both negative and positive guidance for acquiring a renewed mind. The admonition is not to be conformed or fashioned according to the world—trying to fabricate a likeness to everyone else and seeking to identify with prevailing standards, customs, and lifestyles of the present age. "Don't let the world around you squeeze you into its own mold" (Romans 12:2, Phillips).

It sometimes seems that Christians and churches today are in a rush *to fit in* with pop-culture. They are conforming to a fleeting standard that will soon pass away. A believer that is an earthly chameleon—blending in with the world—can never acquire a God-mind. Remember, you are called to be set apart!

The Word of God stresses that it is imperative to be *transformed*—changed in the inner being, in your thought process and priorities. The journey towards God-mind begins with regeneration, accepting Christ as your personal Savior. Once God-birth occurs, you are challenged to have a renewed mind—out with the old and in with the new. "Grow in the grace and knowledge of our Lord and Savior Jesus Christ" (2 Peter 3:18).

As noted before, the word *transformed* (*metamorphoō*) is obviously the source of the biological word *metamorphose*, that which happens when a caterpillar becomes a butterfly. The obligatory, self-imposed action is for you to change your mindset in order to accommodate new thought patterns—a spiritual metamorphosis.

To acquire a God-mind, decisions and judgments require a radical change. To have a renewed mind and discover the will of God, you must be released from the world, its ways, and its fashions (see 1 Peter 4:4). God will not transform your mind against your will; however, a transformed mind is imperative for acceptable service and worship—for a fulfilling and effective God-life (see Romans 12:1).

When earnestly and humbly seeking a renewed mind, God will impart His own mind (understanding) to you. This is not a matter of academics, but rather, a divine revelation. A renewed mind—a God-mind—must come from Him, He alone can reveal His mind.

Six Steps to a Renewed Mind

Let's consider practical, effective steps to achieve a renewed mind, a God-mind. I heard a bible teacher say, put on the mind of Christ and have a renewed mind. The question is: *How can this be done?* What must I do to function with a God-mind? The following steps will answer that question.

STEP ONE: Allow the Word of God to be a literal guide to your mind in all things.

The Word of God is the roadmap, the compass, and the indispensable light to guide you through life. When you faithfully and carefully study the Word of God, you discover the mind of God—His thoughts, His precepts, and His judgments.

Once you discover the mind of God, you are equipped to renew your mind and have God-mind. When a pilot flies his plane by the authoritative instructions of an air traffic controller, he must yield completely to what the controller sees. This is because the radar reveals much more to the controller than the pilot could ever hope to observe. When the pilot is instructed to change vectors (compass settings), he must do so immediately. He knows that the controller exists for his safety and the satisfactory completion of the flight; so the pilot willingly yields to the informed best judgment of the controller.

Likewise, when you desire to have a God-mind, you must yield to the inspired, inerrant Word of God, and the guidance of the Holy Spirit, because God directs you based on perspectives far wiser and better informed than you could ever hope to attain.

STEP TWO: Set your mind to obey the Commandments of God.

It is not enough just to hear the Word of God; you must obey His commandments. Too many Christians go to church, hear a sermon, and leave, only to continue living the way they were before hearing God's Word.

"Be doers of the Word [obey the message], and not merely listeners to it... he who looks carefully into the faultless law... and is faithful to it and perseveres in looking into it, being not a heedless listener who forgets, but an active doer [who obeys], he shall be blessed in his doing—in his life of obedience" (James 1:22, 25, AMP).

Keeping the commandments of God is not an option—it is a *duty*. When you diligently seek to obey His commands, you have everything to gain and nothing to lose. God says He will show mercy and lovingkindness when you love Him and keep His decrees (see Exodus 20:6). Jesus said, "if you love Me, you will keep My commandments" (John 14:15). The only *if* in keeping the commandments is the measure of the quality of your love for God.

Luke records a socio-cultural illustration that Jesus used in emphasizing the believer's responsibility to obey God and keep His commandments. Jesus said that a master does not invite the servant in from the fields to sit at the dinner table. "Will he not rather say to him, 'Prepare something for my supper... and serve me... afterward you will eat?' ... Does he thank that servant because he did the things that were commanded him? I think not. So likewise, when you have done all those things that you are commanded, say, 'We are unprofitable servants. We have done what was our duty to do'" (Luke 17:8-10, NKJV). This strong statement emphasizes the unmeritorious *duty* of the believer to obey the commandments of God.

Keeping God's decrees should be an unmatched *delight* for you. Jesus cites your kingdom relationship with the Sovereign God, who gladly blesses His obedient servants (see Luke 12:35-37). You should honor God's Word and keep His commandments because you love Him. The result of your obedience will be in manifold blessings from Him.

The first Psalm begins, "Blessed." Actually, the original is plural. Blessedness belongs to the one "who does not walk in the counsel of the wicked... his delight is in the law of the LORD, and in His law he meditates day and night" (verses 1-2). When you determine to keep God's commandments, you find joy in the Lord's principles and enjoy obedience. You meditate, ponder, digest, and celebrate the Word of God, because it is your daily bread.

~~~~~~
Meditate, ponder, digest, and celebrate the Word of God.
~~~~~~

In the commandments, you discover the mind of God—His values, His perspective, and His desires. God is love, and you are to love keeping His decrees. Furthermore, through a conscious keeping of His commands, you discover God-mind and God-love. For instance, "you shall not murder" (Exodus 20:13), is a corollary to, "you shall love your neighbor as yourself" (Leviticus 19:18), and "love your enemies" (Matthew 5:44). Keeping God's commandments is both a duty and a delight.

STEP THREE: Keep an open mind (an appetite to learn, and willingness to change).

A renewed mind implies radical alteration—a renovated thought process. The transforming of the mind may be stressful or difficult; even emotionally and intellectually painful. It often begins with a struggle in which the believer must bring his body into subjection in order to obey God (see 1 Corinthians 9:27). Having an open mind does not imply casual awareness, but a rigorous effort to develop a God-mind.

When you hunger for a renewed mind you will voraciously study the Word of God with the goal of obedience. "Every Scripture is… profitable for instruction, for reproof and conviction of sin, for correction of error and discipline in obedience, and for training in righteousness [that is, in holy living, in conformity to God's will in thought, purpose, and action]" (2 Timothy 3:16, AMP).

As the revelation of the mind of God is made manifest, the thirsty believer applies the truths learned. This application means appropriating and practicing the mind of God—living with a God-mind. A willing student has a mind receptive to the Lord, whether sitting in the presence of a godly teacher or preacher, or in private study of God's Word. A learner is open to the revelation of God-mind in the God-breathed Scripture.

STEP FOUR: Develop a disciplined mind of "thou shalts" and "thou shalt nots" for life situations.
"Be careful how you walk, not as unwise men, but as wise" (Ephesians 5:15). The renewing of the mind begins by establishing boundaries, erecting a mental fence, and placing a "posted" sign: "Do not trespass!" You are to "walk circumspectly" (Ephesians 5:15 NKJV). The word *circumspectly* means *accurately* or *carefully*, live within limits or guidelines. Draw a biblical circle around your life—define and limit your thoughts, activities, and relationships.

A disciplined mind is prudent, observant, and considers all circumstances and possible consequences of your actions and words. This is evidence of a God-mind.

STEP FIVE: Renew your mind, forget the past, and forge ahead.
"Forgetting those things which are behind and reaching forward to those things which are ahead... as many as are mature, have this mind" (Philippians 3:13, 15 NKJV).

A renewed mind is directed to look forward and forget the past. Both achievements and mistakes of the past can distract your mind from "the goal... the upward call of God in Christ Jesus" (Philippians 3:14). The basic need for approval, acceptance, and prominence may tempt you to glory in past accomplishments. Human nature is often enticed to use prior success or recognition as a platform for self-flattering ego building. In the very nature of self-centeredness, your eyes are taken away from the goal. Don't rest on what you have accomplished, focus on what God wants you to achieve!

Likewise, focusing on past sins, wayward acts, or worldly lifestyle will be fatal to achieving a renewed mind. The devil is intent on your rehearsing the sins of the past—this is a hindrance in developing a renewed mind. When you have confessed acts of sin with a sincere and repentant heart, God removes your transgressions from you—they are gone! God has forgotten them and you should also.

Keep in mind that unreleased guilt over past transgressions can turn into the "sin which so easily entangles us" (Hebrews 12:1). The renewed mind has no closet where skeletons are kept and remembered. Get rid of them! Put them under the blood of Calvary and clean house (see Ephesians 4:20-24). Forgiven! Bygone failures will not impede your renewed mind today.

STEP SIX: Submit your mind to the will of God on a daily basis. There is a difference between the long-term *goal* for your life, and *God's will* for your day-by-day pilgrimage.

Take a few moments to think about long-term goals vs. God's daily will for you:

A long-term goal is stated and known.
God's will for you is an ongoing revelation.

A long-term goal is for to me, to live is Christ (Philippians 1:21).
God's will for you is, How can I become more like Jesus today?

A long-term goal is "the upward call of God in Christ Jesus" (Philippians 3:14).
God's will for you is to know every dimension of Christ on your upward journey.

A long-term goal is the finish line, the ultimate achievement, a Christ-like life.
God's will for you is the roadmap in route to the goal.

A long-term goal is "looking unto Jesus, the author and finisher of our faith" (Hebrews 12:2 NKJV), to have His mind, and be molded into the likeness of His person.
God's will for you is to follow Jesus who left an example for daily living. To "follow in His steps" (1 Peter 2:21).

~~~~~~~~~~~~~~~~~~~~~~~~~~~~~~~~~~~~~
The will of God is a daily discovery,
unfolding God's life-plan for you.
~~~~~~~~~~~~~~~~~~~~~~~~~~~~~~~~~~~~~

God has a will (life-plan) for everyone. The eternal, all-knowing God *predestines* or wills a *destiny* by divine decree—a God-walk for every person! Every decree is positive and productive. People in their freewill often deny or reject the Lord—casting away the *destiny* designed for them by God, and thus suffering the consequences of insignificance and purposelessness.

God had a will and life-plan for Isaiah from his mother's womb (see Isaiah 49:1). He also had a destiny for Jeremiah, "before I formed you in the womb I knew you, And before you were born I consecrated you; I have appointed you a prophet to the nations" (Jeremiah 1:5). Paul the apostle testified that God "set me apart, even from my mother's womb, and called me" (Galatians 1:15).

God rarely reveals His will or life-plan in its entirety. For most, if not all of us, seeing the whole roadmap or life-plan would perhaps be daunting or even defeating. To Isaiah, Jeremiah, Stephen, or Paul, their full life-plan could have produced some hesitancy to follow God's will because in each life there were testings, difficulties, hardships, persecutions, and executions—yet, all in God's will and for His glory.

God's will is a daily discovery; it is the revelation of an unfolding plan. You can read any story in the Bible and see how the Lord slowly but surely revealed His plans to His people. Think about Joseph—favored by his father, hated by his brothers, sold into slavery, unjustly imprisoned in Egypt, trusted by Pharaoh, empowered to provide for his father and family during the great famine, and renowned as a patriarch of the faith (see Genesis 37-41).

In God's mercy, He leads you one step, one day at a time. As you have the capacity to receive it, He reveals His life-plan for you.

- **Stop and read again the six steps to a renewed mind and measure yourself. How many steps have you taken?**

Prayer for a Renewed Mind

To think God's thoughts with a God-mind, it requires a renewed mind. Before you can change your actions, sentiments, judgments, and viewpoints, you must change the way you think. With a renewed mind, a God-mind, you can live in God's will and achieve your God-ordained destiny. Yet, the thrilling and satisfying reward of pursuing with such singleness of purpose is knowing that you can have full and thorough knowledge of His will in your daily walk.

"I thank my God... for the grace of God which was given you in Christ Jesus, that... you were enriched in Him in... all knowledge" (1 Corinthians 1:4-5). Through God's grace, you can be filled with an accurate knowledge of God's divine plan for your daily life achieved through spiritual wisdom. Think about it, God's will is possessive—it is His will to disclose Himself to you. This is not academics; it is revelation, which comes by the Holy Spirit. "When He, the Spirit of truth, comes, He will guide you into all the truth" (John 16:13).

With the knowledge of God's will and through spiritual (Holy Spirit) wisdom, you have the ability to discern God's life-plan, or course of action. You are enabled to "Walk in a manner worthy of the Lord, to please Him in all respects" (Colossians 1:10). This is a portrait of a renewed mind, which is ever increasing in the knowledge of God. A renewed mind is not knowing about God, but experiencing a firsthand knowledge of God. Keep in mind, the will of God is never in conflict or in variance to the Word of God. Prayer and obedience to the Word of God are keys to discovering God's will. Knowledge of God's will comes from God—He alone reveals His mind. God's will always exalts the Lord Jesus Christ.

Renewing your mind is above all very personal—it is your thought process—how you think, speak, and act in every day life. It is your responsibility to think and operate with a God-mind—to order your life with the value system and mindset that harmonizes with the mind of God—and to live in complete agreement and obedience to His life-plan for you.

Thinking on this I heard God say…
Follow Me.
"Yes, Lord, I'll follow You. But, Lord…"
Yes.
"Where to? Where will I be going?"
With Me.
"What will I do?"
What I would do.
"What will I say?"
What I would say.
"How Lord? How can I…"
With a renewed mind, beloved, with a God-mind.

- **Is there a transformation occurring in the way you think?**

- **Are you in the process of renewing your mind to a God-mind?**

SECTION EIGHT

GOD-WISDOM

"If any of you lacks wisdom,
let him ask of God"
(James 1:5)

I am moved by the words of the song, "You'll Never Walk Alone." This lyrical epic by Rodgers and Hammerstein grows in emotion, and then rises with affirmation of assurance: "When you walk through the storm… Walk on, walk on, with hope in your heart… and you'll never walk alone."

Storms—storms of indecision, uncertainty, questions, and other challenges are common to all of us. God does not intend for you to walk through your storms alone. You'll never have to walk alone— God will be with you and share His wisdom for your life issues; it's His promise to you.

Spiritually mature followers of Christ have discovered how to live their life with God-wisdom. They've learned how to appropriate His wisdom for everyday challenges. You can too! What are your challenges? Are they too big for God? No! Not on any day, in no way. It doesn't matter what your challenge is, you can trust God for the right words, attitude, and response. Turn the "woe is me" into "Christ in me."

Wisdom is accumulating knowledge, comprehending truth, and with insight and discernment, applying it to your life. *God-wisdom* is acquiring knowledge from God's Word, understanding its truths, and enabled by the Holy Spirit, applying divine teachings to your everyday life. While "wisdom" is defined as accumulated learning, God-wisdom comes from an intimate relationship with Almighty God that governs your thinking, behavior, and decision-making. You learn how to function with the wisdom of God. Yes, *His wisdom*!

Are you ready for a turning point in your Christian pilgrimage? Are you willing to abandon your habitual thinking and let God-wisdom be the governing principle in your life? Through His Word and the Holy Spirit, you can have the very wisdom of God in life's choices.

In Christ, you have a God-given ability to manage your life— deciding what is God-honoring and what is not. I am not talking about theoretical knowledge, but discernment of what is right and wrong from God's perspective. It is no longer you who live, but *Christ in you*. Simply put, you have an opportunity to reveal Christ in the whole of your life. Intellectually enlightened (Word of God) and spiritually illuminated (Holy Spirit), you can exhibit God-wisdom. You never have to walk alone.

"Wisdom is the principle thing; therefore, get wisdom." (Proverbs 4:7, KJV)

At last, we have come to the sum and substance of God-life. Let's review, asking the fundamental question: "Have you had a God-birth—have you been born again?" God-life begins with your personal relationship with the Lord God. Then, the operational question: "Are you living a God-life?" It is crucial that you have an honest self-awareness, to know yourself.

Here's a thought to ponder: You can't be all that God wants you to be until you understand yourself. And, you will never have true self-knowledge and self-awareness until you contemplate the very presence of God. When comparing how you conduct your life with others, you can be quite satisfied. But, when alone before Almighty God, you'll have an "Isaiah" experience, "woe is me, for I am undone" (Isaiah 6:5, NKJV). It is a daunting and humbling event, and it is decisive in the journey of living God-life.

When facing your flaws and imperfections, your humanness, don't be discouraged. You have every reason to be confident, to live God-life with God-wisdom, because God has already equipped you with everything you need—His Word and His Spirit. Keep in mind, you are a born again child of the heavenly Father, and He wants you to function with His wisdom. As His child, you represent Him; do it with His wisdom. God did not send His Son to Calvary to make you just an average, non-productive Christian struggling through each day. He wants you to live victoriously.

This section further explores the question: "How can I live a God-life?" And examines: "How can I have the wisdom of God?" While preceding sections of this book focus on specific areas such as inner strength (faith), and external function (talk, walk), for testifying your God-birth, let's learn to apply acquired knowledge to live *Christ in you*. After reading this far in *God-life* it is my prayer that you've opened your heart and mind to new thoughts, and are seeking God-wisdom.

- **Have you had an "Isaiah" experience before Almighty God?**

- **Do you want to live with God-wisdom?**

—Chapter One—

What is the Source of God-Wisdom?

"Where can wisdom be found?
And where is the place of understanding?
Man does not know its value,
Nor is it found in the land of the living."
(Job 28:12-13)

God-wisdom isn't found in the wisdom of the world, it's not a mystery hidden in a book deep in a library, nor is it equated with educational degrees or academic achievement. While profound, it may appear over-simplified; the source of God-wisdom is God Himself. An undeniable attribute of God is His wisdom. "Oh, the depth of the riches both of the wisdom and knowledge of God! How unsearchable are His judgments and unfathomable His ways" (Romans 11:33)!

Our Heavenly Father is the God of infinite wisdom. Consider what Job said in this hymn of wisdom, "Where can wisdom be found? And where is the place of understanding?... Where then does wisdom come from? And where is the place of understanding?... God understands its way; And He knows its place" (Job 28:12, 20, 23).

Theologians refer to the omniscience of God—His incomparable awareness, insight, and understanding. The consummate wisdom of God is complete in all things both animate and inanimate. God's wisdom is incomprehensible whether it was in a time pre-existent to all known things, during the history of humanity, in the happenings of today, or that, which is yet to be.

Think with me, "He counts the number of the stars; He gives names to all of them" (Psalm 147:4). And, "The LORD knows the thoughts of man" (Psalm 94:11). God's wisdom is superior to mankind, "'My thoughts are not your thoughts, neither are your ways My ways, declares the Lord. ' For as the heavens are higher than the earth, so are My ways higher than your ways, and My thoughts than your thoughts'" (Isaiah 55:8-9).

What is the source of God-wisdom? God is the eternal source of all wisdom; His resources are unlimited. The awesome truth is He wants to impart His wisdom to you. He wants you to live with God-wisdom.

Jesus Lived God-Wisdom
"Christ the power of God and the wisdom of God…
you are in Christ Jesus who became to us wisdom from God."
(1 Corinthians 1:24, 30)

The preeminent and magnanimous manifestation of the wisdom of God is a person: the Lord Jesus Christ. The wisdom of God was manifestly operative in Jesus, the incarnate person of God-wisdom. First, the divine revelation of the Lamb of God, the Son of God, who bore our sins on the cross, is the disclosure of God's wisdom in the provision for forgiveness of our sins. Thus, the cross of Calvary is both the power and wisdom of God. Jesus, the Son of Man, is the supreme example of living your life exhibiting God-wisdom.

Let's look at examples of God-wisdom in the life of Jesus.

In early childhood, Jesus was committed to His heavenly Father's business.

"Why is it that you were looking for Me? Did you not know that I had to be in My Father's house" (Luke 2:49)? God-wisdom knows, understands, and makes a commitment to the Father's business.

Jesus exemplified God-wisdom in how to thwart temptations of the devil.

"And the tempter came and said to Him... He [Jesus] answered and said, 'It is written, Man shall not live on bread alone, but on every word that proceeds out of the mouth of God'... Then the devil left Him" (see Matthew 4: 3-11) God-wisdom uses the Word of God to defeat the Adversary.

Jesus drew spiritual insight and God-wisdom through prayer.

"He... would often slip away to... pray" (Luke 5:16). God-wisdom is available when you ask your heavenly Father.

Jesus exhibited God-wisdom when He forgave the sinful, immoral woman who anointed His head with perfume and His feet with tears.

Jesus said, "Her sins, which are many, have been forgiven" (Luke 7:47). God-wisdom forgives; seventy times seven, and more.

Jesus revealed God-wisdom when He said that He came to save mankind.

"For the Son of Man has come to seek and to save that which was lost" (Luke 19:10). You apply the wisdom of God when you seek to share an effective witness to a lost person.

Jesus demonstrated the God-wisdom of a servant-minister.

"Whoever wishes to become great among you shall be your servant... the Son of Man did not come to be served, but to serve" (Matthew 20:26, 28). When you display the God-wisdom of servanthood, you stand out as one-of-a-kind in the body of believers.

Jesus was the embodiment and personification of God-life revealing God-wisdom in every area and in every situation of His life. In his earthly lifetime, Jesus applied God-wisdom perfectly. He left you an "example for you to follow in His steps" (1 Peter 2:21). In Christ, the Son of God, "are hidden all the treasures of wisdom and knowledge" (Colossians 2:3). When you receive Jesus Christ as Lord and Savior, there is a limitless potential for living a life governed by God-wisdom.

Study the life and words of Christ—the challenges he faced with Satan, enemies, politicians, followers, and even friends—all are applicable lessons for today in how to live with God-wisdom.

The Holy Spirit Facilitates God-Wisdom

Jesus promised, "I will give you utterance and wisdom" (Luke 21:15). A literal translation of this blessed promise of our Lord is, "I, myself, will give you utterance |words| and wisdom." How can this be? How can you receive the words and utterances of God-wisdom? The Bible declares, "the thoughts of God no one knows except the Spirit of God" (1 Corinthians 2:11). What then? Is it sacrilegious for mortal man to pursue God-wisdom? No, not at all.

The glorious possibility for exercising God-wisdom is yours! Jesus promised, "The Helper, the Holy Spirit, whom the Father will send in My name, He will teach you all things, and bring to your remembrance all that I said to you" (John 14:26). Remember, the Holy Spirit is described as Helper, literally, One called alongside to help. "Now we |you| have received... the Spirit who is from God, that we |you| might know the things freely given to us |you| by God" (1 Corinthians 2:12).

An unending blessing resulting from your God-birth is His indwelling residency. He will empower you to apply God-wisdom to difficult and simple issues. The Holy Spirit is your inward Guide giving you understanding and revelation, a daily discovery of God-wisdom.

Have you ever paused to consider the difference and blessed advantage that believers today have that Old Testament believers did not have? You have the witness and life of Christ to follow and the presence of the Holy Spirit to help you! In the Old Testament, the Israelites continuously made the same mistakes—forgetting God and sinning against Him. How different it should be today. We are continually prompted with God-wisdom by the Holy Spirit through conviction and discernment.

A Helper in His Time of Need

Smiling and overjoyed, a church member rushed up following the morning worship service and said, "Let me tell you how God helped my grandson pass a test!" She was radiant as she told me a wonderful account of how God meets our every daily need, no matter how small.

Her grandson, Tommy, a high school student whose parents were divorced was returning from a long weekend visit with his father. The flight from Denver to Atlanta would give him time to catch-up on homework neglected during the busy weekend. He opened his backpack, pulled out his algebra book, and started preparing for an exam the next morning.

Struggling, sighing, and thoroughly frustrated, Tommy turned the pages of his Algebra book back and forth, then shaking his head, closed the book, and looked out at the night sky.

"Excuse me," a soft, caring voice broke the silence, "May I look at your assignment?"

"Be my guest," the discouraged boy said. "It says Algebra, but it's Greek to me!"

"Would you like for me to help you?" the fellow traveler asked.

"Would I? Sure!" the dejected high-school student eagerly said. "I'm stuck, and I have a big test in the morning."

God's favor had placed a college professor of mathematics next to Tommy. One- on-one teaching for the next two hours and algebra began to make sense. Tommy couldn't wait for the exam! He was ready.

What a beautiful expression of grace! A helper placed alongside Tommy enabling him to have knowledge, understanding, and wisdom for his assignment. Look around, what help has God placed next to you?

The ministration of the Holy Spirit, as your Helper, imparts the wisdom of God. He does this in a variety of ways—through prayer, the Word of God, preaching, testimonies, and a variety of other ways. With Tommy, the Holy Spirit placed help in the seat next to him.

- **Are you aware of God's intervening help for you? List some examples.**

- **Are you available to "go alongside" and help someone that God places next to you?**

—Chapter Two—

How Do I Attain God-Wisdom?

"The LORD gives wisdom; From His mouth [words]
come knowledge and understanding.
Wisdom will enter your heart, and knowledge will be pleasant to
your soul; discretion will guard you,
understanding will watch over you."
(Proverbs 2:6, 10-11)

A logical progression is from *knowledge* to *understanding* to *wisdom*. However, at times in Scripture, these three terms are interchanged or even transposed in their order. God's intent is for His own to have God-wisdom, which incorporates knowledge and understanding.

An Urgent Prayer for Wisdom

Paul prayed for the believers at Colossae that they would "be filled with the knowledge of His will in all spiritual wisdom and understanding" (Colossians 1:9). This pastoral prayer warrants a closer reading. Paul, while a prisoner in Rome, sent a message of encouragement to believers that they would have a more mature Christian life, or manifest God-wisdom.

The basis of spiritual wisdom and understanding is found in the opening phrase of Paul's prayer: "That you may be filled with the knowledge of His will." In the "real time" of the writing of this letter, there was an arrogant pseudo-intellectual mindset (Gnosticism) of false teachers in the church at Colossae that claimed superior knowledge. The exclusiveness of Gnostic teaching was an attack on Christian faith. This teaching held that all matter was evil and deliverance came through *knowledge* (*ginōskō*) alone. Paul's urgent prayer was for the believers to have (*epiginōskō*) *full knowledge* or *know fully* God's will (His way of life). The false teachers of Gnosticism were boasting of a life with greater wisdom, with secret knowledge of mysteries and revelations. God-wisdom is far superior.

Let's look more closely at three fundamentals of God-wisdom that will set you apart as a follower of Christ: Knowledge, Understanding, and Wisdom.

Knowledge

To have knowledge is to be cognizant of a body of truth through experience, or the apprehension of specific information and/or facts. The Bible is the primary source for instruction concerning practical everyday living. It holds a wellspring of knowledge—not just history and writings of a people—it is where we discover the revelation of the Lord God of heaven and earth. The Bible is an extraordinary volume of truth.

The Holy Bible is authoritative and through it, God reveals His wisdom. "All Scripture is given by inspiration of God" (2 Timothy 3:16, KJV). The Holy Spirit communicated or inspired those who recorded God's words, and the Word is inspired (*theópneustos*), breathed out by God. "No prophecy was ever made by an act of human will, but men moved by the Holy Spirit spoke from God" (2 Peter 1:21). Scripture is the source for the knowledge of God-wisdom.

Someone said to me, "I have never heard God speak." If you want to hear from God, turn to His infallible, inspired Word and He will speak living words of knowledge and truth to you.

"Knowledge will be pleasant to your soul" (Proverbs 2:10). The knowledge spoken of is from the mouth or words of the Lord. Knowledge of the Word of God is indeed "pleasant to your soul." Mankind does not *have* a soul; you *are* a soul. It is the very core of your personhood, the center of your will, your inner person—that which desires, perceives, and plans. What a fulfilling experience to direct your life with acquired knowledge from God's Word. To live God-life, absorb life-changing knowledge from the Word of God.

~~~~~~~~~~~~~~~~~~~~~~~~~~~~~~~~~~~
"Take my instruction, and not silver,
and knowledge rather than choicest gold."
(Proverbs 8:10)
~~~~~~~~~~~~~~~~~~~~~~~~~~~~~~~~~~~

Acquiring knowledge is a lifelong process from the day of your birth. It manifests an acquired maturity and is mind (soul) altering. The knowledge of history can be invaluable in managing your life. The knowledge of science can greatly benefit your health and existence. *To live Christ*, to have God-life, you must be filled with the knowledge and instruction of God's Word. While God says to seek His instruction and knowledge rather than silver and gold, most seek silver and gold.

Life-Changing Book
A small plane flying over remote mountains of South America developed mechanical difficulty and crashed. There were no survivors; one of the fatalities was a Christian missionary. Two years after the tragedy, natives came to one of the villages on the edge of the deep forest seeking someone to explain a book. The book was the missionary's Spanish New Testament. One of the natives salvaged it from the wreckage and could read but a few words. With this very limited knowledge, several from the village had prayed to Jesus and were anxious to know more. The Bible provides precious life-changing knowledge.

Understanding

Understanding is intellectual comprehension—the ability to perceive and discern, to make the right choices. To make decisions with God-wisdom you must not only know God's Word as truth, but also understand its message. There is a marked difference in rote memory of Scripture and comprehending the message.

~~~~~~~~~~~~~~~~~~~~~~~~~~~~~~~~~~~
"Incline your heart to understanding."
(Proverbs 2:2)
~~~~~~~~~~~~~~~~~~~~~~~~~~~~~~~~~~~

Solomon's Wisdom

The Lord spoke to Solomon, "Ask what you wish me to give you" (1 Kings 3:5). Let's take a minute and reflect on King Solomon's prayer for understanding and wisdom.

"And Solomon said: You have shown great mercy to Your servant David my father, because he walked before You in truth, in righteousness, and in uprightness of heart with You; You have continued this great kindness for him, and You have given him a son to sit on his throne, as *it is* this day. Now, O Lord my God, You have made Your servant king instead of my father David, but I *am* a little child; I do not know *how* to go out or come in. And Your servant *is* in the midst of Your people whom You have chosen, a great people, too numerous to be numbered or counted. Therefore give to Your servant an understanding heart to judge Your people, that I may discern between good and evil. For who is able to judge this great people of Yours?" (1 Kings 3:6-9, NKJV).

What can you learn from Solomon? To begin, "Solomon loved the LORD" (1 Kings 3:3). Understanding begins with submissive reverence to the God of all Creation. It comes through your personal relationship of love and devotion to your heavenly Father. Second, Solomon was *listening* when God asked, "what do you wish?" To better serve God's beloved Israel, not to elevate himself or for selfish gain, Solomon asked for wisdom, understanding, and discernment. Third, Solomon had self-understanding: "I do not know how to go out or come in" (verse 7). He recognized he lacked the skills or the understanding needed to accomplish his daily responsibilities as King. Fourth, Solomon sincerely prayed. His prayer request was "give to Thy servant an understanding [hearing or obedient] heart... to discern between good and evil [right and wrong]" (verse 9).

The Lord God was faithful to His promise to Solomon and abundantly generous: "God gave Solomon wisdom and very great discernment and breadth of mind" (1 Kings 4:29). His wisdom exceeded that of all the wise men of the East—Babylonia, Assyria, Egypt and all the surrounding nations (see 1 Kings 4:30-32). He authored most of Proverbs, Ecclesiastes, and the Song of Solomon. He was gifted to transfer profound truths of God and put them in easily understood words.

When Solomon stood before the altar of the newly constructed Temple, he led in a prayer of dedication. Spreading his hands toward heaven, he prayed: "LORD, God of Israel, there is no God in heaven above or on earth below like You" (1 Kings 8:23, NKJV). Solomon had a deep reverence and awe of his Lord, an exalted view of Jehovah God.

Our youth choir was singing, "Our God is an Awesome God!" Listening, I thought how fundamentally important it is to have a conscious sense of the awesomeness of God! "The fear [awe, reverence] of the Lord is the beginning of wisdom" (Psalms 111:10). Understanding God begins with a worshipful reverence and humble spirit.Do you consider the challenge to acquire God-wisdom for life's challenges to be unreasonable if not unattainable? It is not! God never asks for you to do what He will not help you to do. Not to do what He asks is a disappointment to Him. Hear His emotion of regret when He said to His people of Judah: "My people are foolish, they know Me not; they are stupid children, and they have no understanding" (Jeremiah 4:22). God's desire for Judah was for them to know, to understand, and to live for Him. His desires for His people have not changed.

Seek Understanding

It was the first day of a graduate school class and the professor came to the lectern to begin the first session. He said, "During the next weeks, I pray we both can experience understanding—I want this class to be more than an exercise of transferring class notes from my notebook to yours without going through the mind of either."

Biblical understanding is gaining the knowledge of God's notebook (the Bible), comprehending its truth, incorporating it into your volitive processes, and manifest your acquired perception into your daily life. God's rebuke to Judah was to His own covenant people. They were unwise. They heard the Word, but were without understanding. God has given to you His word (the Bible) so you can know Him, live with understanding, and evidence a God-life.

You may be questioning: *How can I gain an understanding of God's Word?* Listen to the encouragement of the Scriptures. "Those who seek the Lord understand all things" (Proverbs 28:5). The Bible is not a book of riddles and obscure messages. On the contrary, it was given by God so you can have understanding. You, yourself, are His very own. He loves you and He wants you to succeed.

Wisdom

Wisdom is discretionary use of knowledge and understanding. It's much more than amassing facts or a head full of knowledge. Wisdom is the ability to discern and govern your use of reason or understanding. It is prudence in management of your affairs. God-wisdom is the capacity to apply knowledge and understanding of His Word with perception in a manner that will magnify Him.

~~~~~~~~~~~~~~~~~~~~~~~~~~~~~~~~~~~~~
"Wisdom will enter your heart."
(Proverbs 2:10)
~~~~~~~~~~~~~~~~~~~~~~~~~~~~~~~~~~~~~

A Hearing Heart

King Solomon was respected in the world of his day as a wise monarch. We have just discussed that Solomon's wisdom was a gift from God in answer to his beseeching prayer. God answered his prayer because Solomon had a discerning or understanding heart (see 1 Kings 3:11-12). The word translated discerning or understanding means *hearing*. Solomon had a hearing or obedient heart, soul, and mind. He listened to God. God will do for you what he did for Solomon.

A mother quietly slipped out of the worship service and headed to the church nursery. As she neared, she recognized her baby's cry. When the nursery worker asked, "How did you know your baby needed you?" She thoughtfully replied, "I suppose that I have a hearing heart attuned for my child."

That's it! Keep a hearing heart for the still, quiet voice, or even inaudible prompting of God. God-wisdom is lifelong "hearing" and taking appropriate action. An arrogant, know-it-all, unteachable individual is going headlong into a spiritual pitfall. A hearing heart always listens, learns, and responds. God does and will speak to your hearing heart. Take time to hear His voice.

- **When you pray, read the Bible, or listen to God's Word taught, do you have a hearing heart?**

Unequaled Wisdom

"One greater than Solomon is here" (Matthew 12:42, NIV). When Jesus was only a child, He exhibited exceptional wisdom concerning Scripture. He was "in the temple, sitting in the midst of the teachers, both listening to them, and asking them questions. And all who heard Him were amazed at His understanding and His answers" (Luke 2:46-47). God-wisdom listens, asks questions, and from understanding gives prudent answers.

At age 12, Jesus was not a fully mature man in a child's body. He was a child, taught the Scriptures from birth, who worshipped God, and developed a meaningful prayer life. He was at home in the Temple. And with God-focused, Scripture-based conversation, he "kept increasing in wisdom and stature, and in favor with God and men" (Luke 2:52). The neighbors and fellow townspeople of Nazareth were amazed at His wisdom. They reasoned: "Is not this the carpenter, the Son of Mary?" (Mark 6:3). Or, "Is this not one of Mary's boys?" They knew Jesus had never attended a school of Rabbis, nor had teaching credentials. They were perplexed, they didn't understand: where did He get His training? How did He get this wisdom? In their quandary, they actually identified the source: "What is this wisdom given to Him?" (Mark 6:2). Jesus was an instrument of God—the wisdom of Jesus was a God-wisdom.

The knowledge of how to live with God-wisdom is available to you. It is much more than simply seeking to know what to do or say. It is the comprehension of Christ living in you, *I no longer live… Christ lives in me.* If you choose to live unto yourself, you will suffer a spiritual defeat, because you can't go beyond the barriers of your mind. Christ in you, you can have the mind of Christ to break the barriers. The previous section, God-mind, is so very important in living with God-wisdom. If you don't *think* you can have victory over life's challenges, you can't; the victory is lost. Christ can overcome; He will give you God-wisdom.

—Chapter Three—

Do You Function With True Wisdom?

"Give your heart to the heavenly things,
not to the passing things of earth."
(Colossians 3:2, Phi)

The ongoing, unending struggle within the soul of believers is evidenced by two wisdoms: *temporal* and *true*. These two wisdoms are poles apart, they are extremes, and both are evident in the body of faith. Your soul, who you are, is the reservoir of your principles for decisions, desires, affections, emotions and will. It is in your soul where the choice between the two wisdoms is made.

All too often believers vacillate; they try to function dually with both *temporal* and *true* wisdom. This generates confusion, doubt, and uncertainty when making life's choices. James describes these believers well: "One who doubts is like the surf in the sea driven and tossed by the wind. For let not that man expect that he will receive anything from the Lord, being a double-minded man, unstable in all his ways" (James 1:6-8).

We call this kind of person wishy-washy, or inconsistent in their decisions. *Double-minded (dipsuchŏs)* is literally *two-souled*. The portrait of a double-minded person is that of wobbler; they seek godliness while trying to hold on to things of the world. Remember

John Bunyan's "Mr. Facing-both-ways?" They struggle through life without true wisdom—God-wisdom.

Temporal Wisdom, Not from God

The Word of God gives a clear description of temporal wisdom that is not from God. This wisdom does not come down from above, but is *earthly*, *natural*, or even *demonic* (see James 3:15). These characterizations profile the temporal wisdom of man apart from God and His Word.

Earthly Wisdom

A wisdom that is not from God—*worldly* or *earthly* wisdom—avariciously and covetously cares for and seeks the things of this world. Can Christians operate with a earthly wisdom? Yes! Christians who choose to live by worldly wisdom are committed to the ways and measures of every day life in the worldly culture. They are aggrandized, influenced, and enamored by the acclaim and values of mainstream. They are secular-minded with earth-bound standards.

The Bible says they are "opponents [who] ignore the cross of Christ [being crucified with Christ] whose appetite is their god, and who are proud of what they should be ashamed of, their minds (souls) are absorbed on earthly things" (Philippians 3:18-19, my translation). The earthly minded are in opposition to the heavenly minded.

- **Are your standards of wisdom worldly? Are you operating in self-centered wisdom and ways of the world?**

By secular standards, worldly or earthly wisdom isn't necessarily non-productive; it may be a success strategy. It seeks recognition, success, publicity, and is focused on immediate gratification. It's like a well-known and brilliant linguist who specialized in Biblical languages, but was consumed with seeking personal recognition and approval. He constantly submitted press releases, articles, and more—all soliciting attention and affirmation of his work. He oper ated in the earth-bound mode of worldly wisdom, not the lasting benefit of a superior linguistic ministry.   .

Natural Wisdom

Natural Wisdom is wisdom with characteristics pleasing to the senses, and is focused on feelings. The word translated *natural* (*psuchikŏs*), relates to the *soul* (*psuchē*) or mind-set of one who chooses to live the self-absorbed natural lifestyle. Natural wisdom is operating with the thought process that springs from a wisdom that evolves from unchecked human and common desires and affections. Have you ever said or heard said, "He is only doing what comes naturally?" Christians and even church leaders fall folly to pursuing their own advantage; devoted to nothing higher than self-indulgent advancement and self-absorbed boasting. Their life is all about them.

True, every believer is indwelt by the Holy Spirit, but sadly, many believer's actions and decisions are based on natural instincts, selfish concerns, and ambitions. They are void of spiritual enlightenment, untouched by the revelation of: *It is no longer I who live, but Christ lives in me* (Galatians 2:20).

Tent Revival

God led several members of our church to pray about having a tent revival. The feeling was that evangelistic services conducted in such a venue could reach some for Christ who would not likely attend a revival held in our sanctuary. There was a *natural* opposition to the idea from some well-meaning church members. Some of the objections were: it's not in the budget, it's an outdoor tent event in August heat, and it's too risky to move the church piano. These and other resistances opposed an out-of-the-ordinary evangelism effort.

Well-intentioned members had understandable questions, but their thinking was flawed with temporal wisdom. They were focusing on natural concerns, not eternal benefits. The church business conference approved the tent revival, but stipulated the event had to cover all expenses.

The tent went up, the revival began, and people came. Carloads of young people attended every night from a nearby Christian

College. They sang, gave testimonies, and played musical instruments. Crowds showed up... the tent over-flowed... and more came. Each evening there was a cool breeze... life-changing decisions were made... God was glorified! And, you guessed it; the offering far exceeded the expenses.

Demonic Wisdom

"Wisdom not from God may be *demonic"* (James 3:15). How can a Christian's actions with temporal wisdom be demonic or devilish? James is not saying believers are demons, but rather, living according to the wisdom of the world, they can be used by the devil. Demonic wisdom serves the purposes and interest of Satan who is opposed to divine wisdom.

In short, purely human interest by good people may serve the devil's purposes. God-wisdom is not man-centered—doing things by your feelings or earthly thoughts—but rather, by the Word of God and inspiration of the Holy Spirit. When God becomes superficial in your life, little more than a religious expression, the devil can easily use a wisdom that does not "come down from above." God-life is much more than a simple belief in God. God-wisdom is Christ, the wisdom of God, living in you.

True Wisdom, From God

Wisdom is defined as having sound (well-grounded) and prudent (far-sighted or circumspect) judgment. One definition interprets wisdom as "possessing inside information," operating with insight. Look again at God's Word. "If any of you lacks wisdom, let him ask of God, who gives... generously and without reproach, and it will be given" (James 1:5). What better way is there to get inside information with insight? Enlarge your vision, God is ready to give you true wisdom; don't settle for less.

~~~~~~~~~~~~~~~~~~~~~~~~~~~~
If you lack wisdom, ask God.
~~~~~~~~~~~~~~~~~~~~~~~~~~~~

Amazing Grace

"Isn't that melody Amazing Grace?" A memorable experience of witness occurred when a fellow staff member and I were touring Mainland China. We were having dinner in a beautiful restaurant and were somewhat oblivious to the pianist and soloist providing pleasant background music. Suddenly, we realized that over the hum of diners and clinking silverware was the sound of a familiar hymn. Though we didn't understand the language, we recognized the melody—why, it was Amazing Grace!

She was unafraid, single-mindedly communicating her faith to those having dinner. A Chinese Christian explained that she was communicating to us that she was a sister in Christ. The Chinese lyrics were changed and perhaps were not the words of "Amazing Grace," but the message was clear. While prohibited by law to share her faith, God-wisdom found a way to witness through the tune of a beautiful hymn known worldwide.

Such prohibitions seem surreal to us. China has a tightly controlled society. To illustrate, we stayed in an "approved" hotel for foreigners. There was armed security visible in the lobby. And, every time exiting the elevator or leaving my room, a man in a closet-sized room would lean out a Dutch door and observe my movements.

You're aware of the "underground church" in China. Church buildings are few and far between, and the public services usually are monitored. Undefeated, they've organized "house churches." Unadvertised, they quietly gather in small groups. Countless believers worldwide fearlessly and boldly celebrate and share their faith in spite of a threat of brutal punishment or even death. Like the Chinese singer in the restaurant, they have called upon God for His wisdom in how to share their witness. We need to lift up in fervent prayer these courageous believers of the body of Christ in China and throughout the world.

Fruits of God-Wisdom

A fruit-bearing Christian has spiritual maturity that comprehends the wisdom of God and applies it wisely, judicially, and with under-standing. This is a vitally important aspect of God-life—developing a growing awareness that God has equipped you with everything you need to live God-life. You are a child of God, created with a new nature; a new creation with Christ's nature. His wisdom will enable you to bear God-honoring fruit in every life challenge.

God wants you, His very own child, to show His wisdom in every situation. You can start trusting Him for wisdom that comes from above—God has promised and He will respond. It may not always be easy to exhibit His wisdom, but it will always be available. "He who began a good work in you will continue... developing [that good work] and perfecting and bringing it to full completion in you" (Philippians 1:6, AMP). Aspire to be all He has planned and will teach you to become.

Seven Fruits of True Wisdom
James gives a pyramid of seven characteristics of God-wisdom; they shadow the very presence of God (see James 3:17). Each should be observable in your daily lifestyle and in your interactions with others.

Pure (*hagnŏs*) and Holy (*hagios*)
Aim to live a clean, separated, and chaste life. Both pure and holy are from the same root in Greek, and signify an undefiled or separated life. They both have moral implications. When you strive to be pure, you are committed to living with God-wisdom. Are you actively purifying (separating) yourself, as your Lord is pure (see 1 John 3:3)? Living a circumspect life—it is much more than a theological or biblical understanding, it is *Christ living in you.*

Peace-loving (*eirēnikos*)
Seek to live peaceably or peacefully, striving for harmonious relationships. "Let us... aim for and eagerly pursue what makes for harmony and for mutual upbuilding (edification and development) of one another" (Romans 14:19, AMP).

God-wisdom comes from the "God of peace" (Romans 15:33). When you are peace-loving, you forgive wrongs, accept differences, and mediate misunderstandings. It is an active, fervent, intentional engagement to bring harmony. Peace-loving is often needed between siblings, with neighbors, in the work-place, and in the church. Peace-loving never holds grudges, seeks to get even, renders "kind for kind," nourishes disagreements, or starts quarrels. "Let us pursue the things which make for peace and the building up of one another" (Romans 14:19).

Gentle (*epieikēs*)

Be patient or forbearing with others. This word is formed from two words, *unto* and *fitting*, together they are the God-wisdom of being equitable, fair, kind, and considerate with others. God-wisdom maligns no one, is not argumentative, or quarrelsome and does not have a "me first" attitude. Be considerate of others when they have needs and hurts. The maxim "A gentle answer turns away wrath" (Proverbs 15:1) should be the watchword and principle for every believer.

Reasonable (*eupeithēs*)

Stay approachable, rational, and fair, but not passive. It is willingness to yield to credible information or be compliant and responsive to justified explanations. It is the ability to change your mindset. This doesn't mean you are weak, an easy push-over, or void of basic convictions; but you have openness to others and ability to sort out truth.

Reasonable in Greek also implies obedience and compliance. God-wisdom compels the believer to obey the will of God. It also expresses a willingness to obey those in authority by being amiable to the laws of the land.

Mercy (*eleos*) and *Good Fruits*

Mercy and good fruits is a cause and effect of those who live their daily lives with God-wisdom. Mercy, whether divine or human, is an active, outgoing, caring expression of compassion. "God, being rich in mercy, because of His great love with which He loved us [you]... made us [you] alive together with Christ" (Ephesians 2:4-5).

Because God loved you with an initiating action of mercy (cause), He made a way for your salvation (effect), even when you were dead in your trespasses and sin. Living in God-wisdom necessitates being proactive with mercy towards others.

Good fruits or works are the effect of intentional mercy you show towards others. Those who actively employ God-wisdom initiates practical expressions of mercy seeking to alleviate suffering, aiding those in distress or those who have special needs (see James 1:27). Good fruit—all kinds of loving-kindness—will be initiated by those who are governed by God-wisdom (see Philippians 1:11).

Unwavering (*adiakritŏs*)
Stand firm without partiality, without disparity, or without variance. As we saw earlier, a follower of Christ must not be double-minded. God-wisdom is impartial when relating to others, not vacillating when dealing with different individuals. God-wisdom is not one way now, and another way tomorrow.

Without *hypocrisy* (*anupokritŏs*) is to be sincere and without dissimulation. Hypocrisy is role-playing; adopting a role that covers or obscures reality. Adlai E. Stevenson said, "A hypocrite is the kind of politician who would cut down a redwood tree, then mount the stump and make a speech for conservation." God-wisdom has no place for hypocrisy; it always is seen with unmasked sincerity.

Who Bears God-Wisdom?

The Church is to Manifest God-Wisdom
The result of preaching the "unfathomable riches of Christ" is the birth and growth of the church. In the New Testament, the Greek word *ekklesía* (*called out* or *assembly*), was used by Jesus for church. "I will build My church" (Matthew 16:18).

Church in the New Testament is primarily the local assembly of believers. It is also used for the regenerate of all times and ages. The latter is referred to as the universal church, or all true believers—the body of Christ (see Ephesians 1:22-23, Hebrews 12:23).

From across the face of humanity, the church has been reconciled (thoroughly changed) into one body through the cross (see Ephesians 2:16). All in Christ are "fellow-heirs and fellow-members of the body, and fellow-partakers of the promise in Christ Jesus through the gospel" (Ephesians 3:6).

The purpose of the Church is not only to win the lost to a saving faith, as fundamental as that is; but also, to glorify God by manifesting God-wisdom. "The manifold wisdom of God might now be made known *through the church*" (Ephesians 3:10, emphasis mine).

The church is not an end in itself, but a means to make apparent the wisdom of God. It is a vehicle or medium to make known to a sinful world the grace of God as seen by believers living with God-wisdom. God works *through* godly men and women who have saturated themselves with His Word and provide wise answers to life's questions.

Look again at Ephesians 3:10: "The manifold wisdom of God." The word *manifold* (*polupoikilos*) means *highly varied* or *multicolored*. From the most diverse backgrounds the wisdom of God is displayed in the body of Christ, the church. The "called out" believers are from varied backgrounds, languages, cultures, and races; yet, in their diversity are one in Christ. He breaks down all barriers and the body of believers becomes brothers and sisters of "the Way."

Mt. Pisgah

In the last thirty years, I've been privileged to be interim pastor of this unusual church four times. In the worship service, I welcome everyone to God's House, where the *body of Christ* worships. Mt. Pisgah is exemplary in this wonderful truth. It is a church body that genuinely loves each other in Christ. They are young and old, well funded and not, different races and cultures, native and immigrant— all one in Christ. Diverse, but united in Christ, they are multi-splendored. God-wisdom is not identifying yourself by *who* you are, but by *whose* you are—one in the body of Christ.

Let's focus a minute on "the manifold wisdom of God *might |or may|* now be made known through the church" (Ephesians 3:10, emphasis mine). "Might" speaks of the possibility that the church can make known the wisdom of God. "May" implies that the church has permission to make known the wisdom of God. Either interpretation refers to the will or decision on the part of the church to exhibit God-wisdom.

Is the manifold wisdom of God evidenced in all churches? No! Can all churches display the wisdom of God? They might, or may do so under the leadership of God's Holy Spirit. The polity of a church should be more a theocracy than a democracy. The local church should enmasse submit to God's will and His Word in every decision made.

- **Are you contributing God-wisdom in your church?**

You Are to Be Filled With Wisdom

Without question, pastors and ordained ministers are to function with the wisdom of God. But, what about the congregation? What about you? God has promised to make His wisdom available to you liberally and magnanimously.

The Cross and Beyond

A belief system that begins and ends with Christ's death on the cross is a limited understanding of Scripture. I hasten to add, a belief system that *does not* begin at the Cross of Calvary is worthless. The cross is the heart of the gospel (Good News) and the central thesis of Christianity. "God forbid that I should glory, save [except] in the cross of our Lord Jesus Christ" (Galatians 6:14, KJV).

The cross is the irrefutable declaration of the love and wisdom of God. "God in His wisdom was pleased through... preaching [of salvation, procured by Christ and to be had through Him], to save those who believed" (1 Corinthians 1:21, AMP). *Preaching* (*kērugma*) does not refer to the act of preaching, but to the content of the message. God's wisdom in the salvation of sinners is by the cross of Christ, even though worldly wisdom calls it foolishness. The scope of the message of salvation is that God saves the lost through the crucified Savior. Salvation does not come by exercising wisdom; it comes to them that believe. God-birth graces you with eternal life; now, what about God-life?

Look at Paul's message in 1 Corinthians 1:24: "Christ [is] the power of God [life deliverance] and the wisdom of God [life principles]." God-wisdom dictates that you are to "grow in the grace and knowledge of our Lord and Savior Jesus Christ" (2 Peter 3:18). *Grow* is a present tense imperative not up for debate; it is not optional. Peter stresses that maturation is evidence of your faith and your God-wisdom. God knows your potential and He has an incredible goal for you—to live a God-life. Possible? Yes, because God "has given to us all things that pertain to life and godliness... that through these you may be partakers of the divine nature" (2 Peter 1:3-4, NKJV).

Jesus promised that after your God-birth, the indwelling Holy Spirit, the Spirit of Truth, will empower you to show forth God-wisdom in your life (see John 14:16-17). Salvation in Christ is so much more than assurance of Heaven, it is *living Christ*. The norm of mediocrity is unacceptable; you are called to live in His image.

Christ living in you, what a thought! It can be a reality in your life. The magnitude of this unqualified truth is seen in Colossians 1:19: "In Him the complete being of God... came to dwell" (NEB). The completeness of deity, all the fullness, the very essence of God in Christ dwells in you. God-wisdom is available! Don't settle for status quo, God has so much more for you. He will share Himself with you.

Spiritual understanding is the ability to grasp the meaning of and comprehend the Scriptures. Pray with the psalmist: "Give me understanding, and I shall keep [Your] law" (Psalms 119:34, KJV). Luke records that Jesus met with His disciples and "opened their understanding, that they might understand [comprehend] the Scriptures" (Luke 24:45, KJV). Christ came not only to save us from our sins; but also that "we know that the Son of God has come, and has given us understanding, in order that we might know Him who is true" (1 John 5:20).

Spiritual wisdom (God-wisdom) is the ability to use and apply spiritual understanding in life situations. You should pray daily for this wisdom: "For the Lord gives skillful and godly Wisdom; from His mouth come knowledge and understanding" (Proverbs 2:6, AMP). The gifts of perception and discretion are vital in living a God-life with God-wisdom. Jesus said, "The words (truths) that I have been speaking to you are spirit and life" (John 6:63, AMP). Stop and think about what Jesus said. The very Son of God, with the breath of God, spoke life-giving words. The very life of God was in His words.

Do you want to live a God-life? Then, "know the things freely given to us by God, which things we also speak, not in words taught by human wisdom, but in those taught by the Spirit, combining spiritual thoughts with spiritual words" (1 Corinthians 2:12-13).

There was life beyond the cross for Jesus, a glorious life! And there is life beyond Calvary for every believer, a splendorous life. The potential of applying Biblical truth and understanding with God-wisdom in your life can be reality. Believers living a God-life, applying God-wisdom, being *filled up to all the fullness of God* is glorious!

Paul prayed for the believers at Ephesus that "the Father of glory, may give to you a spirit of wisdom and of revelation in the knowledge of Him" (Ephesians 1:17). Paul realized that if Christ was to live in you, He must be the Lord of your life and you must function daily with God-wisdom. Don't settle for mediocrity. God-wisdom is waiting for you.

Today's call is: "Who among you is wise" (James 3:13)? Who is wise? Or who has God-wisdom, is a charge for self-examination. God-birth changes who you are. God-faith gives you a tenacious expectancy; an assurance that God will provide you with His wisdom. God-wisdom changes how you live. Have an undaunted and courageous faith. Anticipate that God will give you wisdom.

- **Pray this prayer daily: "Lord Jesus, fill me with spiritual wisdom and understanding, I seek to do your will and be all you saved me to be."**

How is God-Wisdom Received?

God's astonishing desire for you is to "be perfect and complete, lacking in nothing" (James 1:4). What a gracious, loving, caring LORD our God is! His will for you is to live God-life, to be *perfect* (*teleios*), or attain spiritual *maturity*; and to be *complete* (*holoklēros*), *whole* and *without defect* in every part. In other words, "that every grace present in Christ should be manifested in the believer."[i] To be a complete believer you must function with God-wisdom.

Think about it: to have God-wisdom is to have *nothing lacking*. What a challenging thought! For you to have acquired all that God in His discretion has allotted for you in Christ—nothing lacking, nothing wanting. The question is: *How can I obtain God-wisdom for my daily trials?*

The need is obvious and critical: You cannot avoid observing the stark contrast between a spiritually mature Christian who is functioning with God-wisdom, and a spiritually immature believer. Sadly, masses of today's church members and even some leadership fall into the latter category. This is true when there is little or no distinguishable difference between a believer and unbeliever. Large numbers of professed believers never or infrequently attend worship services. Many Christians marginalize their witness because of their worldly lifestyle.

In every way there is a flagrant need for believers to have and manifest God-wisdom in day-to-day contacts and issues. There is a crying out for God-wisdom to regulate conduct by establishing a moral, ethical, and spiritual foundation that shapes the whole Christian. Without God-wisdom you cannot live the Beatitudes (see Matthew 5:3-12), pray the model prayer (see Matthew 6:9-13), nor follow or imitate God (see Ephesians 5:1).

Are you asking: *What am I to do*? If you're ready to live with God-wisdom, the next pages will be important.

The Initiative of Discovery
"If any of you lacks wisdom" (James 1:5).

Does this apply to you? Do you sense a need for God-wisdom? *If* can be a mountainous obstruction for obtaining God-wisdom and being all that God desires for you to be.

If you meditate daily on the Word of God until the words fade and the message becomes personal.

If you have clear, uninhibited insight into life's challenges from God's perspective.

If you seek to live subject to the will of God.

If is the hinge of the doorway to God-wisdom. Open the door. God-wisdom doesn't come automatically, it must be pursued; it doesn't fall down out of the sky.

- **Do any of the "if" questions apply to you?**

The Route of Discovery
"If any of you lacks wisdom, let him ask of God,
who gives to all men generously and without reproach,
and it |wisdom and more| will be given to him" (James 1:5).

Ask God! Your God is a giving God; in fact, a literal translation of this verse is "ask the giving God." He is a God who gives generously and unreservedly to those who ask. Don't stop short of living God-life by thinking, "I can't; it's too hard, it's beyond me." Don't be satisfied with life as it is. God has much more in store for you than you can imagine. There is no end to the abundance of God's gifts. And, He gives "without reproach," or without censure or limitation. Ask and it will be given.

Pause for a moment, you can hear Jesus saying: "Ask, and it shall be given to you" (Matthew 7:7). *Are you asking for God-wisdom?* You may be thinking: "Asking is too simple! Surely there is more to discovering God-wisdom." Well, there is a condition; you must ask in faith, believing God. You're asking, "must be in faith... with no wavering, no hesitating, no doubting" (James 1:6, AMP). You can expect God to answer your prayer for wisdom not because of *who you are*, but because of *whose you are.*

When asking for God-wisdom, you're asking for part of God Himself. Such a prayer is not casual or incidental, but it is a soul-emptying, life-altering proposition with God. The mark of a mature believer, a complete believer, is to ask God for wisdom with unwavering faithing and with thanksgiving for an anticipated response.

God Says: "If You" then, "I Will"

Proverbs is recognized as wisdom literature; verse after verse reveals wise and insightful truths. Above all, it is a practical book, focusing on everyday life. Have you noticed that the Bible often has an *if-then* formula for God's blessings?

A classic example is found in 2 Chronicles 7:14: "If my people will... then I will."

Turning to the wisdom literature, let's look at Proverbs.

Proverbs 2:1-4
If's loom from the page in critical requisites for functioning with God-wisdom.

If you will receive and treasure God's Word, and be attentive to its wisdom and understanding (verses 1-2).

If your desire or yearning for God-wisdom is the unwavering focus of your prayer, your cry for discernment (verse 3).

If you seek God-wisdom as intently as you would seek lost money or something of value (verse 4). The intensity of this quest was illustrated by Jesus in His parables of the lost son, sheep, coin (see Luke 15:8-10).

Then is the blessed answer that comes when requisites are met. Two results, or then's, are answered in your prayer for God-wisdom.

Then knowledge, discernment, and wisdom of God's ways will be yours (verse 5).

Then moral discretion and a righteous lifestyle will be seen in daily challenges (verse 9).

God-wisdom is for everyday use; it's not a lofty acclaim, but it is living *Christ in you.* It is having the knowledge and understanding to manifest Christ in every way.

Inseparable with the soul cry for God-wisdom is the Word of God. As we discovered in God-mind, His mind and judgments are revealed in His words. The Lord speaks and shares His wisdom with you through Scripture. Too often, we resolve conflicts, make decisions, and handle life situations in an emotional or reactionary manner. The challenge is to go deeper, reach beyond yourself, and appropriate wisdom from the inspired Word. Remember what Jesus did? He let the Word of God speak for Him (see Luke 4).

To function with God-wisdom, the Word of God must be implanted in your heart (see James 1:21). It is not just accepting the Bible as the Word of God, or just receiving it as God's truth, but it is to be embedded or rooted in your heart. The word of truth is the gospel, and much more. It is God's message to you as to how to live a mature and complete life, lacking nothing. The ingested Word is to be received, reviewed, and recalled until its message is amalgamated and merged into your very being. The James 1:22 challenge is to be a doer of the Word, not merely a hearer.

~~~~~~
"Let your roots grow down into Him [Christ]
and draw up nourishment from Him.
See that you go on growing in the Lord,
and become strong and vigorous in Truth."
(James 1:22, Tay)
~~~~~~

Word-doers

A missionary returned to the states and shared a gripping account of his visit with indigenous native believers. He observed that believers carried a single page of the Bible on their person. The natural assumption would be that the purpose was to memorize a passage of the Bible. Not so, it was far more compelling. The missionary shared that each believer took a page of the Bible and kept it until they could live it. Then they would get another page. Living the Scripture, Word-doers, that's it!

Discover God-wisdom and you will be lacking in nothing. There is an enormous difference in learning Scripture and living Scripture. Living a God-life with God-wisdom does not happen by taking a course or pursuing a degree; it is not a matter of head knowledge. If this were true, we should all take a seat in a library and spend our time reading a stack of books. God-wisdom is not academic; it is a personal pilgrimage of a child of God.

- **Are you a Word-doer? Are you seeking to live a God-life?**

And now, we come to the close of our journey in discovering how to live a God-life. Has God helped you to understand what it means *to live is Christ?* Can you proclaim: I've been crucified with Christ; and *it is no longer I who live, but Christ lives in me?*

God lives in you, manifest God-life! It is all of God. With importunity, petition God—seek to know Him, His thoughts, and His ways. It is His joy to give Himself to you as you ask. "Your Father who is in heaven [shall] give what is good to those who ask Him" (Matthew 7:11).

God-birth, God-faith, God-shine, God-talk, God-rest, God-walk, God-mind, and God-wisdom all work together for a mature God-life. A journey is waiting for you. The good news is, it's never too late to make the life-altering decision to live God-life. Decide today to let your Lord and Savior live through you, become more Christ-like.

God-life is a choice; it's up to you.

ENDNOTES

Section One

i James Orr, ed., *The International Standard Bible Encyclopedia,* Vol. 2, (Grand Rapids, MI: Eerdmans Publishing 1939), 1011.

ii F. B. Meyer, *The Epistle to the Philippians* (Grand Rapids, MI: Baker Book House, 1952), 109.

iii John R. Stott, *The Message of Ephesians* (Leicester, England: Inter-varsity Press, 1979), 189.

Section Two

i Alan Richardson, ed., *A Theological Word Book of the Bible* (New York: Macmillan Co., 1950), 75.

ii *Webster's Seventh New Collegiate Dictionary* (Springfield, MA: G. & C. Merriam Co., 1965), s.v. "Temporal."

iii Ibid., s.v. "Reality."

iv R. C. H. Lenski, *The Interpretation of St. Paul's First and Second Epistle to the Corinthians* (Columbus, OH.: Wartburg Press, 1955), 773.

v J. A. Alexander, *Commentary on the Gospel of Mark* (Grand Rapids, MI.: Zondervan Publishing House, reprint of 1864 edition), 310.

vi William Barclay, *The Letters of James and Peter* (Philadelphia, PA: Westminster Press, 1976), 297.

vii Sir Anthony Van Dyke, 1599-1641.

Section Three

i   Joseph Addison Alexander, *Commentary on the Prophecies of Isaiah,* Vol. 2 (Grand Rapids: Zondervan Publishing House, 1953), 380.

ii   J. F. Strombeck, *So Great Salvation* (Moline, IL: Strombeck Agency Inc., 1946), 38.

iii   Paul Powell, *The Great Deceiver* (Nashville: Broadman Press, 1988), 32.

iv   Maurice S. Rawlings, *To Hell and Back* (Nashville: Thomas Nelson Publishers, 1993), 16.

v   Ibid. 91.

vi   *Moody Monthly*, July, 1956, p. 64.

vii   William Barclay, *The Gospel of John*, Vol. 1 (Philadelphia: The Westminster Press, 1975), 49.

viii   W. E. Vine, *Vine's Expository Dictionary of Biblical Words* (Nashville: Thomas Nelson Publishers, 1985), sv. "Image."

ix   Robert S. Candlish, *The First Epistle of John* (Grand Rapids: Zondervan Publishing House, n.d.), 49.

x   G. Campbell Morgan, *The Gospel According to Matthew* (New York: Fleming H. Revell CO., 1929), 48.

xi   Jürgen Moltman, *The Spirit Life* (Minneapolis: Fortress Press, 1993), 177.

Section Four

i   C.H. Spurgeon, The Treasury of David, Vol. 6 (Grand Rapids, MI.: Zondervon Publishing House, 1950), 308.

ii   Marvin R. Vincent, *Word Studies in the New Testament,* Vol. 3 (Mclean, VA.: MacDonald Publishing Co., n.d.), 398.

iii   John MacArthur, *The MacArthur New Testament Commentary, Ephesians* (Chicago, IL.: Moody Press, 1986), 36.

iv   P.T. Forsyth, *The Soul of Prayer* (Grand Rapids, MI.: William B. Eerdmans Publishing Company, 1916), 18.

v   Andrew Murray, *The Prayer Life* (Chicago, IL.: Moody Press, n.d.), 15.

vi   Ibid Forsyth.

vii   Page H. Kelley, *Judgment and Redemption In Isaiah* (Nashville, TN.: Broadman Press, 1968), 18.

Section Five

[i] Charles H. Spurgeon, *Spurgeon's Expository Encyclopedia* (Grand Rapids, MI.: Baker Book House, 1952), Vol. 13, 169.

[ii] F.B. Meyer, *The Way Into The Holiest* (Grand Rapids, MI.: Baker Book House, 1951), 81.

[iii] W.T. Conner, *The Faith Of The New Testament* (Nashville, TN.: Broadman Press, 1940), 99.

[iv] "When Jesus Comes," Oswald Smith.

Section Six

[i] Timothy George, *The New American Commentary* (Nashville: Broadman & Holman, 1995), Vol. 27, 73.

[ii] Martin Luther, *St. Paul's Epistle To The Galatians* (Westword, N.J: Fleming H. Revell Co., first published 1535), 527.

Section Seven

[i] Kenneth S. Wuest, *Romans in the Greek New Testament* (Grand Rapids, MI.: Wm. B. Eerdmaus Publishing Co., 1955), 37.

[ii] A. T. Robertson, *Word Pictures in the New Testament*, Vol. 4 (Grand Rapids, MI.: Baker Book House, 1931), 601.

[iii] Billy K. Smith, Frank S. Page, *The New American Commentary*, Vol. 19B (Nashville, TN.: Broadman & Holman Publishers, 1995), 59.

[iv] J. Clyde Turner, *These Things We Believe* (Nashville, TN.: Convention Press, 1956), 1.

[v] Marvin R. Vincent, *Word Studies in the New Testament*, Vol. 1 (Mclean, VA.: Macdonald Publishing Co., n.d.), 636.

Section Eight

[i] W.E. Vine, *Vine's Expository Dictionary of Biblical Words*, (Nashville, Thomas Nelson Publishers, 1985), 204.

Printed in the United States
219240BV00001B/5/P

9 781607 914273